IF YOU FEEL THE DESIRE TO WRITE,
IF YOU KNOW IN YOUR HEART YOU WERE
BORN TO BE A NOVELIST,
BUT YOU ONLY HAVE FREE TIME ON WEEKENDS,
WAIT NO LONGER.
BEGIN THIS SATURDAY . . .
AND ONE YEAR FROM NOW YOUR BOOK CAN BE FINISHED.

Find out what only a writer can tell you . . .

- How to make your writing time sacred. Every minute counts.
- Which books to have on your bookshelf.
- How to think like a writer.
- Why other writers quit after the first chapter . . . but you won't.
- How to start your book in the first four weekends . . . and how just one month will change your life.
- Why "third person omniscient" is the point of view to use.
- What you can learn from sitcoms on TV.
- Why the chapter is NOT the basic building block for your novel.

. . . and so much more

THE WEEKEND NOVELIST

ROBERT J. RAY

THE

WEEKEND

NOVELIST

THE
WEEKEND
NOVELIST

Robert J. Ray

A DELL TRADE PAPERBACK

A DELL TRADE PAPERBACK

Published by
Dell Publishing
a division of
Bantam Doubleday Dell Publishing Group, Inc.
1540 Broadway
New York, New York 10036

Library of Congress Cataloging in Publication Data

Ray, Robert J. (Robert Joseph), 1935–
      The weekend novelist / Robert J. Ray.
          p.   cm.
      "A Dell trade paperback."
      ISBN 0-440-50594-1
      1. Fiction—Technique.   I. Title.
PN3365.R38   1994
808.3—dc20   93-15108
                                                                                    CIP

Printed in the United States of America

Published simultaneously in Canada

January 1994

10   9   8   7   6   5   4   3   2   1

BVG

For Lee Eckert and Joe Ryan,
twin gurus of the marketplace,
who taught me that a writer in
America must be plotter and planner,
inventor and entrepreneur, wordsmith
and clown, tireless quester, and
never-sleeping keeper of the language

Thanks, guys

When we write we begin to taste the
texture of our own mind.

Natalie Goldberg,
Long Quiet Highway: Waking Up in America

Acknowledgments

Several people helped with the making of *The Weekend Novelist*. Early drafts were read by Jean Femling, Deborah Shouse, and Jo Kohn. Later drafts were read by Lora Jansson and Jack Remick. Students in my writing classes gave great pointers on the exercises. At Dell I had invaluable help from Jackie Farber, Catherine Chapman, and Shawn Coyne.

Special thanks to my agent, Ben Kamsler, who thought the book was a good idea from the start; to Natalie Goldberg, who showed me the way of writing practice; to Anne Tyler, for giving me permission to quote from *The Accidental Tourist;* and to my wife, Margot, who enables me, with her real job, to keep on working in the garden of words.

Contents

THE
WEEKEND
NOVELIST

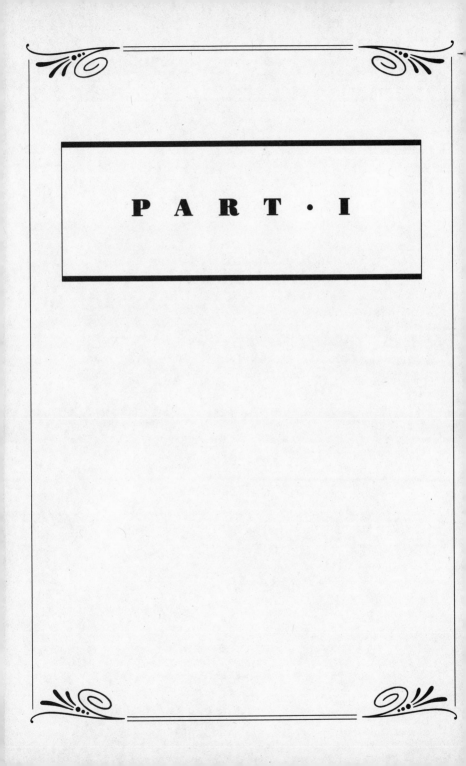

PART · I

Getting Started

When my agent sold my first novel to a major New York publisher, I was wild with joy. The novel, written mostly on weekends while I held down a full-time teaching job, was published eleven months later as a paperback original from Berkley Books. The title was *The Heart of the Game*.

Like many first novelists, I had written a book about something I knew. The subject of my novel was tennis, a game I truly loved. The game, stimulated by open tennis, where legendary professionals competed against gifted amateurs in the grand arenas of the sport—Wimbledon, Stade Roland Garros, Forest Hills—provided a colorful international backdrop for my story. As an avid player and moonlighting tennis instructor, I knew my subject, the strokes, the personalities of the game, the right moves. In the novel itself I tried to capture not only the players and the sport, but also the beauty and courage and grace under pressure when you're out there on the court, alone. When the book appeared, transformed from my thick, well-thumbed typescript into a tidy package for the marketplace, I was so happy it hurt. My hard work at the typewriter had paid off. At last, I was a real writer.

I did not, however, quit my teaching job. I kept on writing, mostly on weekends, while I learned the novelist's craft. I took writing courses, attended writers' conferences. I studied fiction, taking novels apart to see how they were built. I studied film, probing the secrets of scene and structure and pacing. As my skill level got deeper, I wrote better books (six of my novels have been sold in the last six years) and through writing I made friends with other writers. All of us shared a love of words and writing. To us, writing was seductive, a siren song that never winds down into the final coda. We had no choice. We had to write.

The same thing has happened, or will happen, to you. Your first novel will grow like a lotus out of something you know and love: a person, a place, an event, a time in your life, an activity, a book you'd like to emulate. Once you try your hand at writing deep, once you feel the glow of the words, once you feel their power, you won't want to do anything else. Words will wake you from your sleep. Words you never noticed before will amaze you as they shimmer in a new way, as they change shape, as they take you deeper. Because of the words and the joy of writing, you'll steal time from family and friends so you can practice your writer's craft.

The Weekend Novelist will help you make the best use of the time that you steal for writing. As you read through the book, trying out the exercises, giving yourself permission to write the book that's been wanting out all these years, you'll feel better about yourself. Because now you know where you're going with the writing. In fifty-two weekends, you are going to write a novel.

And when *your* agent sells *your* first novel, let yourself be wild with joy.

How to Use the Book

Using this book, you can organize your writing around the weekends. Each weekend has a specific task—character sketch, for example, or writing deeply about your character's past, or writing a wild, uncontrolled dream—and each task makes a building block for your novel. As you work through the assignments, shaping those building blocks, you'll be training yourself to think like a novelist. Everyday details that once slid by unnoticed will become material for your novel. In the local coffeehouse, you'll find yourself listening hard as you eavesdrop for good dialogue lines. At work, you'll cast co-workers as possible characters for your book. In a movie house, you'll discover that your mind is working on two levels: the Old You is here for entertainment and escape; the New You, that writer-in-the-making, is here to study the structure of the film, which you will apply to the structure of your novel.

The first fourteen weekends are designed to teach you the basics of novel writing. You work through the basics in three sections: character, scene, and plot. The weekends after that take you into the structure of the novel—acts, scenes, turning points, high points—and with those in place (or sketched out) you'll move on to write the book.

The process of the weekends is linear. Your work on character flows naturally into scene building, where characters come onto your novel's stage to carry out their agendas. Scene building introduces you to the secrets of scene structure (how action meshes with dialogue and stage setup to produce a dramatic climax). Learning the structure of scenes, the way they are put together, leads naturally on to the next section, the study of plot, a larger structure. The last assignment in the plotting section is to write a scenario, a narrative treatment of your story. This scenario, written in acts or sections, enables you to make an easy transition to writing the book.

You'll write the book in stages, working quickly to explore your discoveries about character and event in a first draft, writing deeper (a meditative state) for your second draft, saving most of the editing until your final draft. There are guidelines to follow for each weekend, strategies to help you move forward, specific goals to help you keep up the pace. If you follow the steps, you'll get there. Discovery makes the journey fun.

How to Structure Your Writing on Weekends

Each weekend focuses on a specific task, a model for you to follow in your work. First, there's a definition of the task and its purpose, plus a writing sample to illustrate the range of possibility. Definition and writing sample are followed by guidelines for writing, specific techniques you can use to work through the weekend. The guidelines lead you directly into the exercises, two or three writings based on the example for the weekend. After the exercises, during the week, I've included suggestions for deepening your understanding of how novels work while you broaden your horizons as a writer. Sometimes you draw a diagram. Sometimes you make a list. Sometimes you'll be asked to read a passage from another novel or from a book on fiction writing. Often you'll be asked to look ahead to the next weekend.

Work Space/Writing Time

You need a comfortable place to write, a desk, a cubbyhole, a room of your own: "On one side was her bed, flanked by the washstand and the looking glass. On the other side was the wicker chair in which she read, a writing table inherited from Stella [her sister], made by the St. Ives carpenter and stained green and brown with a leaf pattern by Stella herself, and, on top of it, her Greek lexicon, always open—also, inkpots and manuscript books in which she was constantly working. The 'literary' side of the room contained Virginia's icons of selfhood, and it was to this side that she escaped, reading in the hours between tea and dinner, writing whenever she could. She began keeping journals in her teens. . . ." (*Woman of Letters: A Life of Virginia Woolf,* by Phyllis Rose)

You need time that is just for writing. Let your family and friends know your schedule. Post the schedule, Saturday 7:00–10:00 A.M.; Sunday, 2:00–5:00 P.M. As the novel grows and you need more time, post a new schedule. Don't answer the phone. Don't answer the door. Don't use this time to pay the bills or worry about your life. This is writing time. It is sacred. Here, every minute counts.

Writing Tools

You need a notebook and something to write with. I write with a Schaefer slim-nib fountain pen, the kind that uses refills. I like the bold look on the page because it means business. My notebooks are spiral bound, bought in six-packs from Pace or Costco or some other discount warehouse. I like spiral-bound notebooks because they open flat, then fold under to provide a stable writing surface for a lap. One writer in my writing practice group prefers the gray perfect bound notebook. Another, who writes fast, likes the steno notebook, spiral bound along the top, so he can flip fast and not lose his rhythm.

On the front of your notebook, write the start date and the topic:

My Novel, Techniques, October 28, 19——

You'll fill several notebooks doing this first novel. Dates on the cover and on each piece of writing help you locate your writings. If you're writing hot, filling several pages at a sitting, you might lose track of what you've written. So you go back, paging through, to number each page. Make a table of contents and paste it up front in the notebook.

The notebook is the place where you store your creativity. It's a place for shelving, a storage closet for lists, ideas, images, jottings, plot diagrams, dialogues, scenes yet to write, inspiring quotes. In your writer's notebook, you can explore, seek, play, fly, dream. Writing in the notebook, you teach yourself the meditative discipline so crucial to the writer's art: to observe with words. Cherish the notebook.

In addition to your notebook, you'll need a word processor or a typewriter. Some writers stay with the notebook through their first draft. Others enter their day's writings into a word processor. Whichever you choose, computers make the mechanical tasks so easy, you owe yourself a trip to the local computer store.

Word-processing software, once mind boggling, is now easy to use. It's a good idea to check out software—the program that turns your computer into a word processor—before you buy. Ask your friends what they use. Try out their software. How easy is it for you to write with? How easy to edit? How easy to move big blocks of type? How easy to move from page one of your manuscript to page one hundred?

Computers are super for editing, for shifting big chunks of words around, and for producing professional-looking copy. Computers set you free. When you finish a hot scene, you sigh, stretch, and take a break. While you're drinking coffee or concocting a pot of goulash, your computer prints the scene. For a writer that is absolute luxury.

Books for Your Bookshelf

As a model to study, we'll be using Anne Tyler's 1985 novel, *The Accidental Tourist* (paperback edition). It's tightly written, with rhythms

that echo deeply. It has a classical three-act structure (Aristotle's beginning, middle, and end, widely used in film and theater) and three main
characters: Macon Leary is the protagonist; Sarah Leary is the antagonist who opposes Macon; Muriel Pritchett is the helper who saves
Macon from himself. The story made the leap from book to feature film,
which helped make it accessible to a wider audience. There are lots of
copies around. For contrasts to Tyler, we'll be looking at other authors. If
you have time, you might pick up copies of *The Great Gatsby* by F. Scott
Fitzgerald, and *The Sun Also Rises* by Ernest Hemingway. Their differ-
ences, in structure, pacing, and use of language, will provide alternatives
for your work while at the same time illuminating what Tyler does in
Tourist.

Writing is mind work, wordsmithing for fun and profit that demands a feeling for language. That feeling comes not only from knowing how words work, but also from knowing where they came from.
English is an exotic language, with words that reach all the way back,
through Middle English, through Old French and Anglo-Saxon and
Latin and Greek, to its Indo-European roots. A good dictionary helps
you get a handle on words and word roots. For tracking word origins, I
like both *The American Heritage Dictionary* and the shorter version of
The Oxford English Dictionary. The *OED* gives you a smidgen more,
usually in quotes from writers. As a writer you automatically become a
keeper of the language. A good dictionary is a must.

Timetables of History is a helpful writer's tool. Each of your characters has a past. With *Timetables,* you can select details (popular music,
films, world events) that deepen the past of your character. Details
bring us close. Details make the setting feel real.

For a study of form and technique, I recommend three books for
your shelf: *The Art of Fiction* by John Gardner; *The Art and Craft of
Novel Writing* by Oakley Hall; and *Writing Fiction* by Janet Burroway.
Gardner and Burroway are available in paperback. Hall's book is available from Writer's Digest Books.

For fun mixed with edification, I recommend *The Woman's Encyclopedia of Myths and Secrets* by Barbara Walker. This is a beautiful
book, carefully researched and tightly written, that upends standard

myths (Freud's misshapen view of Oedipus) while offering insights about turning points in popular literature.

For insights on structure, I recommend four books. The first two, *Screenplay* and *The Screenwriter's Workbook,* are by Syd Field. With his analyses of film structure, three acts turning on plot points, Field offers good insight into the inner workings of the novel. Joseph Campbell's classic, *The Hero with a Thousand Faces,* offers the Cosmogonic Round (a counterclockwise circle) as an alternative structure for your novel. Maureen Murdock's book, *The Heroine's Journey,* reverses Campbell, sending the heroine around the circle going clockwise.

For writing practice, I recommend *Writing Down the Bones* by Natalie Goldberg. Writing practice is what it sounds like—practicing your writing. If you are a writer, you must practice your craft. Violinists practice. Pianists practice. Swimmers, divers, runners, tennis players, actors—they all practice. Writing practice is working out with words. You forget form. You forget spelling and grammar and saying the right thing. You keep the hand moving while you go for hot spots in your memory bank. Many of the exercises in this book use writing practice as a base.

For a better understanding of the world of the writer, read *Max Perkins: Editor of Genius,* by A. Scott Berg, and *The Writer on Her Work,* edited by Janet Sternberg. The Perkins biography includes some inspiring stories about legendary writers (Thomas Wolfe, F. Scott Fitzgerald, Ernest Hemingway) who still profited from editorial counsel. The Sternberg book (volume two is just out) contains essays by women writers on the creative process.

For sheer inspiration, read *If You Want to Write* by Brenda Ueland. It's super.

How to Think Like a Writer

Your big gift as a writer is creativity, images bubbling from your unconscious to make the jottings you store in your notebook. Your big weapon is tenacity, the will to keep going, the strong fingernails you need to hang tight to the sheer cliff-face of writing when you feel yourself slipping.

You don't need a huge vocabulary. Just use the one you have with energy and efficiency and honesty, letting your voice come through. You do need drive and determination and a sense of humor about your work. Most of all, you need to stay *open*. Open to ideas and insights, open to form and techniques and new rhythms and new ways of looking at writing. One way to stay open is to bring a character onto your novel's stage and see what happens once she gets there. You sketch her first. You give her a past and some dreams and a place to live and a wardrobe that fits her life-style. As she comes onstage, you take notes. Let's say she lights a cigarette. What brand is it? Light falls across the glass-topped table to illuminate a film of dust. What is the source of the light? When she leaves her chair, where is she going? You follow your character along a narrow street, shadowing her as she turns a corner onto a busy boulevard. Detail—a French *flic* with a dapper mustache, a black Citroën, traffic, trees, blaring car horns—informs you: this is the Champs Elysées. The city is Paris. And, as your character strolls toward a man in a leather vest, a man with tattoos and a diamond earring, this might be the key scene that unlocks the rest of your book. The possibilities are limitless.

You won't know until you write it. For a writer, writing is the best test.

Warming Up

Writing Hot/Writing Cold

Some days you'll write hot. You'll wake up early with an idea that won't wait. You won't brush your teeth or make coffee or read the paper or feed the cat. Moving quietly, so as not to wake the house, you'll steal away to your writing place and you'll fill page after page of your notebook and when you look up it's almost noon and you've written two character sketches, two back stories, one wild dream, and a wonderful dialogue. You've completed a great scene, one you feared you'd never finish. You've sketched a sequence of four more scenes linked to that one. While you're surprised that all this time has passed, you're also gleeful, almost smug, about the work you've done.

Take these days and savor them. They are a gift from the inscrutable cosmos.

On other days, you'll have trouble starting. You'll blame this on the world, the inscrutable cosmos, a quirk, you feel, in the biorhythmic web. You'll blame it on family, friends, work. You feel chilly, cold hands, cold feet. Your brain feels frozen. Ice water runs in your veins. You peer out at the world through eyes crusted with rim ice. There is no sign of a thaw.

Warming Up

When you're cold and you can't warm up, try any (or all) of these stratagems:

• *Mind Mapping*. Mind mapping means you doodle on paper as you map the workings of your mind. There are two basic forms of mind mapping. First, there is the branching diagram Tony Buzan used in his book *Use Both Sides of Your Brain*. In branching you print your main idea on the trunk or main branch. You expand the diagram by printing connecting ideas on shorter branches. Using different colors for different ideas keeps your mind alert.

Second, there is the cluster diagram used by Gabriele Rico in *Writing the Natural Way*. To cluster, you print a word inside a bubble in the center of your page, and then you arrow out to other words inside other bubbles. Connections happen by word association. Mind mapping is good for developing character or scene building or working out whole sections of the story line.

• *Writing Practice*. A writer friend starts every day by writing for ten minutes using the start line, "I remember . . ." The phrase takes her back to her past. Exploring her past frees her mind by settling old scores and soothing old wounds. "I keep thinking I'll run out," she says. "But I'm always surprised that something new comes up." Sometimes, she says, a scene from her past translates into a scene for her book.

• *Writing with Friends*. Writing together with other writers (in class, in cafés, in the park, in someone's home) is wonderful. You pick up energy from the group. Writing regularly, same time, same place, helps you maintain discipline. You make friends. You share your words. Instead of being isolated, you're supported, supportive. Good places to meet like-minded writers might be: creative writing classes; writer's conferences; the library; bookstores. A writer friend in the Midwest tacked this sign up at her local bookstore: "If you have read Natalie Goldberg's *Bones* and wish to join a writing practice group, phone this number. . . ."

• *Reading Aloud*. When you're stuck, warm up by reading good writing aloud. Reading primes the writing pump. Take your time. Breathe deeply. Let your mind curl around the words. Read into a tape recorder and listen to the sound of your own voice enfolding the words. Read poetry aloud. As a writer, one of your main promotional tools is the public reading. One key to reading aloud is to breathe deeply, paying attention to rhythm, taking in oxygen where there are natural breaks, natural pauses. Taking in oxygen feeds the brain. You get better at reading if you practice, if you work at your breathing.

• *Breathing.* Breath is the foundation for writing even the simplest sentence. In *Long Quiet Highway,* a book about writing, teaching, learning, meditation, discipline, laziness, and waking up, Natalie Goldberg writes about discovering the connection between writing and breathing: "Sometimes it [the breath] would be deep, at other times shallow. It felt like the measure of the line when I wrote poetry: short lines, staccato breath; long lines, I'm breathing way down in my belly. I saw, too, that my breath also determined how much I could write at one time, it made language physical, it propelled the sentence."

WRITING TIPS

The Weight of Heavy Investment

Beginning students in my writing classes have this experience: They start out fast writing Chapter One; but before they reach Chapter Two, they loop back for a rewrite of the first paragraph of Chapter One. Instead of writing, pressing ahead, they edit, fussing with words, fixing a sentence, poking at metaphor.

Some writers make it to Chapter Two before they loop back for a big, intensive rewrite. Others make it as far as Chapter Three or Four or even Five. As a beginner forges ahead, however, the pressure mounts, a nagging voice inside your head telling you to rewrite, to change those words. *This book is bad,* the voice says. *Fix it now, this minute, or else.*

If you heed the voice, if you loop back, if you invest your time and energy in the first of the novel, you use yourself up. You avoid some pain, sure, and those first few pages gleam with a high sheen, but if you spend yourself at the beginning, then you won't experience the climax, the wonderful word-symphony of novel writing, that John Gardner talks about near the end of his book *The Art of Fiction:*

> Toward the close of the novel, the writer brings back—directly or in the form of his character's recollections—images, characters, events,

and intellectual motifs encountered earlier. Unexpected connections begin to surface; hidden causes become plain; life becomes, however briefly and unstably, organized; the universe reverses itself, if only for a moment, as inexorably moral; the outcome of the various characters' actions is at last manifest; and we see the responsibility of free will. It is this closing orchestration that the novel exists for.

Heavy stuff, and very true. If you use up all your writing time fussing over chapters one and two, you never find the door that leads to Gardner's closing movement, something you don't want to miss. By hanging about in the opening pages, you won't generate the energy that starts to build, as if by magic, somewhere around the midpoint of your book.

Rewriting is hard work. Because your tenacity increases in proportion to your investment, this looping back to rewrite has serious consequences for the writer. Let's say you do half a dozen rewrites on Chapter One. Let's say that each rewrite takes five hours, precious time for a weekend novelist. Won't this investment of thirty hours make you reluctant to make changes?

I see this happen all the time. Beginners, faced with a highly polished Chapter One and no plot, toss the rewritten drafts into the closet. Some, thinking new is easy, start another book; some try their hand at short fiction; others, those who have spent themselves, give up writing altogether.

Don't let this happen to you. Writing is hard; writing is wonderful; writing is a craft.

You can learn a craft.

Prepare, Prepare, Prepare

When you read a book, you start at the beginning and you read through the middle to get to the end. When you see a film, you see it from beginning to end. When they shoot a film, however, they shoot it out of sequence, and then editors put it together in the cutting room to make a coherent story. Before they begin shooting, filmmakers prepare. Actors, in their hunt for character, rehearse. Carpenters build sets. Script doctors fix scripts. Artists draw storyboards for key scenes. Wardrobe people make ready the costumes. As a novelist, you'd be smart to prepare before you invest too much in rewriting Chapter One.

You start preparing with character work, sketches, back stories to unearth motivation, dreams to open doorways to the interior of a character. You sketch out key scenes. A sketch is like a film-world storyboard for your scene. You set a stage for your novel and you bring on your characters. While they rehearse, trying out lines in your mind, you keep writing. You change the lighting and record their actions as they respond, turning their faces to catch the light. You move them outdoors for an exterior and they have to change clothes. The clothes inform you (and the reader) about life-style, taste, income.

You list possible scenes for your novel: first encounter, first date, first kiss, first intimate moment. And you sketch out a fictional situation.

Loading Your Unconscious

As you prepare the ground for your novel, you load your unconscious. You load in details about your characters so that your unconscious mind, your engine of creativity, can play around with them. Once inside your mind, the details grow. They mutate, cook, take on new shapes. If your character was named Veronica going in, she may emerge from your unconscious renamed Susannah. She went in quiet and subdued, cowed by circumstance, her shoulders rounded. She comes out talking rich and confident, shoulders back, dressed to kill.

You label the detail as you load it. Jimmy, a college boy of twenty-one, enters your unconscious a surly teen, brash, a loudmouth. His only real friend is his grandmother. Playing what-if, you try this: What if Granny died? What would that do to Jimmy? He comes out subdued, confused, afraid. Missing his grandmother, Jimmy begins to search for his heart.

You load your unconscious so that it can dance its way to the end of your story. Knowing the end, you'll press on instead of spinning your wheels retooling Chapter One.

To Escape the Internal Editor, Write under the Clock

Your internal editor, sometimes called the Judge, squats like the Grand Inquisitor inside your head. The internal editor is logical, systematic, careful, cautious, cold, distant, and numbers-oriented. The editor's major worry is appearances, what people will think. If you write under the clock, you distract the attention of the internal editor.

Your internal editor is a censor, an authority figure who locks doors to keep you away from subjects labeled "taboo." The internal editor's weapons are static, criticism, negation, constant yakking, and warning signs. Don't move on, the editor warns, until you have polished up this scene. Trim it up nice so the neighbors won't point fingers. Make it pretty. And don't write about incest, okay? Incest is taboo territory.

Sometimes your editor sounds remarkably like a parent.

You can get away from the internal editor by writing fast, letting the momentum carry you into strange psychic territory, plunging ahead to tackle some of your demons.

You can also evade the editor by slowing down, breathing deeply, printing your words in big block letters. According to Tony Buzan in *Use Both Sides of Your Brain*, printing distracts your internal editor, who focuses on making the letters look presentable.

Editing while you write chokes you, throttles you, dulls your mind, stifles your energy. When you write, write. When you edit, edit.

Writing to Produce Word Pictures

The language of fiction is the language of making word pictures. Word pictures make it tough on you so you can make it easy on the reader. The key to making word pictures is detail, concrete physical detail delivered in concrete, physically descriptive language. In this passage from the opening of Glenn Savan's *White Palace* (the movie starred James Spader and Susan Sarandon), the verb *threw* sharpens the description by turning the sun into an active force in the stage setup: "The evening sun threw a honey-colored rectangle across his glass-topped coffee table, lighting up a new film of dust, though he had only dusted two days ago."

To make word pictures, you learn from studying the craft of professional writers. They did it. You can do it too. You combine a strong verb (*threw*) with solid nouns (*rectangle, table, film, dust*). You add strong modifiers that give the picture color (*honey-colored*) or a certain moneyed look (*glass-topped coffee table*). To produce rhythm, you alternate a strong image (the sun throwing a rectangle across the table) with a weak concessive clause (concessive means "to yield"). The final clause of the sentence, which opens with *though*, eases into a muffled despair—"though he had only dusted two days ago"—as it forms a layer of muted exasperation, as if he were saying, "You can't win!" because he can't control this bit of dust.

It's easy to write weak; it's harder to write strong. To write a good novel, a solid novel with strength and staying power, get yourself into the habit of making word pictures, big ones, small ones, miniatures, every time you write.

Your first word picture is a character sketch.

PART · II

Weekends 1–4
Character Work

Starting with Character

When you start your book, you might begin with a concept, jotting down an idea for a fictional situation: "This is a story," you might write, "about economic success (not only money and a fancy home, but also happiness, family, love, and good friends) after living a life of drab deprivation."

Or you might begin with a close-up that pulls the reader in tight on the detail: "The rag, filthy with dirt and accumulated cinders, left telltale streaks on the gray stones of the hearth."

Or you might begin with the familiar voice of the storyteller: "Once upon a time, in a kingdom to the West, there lived a cinder maid who detested ashes. Her name was Cinderella."

This movement—from idea to image to opening line—is a handy three-step process, one that you can use to start your own work. You clarify the movement, rising up from rags to riches, with a statement of your central idea. You explore the situation with an image linked to the idea. And when you write your opening lines to introduce the character, you echo the voice of the storyteller, perhaps heard in childhood, because you know you can change it later, when you rewrite.

Cinderella is a great character to use as an example for your own work. She has tenacity, drive, and incredible staying power. The theme of her story, rags to riches, provides clear direction for her movement in the story: up from the cinders. The moral—hard work and honesty will get you through—has wide audience appeal.

The Cinderella myth appears in many different incarnations. In *My Fair Lady*, she's Liza, a cocky cockney lass with an accent that inspires Professor Henry Higgins to play Fairy Godmother before she transforms him into her Handsome Prince. In *Working Girl*, a feature film of the late eighties, she's Tess, a sharp secretary from Staten Island who builds her own on-ramp into fast-track high finance on New York's Money Row. The Cinderella character crosses cultural boundaries: in Germany she is little *Aschenbrödel*, in France she is *la petite Cendrillon*.

When you create your women characters, there's a good chance you'll borrow, either consciously or unconsciously, from the character of Cinderella. Here's why:

First, her beauty, concealed by metaphorical cinders, enables her to be reborn when she gets cleaned up. This dressing ritual, the wardrobe change and the makeup job, links Cinderella to a wide range of readers. If you live in society, you know the pressures of dressing the part. Second, under all the layers of costume, Cinderella is afraid. She's afraid of being alone. Her father's dead, gone away. She's afraid she will never love again. She's afraid of the power her stepmother has over her. Without voicing it, Cinderella lets us know by her actions that she wants out. Her father's house, now in the hands of the Wicked Stepmother, is her trap. To solve the problem, to escape the trap, her only course is to land herself a Prince. Third, landing the Prince will give Cinderella her safe harbor.

Let's use this for your character: Cinderella, driven by fear, wants to get to a safe place.

What Do Your Characters Want?

Wants is the key word when you create character. If you can answer a couple of questions early in the writing—What does my character *want*? What's stopping her from getting it?—your deep work on character will pay off fast.

Professional novelists make "wants lists" for their characters. The wants list sets up conflict. Take this simple example: A wife wants her husband to share his grief; the husband, however, wants to stay buttoned up, tight as a high collar on a stiff starched shirt. Their desires, telescoped on the stage of your story into clashing agendas, produce conflict. Conflict produces heat, excitement, drama. Drama, that spark of emotion that kindles the story, making us laugh, making us weep, is what audiences pay good money for. Good drama educates. It provides an escape hatch from the grim stuff of everyday.

Drama for your novel starts with character. What drives her? What does she want? How badly does she want it? What's in her way? What will she give up to get it? How does she handle the obstacles in her path?

Character and Motive

The word we use to talk about character wants and needs is *motive*. Motive comes from the Latin verb *movere*, meaning to move.

A motive is an emotion or a desire or a need that incites a person to act. The wife who wants her husband to share his grief, to open up to her (if not the world), knows in her heart he'll be better off if he agrees to open up. The wife grew up sharing emotions with her young female peers. As an adult, sharing makes her feel better. From her perspective, everyone should share.

The husband, on the other hand, won't open up because he's afraid of spilling his guts. He grew up in a world of male competition where sharing was thought to be sissy. From his perspective, tough guys don't talk, except to keep score.

Their differing perspectives—built on experiences from their respective pasts—produce conflict: the wife's need (to be open, to share) clashes with the husband's need (to be strong, to compete, to be a man).

Clashes like these, while they might seem bland and everyday, make excellent drama for a novel. This particular clash produces the conflict in Anne Tyler's opening scene for *The Accidental Tourist*, which we'll be examining in detail later.

As a novelist, you look to yourself first for answers. You read. You study the world and how it affects you. You live in the world; hence, you have needs. There's someone or something blocking your way to satisfying those needs. To find out about your characters and their needs, probe your own life, your own motives. You need love. How does this need for love feel to you? How does it manifest itself in your feelings? In your actions? Your character needs love. How does it manifest itself in your character's feelings and actions? Are her actions the same as yours? Are they different?

As a novelist, you probe the lives of people around you—parents, family, friends, enemies, neighbors, co-workers—searching for motives. And when you find the right motive, the perfect pitch of a motive, it makes your character hum. A character that hums at a high enough pitch will drive your whole novel.

The perfect motive is often right under your nose. Let's say your mother is a woman who loves to entertain. Nothing stops her from having people to dinner. Nothing thrills her more than throwing a party. Looking closely, you can see the action, party, party, party. But what *motive* lies behind the symbolism of fine china and gleaming candelabra that once belonged to Grandma? What does your mother *want* from this endless chain of parties? Does she want love? Acceptance? One-upping the Joneses? Community? Is she showing off? Is she afraid to be alone?

As a writer, to discover motive, probe *action* in the people around you. Understanding your mother and your spouse and your boss and your lover and your children will help you understand your characters.

Characters and Character Roles

Characters have roles that set up expectations for how they operate in your novel. Your protagonist, for example, is the lead character and most traditional lead characters, like Shane, Bambi, Wonder Woman, Samson, Tarzan, and Cinderella, are good guys. They are heroes. They are heroines. Their hearts are pure. They fight the good fight and they win in the end.

The obstacle, the character who stands in the way, blocking the journey (need, want, desire) of the protagonist, is the antagonist. *Anti-*

means against, and you produce drama in your story by pitting the protagonist (representing good) *against* the antagonist (representing evil).

Cinderella, the protagonist of the story that bears her name, wants to dance at the Royal Ball. Her desire, simple enough on the surface, is opposed by the Wicked Stepmother, an archetypal antagonist whose presence in the world of fairy tale has given the word *stepmother* a bitter taste in the real world.

To make your conflict more interesting, to give it body and depth, you bring on minor characters, lesser lights doing the hard work of playing supporting roles. When your protagonist is outnumbered by a gang of antagonists, you can recruit a helper character to even the odds. Cinderella, outnumbered by the Wicked Stepmother and the Ugly Stepsisters, dials the cosmos for help; in a puff of perfumed face-powder, the Fairy Godmother appears onstage, eager to help. Since it's economical to exploit what you bring onstage, you now explore the character of the Fairy Godmother. She's bubbly, giddy, magical, forget-ful. What if you turned her into a clown, a lovable bungler with a weakness?

To exploit a particular character trait, let's look at the plot of *Cinderella,* where the Fairy Godmother, all in a tizzy about makeup and wardrobe, fails to make it super clear to our heroine that the magic really does run out at midnight. This glitch, a character flaw discovered in the helper, drives the middle section of *Cinderella,* all the way to midnight, the tolling of the royal clock, the transformation of coach back into pumpkin, the end of the dream.

As a writer, examine a character trait, like the on-again, off-again quality of the Fairy Godmother, and you ask yourself this question: How can I make better use of this trait in my story?

What if, for example, your character was a nearsighted waiter too vain to wear glasses? A coach who hated sports? A secretary with computer phobia? An absentminded professor? A dog trainer who hates dogs?

That last example, the dog trainer who hates dogs, gave Anne Tyler the helper character for *The Accidental Tourist*. Her name is Muriel

Pritchett. She's pulled onstage by a problem, a dog belonging to the protagonist, who attacks innocent people. Muriel uses the dog to land the protagonist, Macon Leary, an isolated guy badly in need of someone to crack open his glass shell. If we step back, pulling away for a wider view, Muriel's help resembles the help of the Fairy Godmother in *Cinderella*. *Tourist* takes a new twist on the Cinderella character because of Muriel's motivation: afraid that she will never be loved, that she will never be secure, Muriel sets her intuitive sights on Macon. At the end of the story, when Macon says, *"Arrêtez,"* ordering the Paris taxi to stop for Muriel, he becomes for a moment the Handsome Prince, while she is transformed by her goodness and trust: Fairy Godmother becomes Cinderella.

Finding Motivation for Your Character

Wants, a small five-letter word, is your key for unlocking motive. Motive gives your characters a reason to act. Their actions, what they do, puts them in conflict with themselves, with each other, and, sometimes, with the universe. Conflict drives the novel.

If you take the time to dig down into character, you'll come up with a core motive for the conflict.

To dig into a character, first give her a name, for example, Susie. Then ask questions: What does Susie want? Does she want children? A family? Money? Romance? A house with a white picket fence? A condo on the beach? To marry a politician who becomes President so she can be First Lady?

Answers, written out in your notebook, again in what-if form, unearth motivation: What if Susie was born poor? What if her deep drive is for economic security? What if her first target is a handsome man with money? What if her second target is any man with money, handsome or not?

A few ifs and what-ifs lead you to discoveries about character which point directly to a fictional situation: for example, you find that Susie, who has certain Cinderellaesque traits, wants to escape from her poor-girl past.

OTHER IDEAS ABOUT CHARACTER

Building Character through Discovery

If you've looked at how-to books on fiction, you've probably run across rules for doing things. Most of these rules are handed down from the Greeks, lessons learned from playwrights like Sophocles and Euripides, which were then canonized by Aristotle in his *Poetics,* and subsequently used as yardsticks by critics to measure a finished work.

Aristotle left us with four labels for defining character—*good, appropriate, like, consistent.* "There will always be an element of character," Aristotle says, "if . . . what a person says or does reveals a certain moral purpose; and a good element of character if a person so revealed is good." I like this idea—action revealing moral purpose—but Aristotle slides past me when he tries to define "good element" as the revelation arising from an abstract *good.* Good, he says, is good revealed. While this circular definition, good rising from itself, might be helpful to a critic, its function in the creative process is limited.

One of Aristotle's heirs was novelist E. M. Forster, who wrote a book called *Aspects of the Novel,* in which he compressed the four labels of Aristotle into round characters and flat characters: "The test of a round character," Forster says, "is whether it is capable of surprising in a convincing way. If it never surprises it is flat. Flat characters . . . in their purest form . . . are constructed round a single idea or quality; when there is more than one factor toward them, we get the beginning of a curve toward the round."

In *Writing Fiction,* Janet Burroway does a super job of exploring the character labels from both Aristotle and Forster. After her examination of character labels, Burroway suggests that the way through this labyrinth of labels (and the starchy *rules for writers* that they imply) is to do a lot of preparatory work in your writer's notebook: "Whoever catches your attention may be the beginning of a character. . . . Start with what you observe, the obvious traits of type—age, gender, color, class. Try to capture a gesture or the messages that features and clothing send. Invent a reason for that harshness or that loneliness; invent a past."

Burroway's comment supports the *discovery method* you'll be using to build your novel. To heighten your chances for discovery, you write fast, trading control for the heat of creation. You make lists, sketches, diagrams. You write three sentences while you search for the right one because you don't know until you write it, until you stitch it into the fabric of your novel, whether the sentence works or not. After you write hot, you step back to breathe, to let the prose cool. Then, and only then, do you edit.

Rules, whether inherited from Aristotle or compressed by Forster, don't help you discover much while you're sweating out the writing. Where they do help is in editing and rewriting, the next important step after discovery. Too many writing rules stifle you, stifle your character, stifle your writing. Discovery writings should flow wild and free, like white birds loosed from the cage. If, while you write, you worry about rules for character, the rules will chill your writing hand and freeze your sentences cold.

To energize your discovery process, to give yourself permission to discover, work with what comes up on the page. If you bring a character onstage semirehearsed and only half-dressed, without knowing what she's doing there, don't kill yourself when she flubs a dialogue line. Now that your character is onstage, give her some attention. What is she doing with her hands? If she's adjusting the strings on her tennis racquet, this could be a tennis court. If this is a tennis court, it's summer, it's hot, Midwest hot, blistering sun and heavy humidity. If it's summer, what is she wearing? If she's wearing a designer tennis dress, she could have money. If, however, she's wearing faded Levi's cutoffs, she could be poor. If she's a rebel, she could be dressing in cutoffs to flaunt the all-white dress code. To find out, let her *react* to the situation. How does it feel wearing Levi's cutoffs and a baggy T-shirt when your opponent across the net wears a pretty designer tennis dress? Does it make her smug? Embarrassed? Afraid? Angry enough to play harder?

As you track these characters through the opening pages of your manuscript, trying to *discover* what they're doing here, you keep asking questions: Who are these people? Where are they going? What do they *want*? What's stopping them? How smart are they? Where are they coming from? How well do they know each other? Whose story is this?

In an essay on her work novelist Joan Didion asks similar questions about the characters from *A Book of Common Prayer*. Then she adds: "Let me tell you one thing about why writers write: had I known the answers to any of these questions I would never have needed to write a novel." (From *The Writer on Her Work*, Vol. I)

WHERE TO START

The First Four Weekends

Weekends 1 through 4 introduce you to Character Work, preparing your characters to enter your story, while at the same time giving you a taste of the discipline you'll need to become a writer. There are four tasks, one for each weekend—sketch, back story, dream, wardrobe—all devoted to one character, a Stranger in the Room.

The character sketch on Weekend 1 gives you a set of observed exteriors—hairdo, clothes, build, gestures—and a chance to expand the character's range with a little creative guesswork about home, family, and life-style.

The back story on Weekend 2 drops you through a trapdoor into the character's past. Here, writing to unearth motivation, you probe childhood trauma.

The dream on Weekend 3 takes you through a doorway into the character's mind. As dreamers, we cannot control our dreams. As writers, we can use dreams to better understand our characters through symbols.

Wardrobe on Weekend 4 returns your character from the world of dream and symbol to the world of exteriors, where clothes and makeup define for her a specific life-style and income. If, in the back story on Weekend 2, you discover that your character was born poor, then the lavish life-style in the wardrobe scene (your character is off to a cocktail party, a debut, a royal ball), takes on the logic of cause-and-effect. She wanted it; she got it. Then you ask: What else does she want? She has everything, right? What's standing in her way?

Your first goal in character work is to develop three characters: one protagonist, one antagonist, and one helper. The protagonist is the most important character—she's the lead, the one your readers will identify with—but because the world can be a slippery place, not always under your control, the protagonist may not appear, on command, in your first sketch.

For that reason, keep the window of opportunity open as you write. Develop your characters; get to know them. Line up their motives on your wants list. Cast them into roles and bring them onstage, where action and dialogue and scene will allow you to know them better. Remember that you're just starting out. This is the beginning, not the end. You write fast to get it down and then you see what you've got, making discoveries in your writing now so you can rewrite later with style and precision. Stay open to learning as you go. Keep writing. As Oakley Hall says in *The Art and Craft of Novel Writing*:

> The character must be produced on the page, whole and alive, his breath congealing on the air. It is not necessary that we know instantly what he *is*, for it is the process of learning about him that interests us. As in the representation of any living reality, characterization is rooted in detail. It is the trifles and what they imply or reveal that create the living entity.

• WEEKEND 1 •
CHARACTER SKETCH

A character sketch is a word outline, a preliminary study of a person, drawn from life experience, that you'd like to use in your novel. A sketch is an audition on paper. You measure the person, writing down what you can see. You note each detail—height, weight, figure, hairdo, gesture, et cetera. Work fast. Use buzzwords and catch phrases. A character sketch is not about perfecting your sentence structure, but is an attempt to build a human foundation for characters in your novel. This work will train your novelist's eye, moving you from real detail (concrete observations of living persons) to assumed detail (value judgments that define your fictional characters). This process is what I like to call "creative guesswork." In creative guesswork, you invade the privacy of a Stranger to make writerly assumptions about the life-style of your character.

You do character sketches to practice pulling useful traits from the real world onto the page, where you combine them with character qualities from your reading experience. You might begin with a concrete observation about externals—your Stranger, wearing a designer tennis dress and a Rolex watch, strides to her Jaguar—and expand the sketch with an assumption based on behavior: as your Stranger races to the aid of a victim being harassed in the parking lot, you conclude that she is courageous. Working the sketch, you jot down external details and internal qualities of your Stranger and begin your creative guesswork. For example, your Stranger, a modern-day Cinderella who witnesses the victimization of another, puts aside what she's attained to rush to the aid of the victim. In that moment of action, a story lurks, waiting to be explored.

But there's more. The external details (the watch, dress, and car) tell us that your Cinderella has already gotten a piece of her revenge, a bit of what she wants from life. To create problems for her, you simply sketch an antagonist who wants to take away her ritzy life-style.

Although the character sketch is a quick exercise, it is very important. Writing down the details of your characters places them in your unconscious—we've discussed this already in "Writing Tips"—where they work for you. Fifteen minutes out of your weekend and you've got a snapshot in words of a Stranger who might become a character who might drive the novel that makes you famous.

Example

The sketch below comes from a Stranger in the Room across the aisle from me in traffic school. It took ten minutes. I began with visual details, things physical, and since I was working well that day, I kept the pen moving while I made assumptions about her life-style. I moved right into "creative guesswork." From a ten-minute sketch, this

Stranger blossomed into Susannah Maxwell, a major character for my novel *The Hit Man Cometh*.

Sketch: Stranger in the Room

Height: 5′ 11″/Weight: 140

Sex: Female

Hair: dark blond, shoulder-blade length; swings when she moves

Dress: Peach, calf length, shoulder pads

Body: lean, catlike, lissome, smooth, liquid; drapes herself over the chair; sits with legs out straight, ankles crossed, like a man, lots of confidence

Shoes: white high-heeled pumps

Face: long, like a Modigliani, with a certain aesthetic leanness

Mouth: wide, full, promise of sensuality

Poses:

> hands folded, elbows on chair in front of her, chin resting on hands
> Lies down on chair, reclines, turns chair into a chaise longue or recliner—in a public place, this suggests eroticism.
> Yawns, stretches, writes in a daytimer, opens her purse, pulls out a mirror, checks her makeup, frowns at what she sees.
> Right leg does a dance with the left tap tap tap—shoe half off, hanging from her big toe tap tap tap.

Build: thin through the shoulder blades, slender throat

Arms: tanned, hairs bleached white-blond by the sun

Legs: trim, slender, athletic (she works out)

Imperfections: gap between two front teeth; overbite; weak lower back; loves to manipulate people for her own desires

Age: 32–34

Birth date: December 22, 1953–55; Sagittarius

Birthplace: Midwest/Chicago/Evanston

Home (imaginary): Spyglass Hill

> Fountain, Jacuzzi, waterfall, mezzanine; curved staircase;
> sterile kitchen; chrome, like a four-star restaurant
> French provincial furniture

Favorite room: She lives in her upstairs lair, with computer that spits out election data from across the country from a service called Election Central—small kitchen and fridge here—no one comes in here without her invitation (especially the villain/ antagonist); easy chairs; sun deck for sunning; this room faces the Pacific, rear of house

View out the window: Tennis court to the southeast, swimming pool, party patio

Five fireplaces; one in her lair upstairs

Habits: likes exercise; does not care about cooking

Vehicle: Jaguar, BMW, Mercedes, ten-speed bike

Name the character: Sue, Susannah, Susan, Susie, Suze, Sooze

Motive: What does the character *want*? Security. Freedom from want. Safety. To be held. To be wanted for herself. To be loved.

Guidelines to Doing the Sketch

A sketch is your bare-bones outline, built on specific detail— female, tall, blond hair, peach dress, catlike moves—which builds to creative guesswork, where you allow your imagination to fill out the frame of your outline: a home on Spyglass Hill (Newport Beach, California); a tennis court; a Jacuzzi; five fireplaces; one Jaguar; one BMW; one Mercedes.

Possessions are a clue to life-style. This Stranger gets richer, or seems to, with every new toy added to the sketch. The property, the ritziest location in already ritzy Newport Beach, would have a value of $4–$6 million. The tennis court and Jacuzzi smack of luxury, as do the five fireplaces, and the expensive cars. Her upstairs lair holds secrets. There's a story behind the computer. What's it doing there?

As you sketch in these details, moving from things you can see to things you only imagine in your mind's eye, you build a profile of a person from the outside. You keep the sketch focused on exteriors. It doesn't take a lot of time, ten minutes, maybe fifteen, to write down the details. But there's a lot you don't know yet. You don't know, for example, about family, friends, parents, siblings. You don't know which car she drives. You don't know who else drives these cars.

This is important. Not knowing gives you a reason to know. Not knowing triggers your mind to ask questions that get behind the details: Who drives the Jaguar? Who drives the BMW? Who else lives in this huge house? Who is the villain/antagonist who can't come into this room? Her husband? A friend of the husband? A business acquaintance?

Do several sketches, training your writer's eye to focus on physical details. You will get better with practice and you'll do sketches as long as you're a writer. It's a nice movement: your eye sees, your hand records. The sketch teaches you, again and again, to make use of what's in the world around you. And with each sketch, you're hoping to turn this Stranger in the Room into the character who drives your novel.

WORKING THE NOVEL

Exercises

1. *Stranger in the Room.*
Take your writer's notebook to a public place—a café, a restaurant, a bar, a library, a waiting room, a zoo—and do three character sketches as you eyeball strangers. Use the categories from the chart on the next page: height, weight, hair, dress, body, shoes, face, mouth, poses, arms, legs, imperfections, age, birthplace, birth date, birth sign, home, and so on.

2. *What-If.*
What-if questions set your character in motion. You can ask random questions, out-of-the-blue queries that give your character a

specific problem to solve: What if she was hit by a car? What if she went to a party and met someone? What if she was caught shoplifting? What if she wakes up in jail? In a strange bed?

Or you can ask questions that work in sequence: What if she was born poor? What if she gets revenge by marrying well? What if her husband dies, leaving her in debt? What if the antagonist buys a bank that buys her mortgage loan? What if the payments are exorbitant, even for her? What if the antagonist offers to turn over the loan papers in return for certain favors? What if the favors are sexual? What if she's unwilling to deliver those favors? What if she knows the antagonist from before? Where did they meet? What was their relationship?

Ask the question, then let the answers spin out. What-if questions are good for story development and for character continuity.

3. Casting Director.

Cast your characters now. You've done three sketches. One Stranger looks good for the protagonist. One looks like a super helper/catalyst. The antagonist looks iffy, so you ask more what-if questions. If that doesn't sharpen your character, try another sketch. You will have to live with your characters for another fifty-one weeks, so cast accordingly now. This is the protagonist, you can write, and this is the helper/catalyst, and so on.

Filling in the Sketch
Height/Weight:

Sex:

Hair:

Dress:

Body:

Shoes:

Face:

Mouth:

Poses:

> hands/gestures
> feet/legs
> torso/head

Build:

Arms/Legs:

Imperfections:

Age:

Birth date:

Birthplace:

Home (imaginary):

> exterior/grounds/outbuildings/spas/etc./
> interior/furnishings/carpets/floors/lighting

Favorite Room:

View out the window:

Habits:

Vehicles:

Name:

Motive: What does the character *want*?

Learning from Other Writers

Sometimes your characters behave. You cast them into roles—protagonist, antagonist, helper, victim, clown, et cetera—and they stay happily put. At other times, they change roles as you write. You bring on a helper; she tries to take over the book. As we'll see later on, this happened to Anne Tyler in *Tourist* when Muriel Pritchett took over Act Two.

Sometimes your characters back away from center stage, easing out of the spotlight to take refuge in the shadows. That happened to F. Scott Fitzgerald and his character Jay Gatsby, the Man from the West who wants to capture Daisy Fay Buchanan, the Girl from the East.

The Great Gatsby was done. Fitzgerald sent it to his editor, the legendary Maxwell Perkins at Scribner's. Perkins liked the book, but he found the character of Gatsby vague, dim, shadowy. Gatsby felt older than he was, Perkins said. There was no satisfactory explanation for his vast wealth. The face-off between Tom Buchanan (Daisy's husband) and Gatsby in the Plaza Hotel in New York City—the scene that precedes Daisy's killing of Myrtle Wilson with Gatsby's yellow car—sagged because Tom was forced to spar with an opponent who danced in the shadows.

After wrestling with himself and his character, Fitzgerald came up with more on Gatsby. He enlarged the character in detail. He brought Gatsby's bootlegging profession into the foreground. But it wasn't easy. And in this letter from Fitzgerald to Perkins (quoted in *Max Perkins*, by A. Scott Berg), you can see how close he came to giving up on Gatsby: "My first instinct after your letter was to let him [Gatsby] go & have Tom Buchanan dominate the book . . . but Gatsby sticks in my heart. I had him for awhile then lost him & now I have him again."

Gatsby's character made Fitzgerald famous—even today this is regarded as his best book—but look how close he came to dumping his protagonist. The lesson here is once you have a cast, stick tight to your characters. "I myself didn't know," Fitzgerald wrote to Perkins, "what Gatsby looked like or was engaged in. . . ." A question to ponder: Was Jay Gatsby, Fitzgerald's central character, still in sketch form when he entered the novel that bears his name? Did he come into focus when Fitzgerald probed Gatsby's back story?

You can learn from Fitzgerald's mistake. Work the details to bring your characters out of the shadows and onto your stage. In return, they'll repay you a thousandfold.

DURING THE WEEK

Looking Ahead to Writing the Back Story

To find motivation, you probe the past of the character. To probe the past of your character, you need an entry point, a doorway that gives you access to the past. To give yourself a choice of doorways, take a few moments during the week to make a list of dates for your character. Start with the date of birth. Let's say the age of your character is thirtysomething. The novel you're writing is a contemporary, set in the present time. Choose a number, 35, then subtract from the current year, 19––. The birth date for your character is 19––. Working up from the birth date, you can develop key dates in the life of your character. Here's an example:

> 1957—born, Skokie, Illinois
> 1963—mother dies
> 1969—first sexual experience, boyfriend of aunt, called "uncle"?
> 1972—first love, a rich boy; jilted/hurt
> 1972—first win, tennis tournament, Lake Forest
> 1975—university/political science major/meets villain
> 1978—grad school (choices: Northwestern, Michigan, UCLA)
> 1980—marriage to a wealthy man
> 1981—moves to posh neighborhood (California, Newport Beach)
> 1984—villain and husband do business deals
> 1985—husband borrows $$$$ from villain; (collateral: house)
> 1987—husband dies
> 1988—problem as story opens, villain pressures her for sexual favors, using the house as leverage

A list of dates opens doorways into the past of your character. When you write your back story on Weekend 2, you'll have several possible starting places to choose from.

· WEEKEND 2 ·
BACK STORY

The Stranger that you used for your character sketch has a past, a personal history. The term we use for talking about the past in fiction is *back story*. Back story is what has happened before the character is introduced. You don't need to create an entire history. You write what you need to unearth character motives.

Before she showed up, dressed, to pose for your character sketch, your "Cinderella" Stranger (let's call her Susie) was somewhere else. She took time to bathe and dress and apply makeup. Outside this room where she poses, she has a life. Your job is to use creative guesswork to establish where she came from, not only in space but also in time. What happened twenty years ago that imprinted her psyche, stamping it with a character trait?

Secrets lurk in the past and influence how people behave in the present. When you first spot Susie, she looks spiffy sitting there, composed, tastefully clothed, a person who has it all together. But what secrets is she hiding? What juicy stuff can you create for her past that will provide motivation for her character in your novel?

To find out, you play *what-if.*

What if she went to college and flunked out? What if she was made pregnant by a professor? What if the professor, who was married, got her kicked out of school? Does she still want revenge? To heighten the drama, you deepen the pain. What if she had an abortion that almost killed her? Or try a logical extension of the "Cinderella" Susie character of your character sketch—her blue-collar background. What if she ran out of money and the only way she could make it through school was to sell her body? What if she sold her body, not out of economic necessity, but because she scorns men? What if she takes money from men to exact her own special revenge on the entire male race? Why is she getting revenge?

The *what-if* boils down to motive. Writing back story is a process of constructing character motivations. You unearth motives for your characters the same way a psychotherapist would unearth them for your mother or yourself. You ask questions. You dig into the past and find trauma.

Trauma in childhood leaves us helpless and afraid. Fear makes us cold. We can't move. We cry a lot. We withdraw inside ourselves by building our own protective box. We sit inside and observe the madness of the world from a position of relative safety. We think about getting even: *When I grow up,* we think, *I'm gonna show them. . . .* We think about getting away: *When I grow up*, we think, *I'm gonna get so far away from here....* The ways we cope with trauma determine our character traits. If we run from our trauma, we may be cowardly, distant, skittish; depending on the severity of the offense, any number of traits might surface.

If you get stuck when writing back story, think of trauma. It will put you back on the track to discovering motive.

Example: Susie's Back Story

Her mother died when Susie was six, so she moved out of the house in Skokie and went to live with Aunt Rosa in Chicago. Her brother Lonnie went to live with Gran—that's where Susie wanted to go because Gran lived in the country in Wisconsin—but Lonnie died in an accident on the ice that next winter, leaving Susie sad and alone.

So her mother died and she switched schools and left her old friends and sleepwalked through life. She was an ugly duckling with straggly hair colored dishwater-blond and buckteeth and hand-me-down clothes. One night when she was eleven she got a toothache and lay in bed crying, biting the corner of her pillow to push back the pain.

Her uncle Gabe raped her when she was twelve. It was Labor Day, the last Monday before school started, the last day of summer. Uncle Gabe was not really her uncle, just a friend who sometimes stayed all night in Aunt Rosa's bedroom. Uncle Gabe had thick hands and square fingers and he smelled of whiskey and cigarettes and stale sweat. A long hank of hair, black and slick with hair oil, hung down across his forehead to the left eyebrow. He'd been staring at Susie all year, but staring more this summer when she wore the cutoff jeans so her legs would turn brown in the short northern summer. She wore cutoff jeans and a shirt with the sleeves torn out and shoes with no socks and her hair in a ponytail that she could feel swinging behind her back. She went around the house humming "Age of Aquarius" from *Hair*. She fell in love with Robert Redford after seeing him play Sundance in the movies. That summer when she was twelve she got a job in the library reshelving books that paid twenty-five cents an hour. She was thrifty. She knew how to save. But she did not know how to stop Uncle Gabe when he found her in the bathroom where the door lock was broken on that Monday afternoon, the last day of summer, the last day of her innocence, coming in to relieve himself smelling of beer and finding her on the john with her cutoffs down around her ankles so she couldn't move and seeing him grin, big teeth and ugly lips, and freezing because she saw in his eyes a line of women like robots lined up for Uncle Gabe, their bottoms exposed, their faces hidden, and when he grabbed her and turned her around she couldn't scream because he was choking her with his strong square fingers stuck into her throat, making her cry, and then she was where he wanted her, hands cold on the round edges of the lavatory, tasting her own tears and behind her the sound of Uncle Gabe's zipper and over that his breath coming through his nose which always needed blowing and she could tell he'd had practice doing this and all she wanted was to escape, split, get away, leave this awful ugly shitty . . .

Guidelines for Writing the Back Story

Again, your shortcut to finding motive is to go directly to childhood trauma. Think of yourself as a writer in search of motive (Susie hates men because she was raped as a child), and not as a parent mooning over a child or a therapist trying to help a patient. Assume the writer's attitude: curious, open minded, professional, slightly hard edged. Watch the internal editor. Work fast now. You can rewrite later.

Follow this pattern when you write your back story. Begin with an overview, then move in closer to the trauma. In the writing, include cause and effect—when Susie is six, her mother's death forces her to live with her aunt; the aunt, we find out, has boyfriends; the trouble starts here. Add lesser but influential traumas to fill out other traits of your character sketch: Susie's toothache at age eleven, with no one to comfort her, tells us Susie is a brave kid.

In the first couple of sentences we zoom across the years, from ages six to eleven to twelve, to arrive at Labor Day of Susie's twelfth year. The "doorway" to this moment in Susie's life came from the chronology entry in the notebook that we made last weekend: *1969— first sexual experience, boyfriend of aunt, called "uncle"?*

There are other back-story doorways—the death of Susie's mother; falling in love; being jilted by a rich boy; the death of Susie's husband—but choosing a rape at the age of twelve provides the writer with the ultimate act of violation. It's awful and it's ugly, but because of the deep trauma, it's the perfect place to start focusing on back story for the character. This kind of experience, buried in the back story, unearthed by what-ifs, drives the character, who, in turn, drives the book.

In our Susie example, the writing moves from the early highlights of Susie's life to focus on the rape itself—fear and ugly foreplay and the helplessness of the Susie character. In this example, the adult has power over the child, something most people recall from their own lives. Watching Uncle Gabe move in, we have the impression, implied though unsaid here, that Susie will get no help from Aunt Rosa, that the molestations will continue until Susie escapes from this ugly world. We use sensory detail to close in on the event. Biting, smelling, and sound help to sharpen the word picture. Details about Uncle Gabe's appearance—whiskey smell, cigarette smell, hair slick with oil, thick hands, square fingers—narrow the focus as we edge toward the moment in the bathroom. In a close-up of Gabe's eyes, Susie sees her fate symbolized in the women lined up for Gabe's pleasure. As Susie grips the edge of the lavatory, her hands are *cold*, one more sensory detail.

Back Story Research

For the cultural detail and historical continuity—the references to the "Age of Aquarius" and Robert Redford—you can research the year 1969 in *Timetables of History,* mentioned as one of the books for your bookshelf. The chronology you did during the past week locates Susie's birth date in 1957, which makes her twelve years old in 1969. *Hair* was big that year—"Age of Aquarius" was the hit song—and in another cultural groove altogether, Robert Redford played Sundance in *Butch Cassidy and the Sundance Kid*.

The back story stops before the rape itself. You want to focus on fear and foreplay and the helplessness of your character. In this example, the adult has power over the child, something that you probably recall from your own life.

In the back story, you probe the darkness that lurks in all of us. In the book, you work out the effects of that dark memory. If you were to include this scene in the book, you might want to amplify the details from *Timetables:* she has an argument with someone about her crush on Robert Redford. Uncle Gabe smashes the radio because he gets tired of hearing songs from *Hair*.

WORKING THE NOVEL

Exercises

1. *Chronology: Dates as Doorways*.
Make a chronology of key dates for each main character.

During the previous week, you were asked to jot down key dates for one or two characters. Key dates give you doorways into the past, and it's a good idea to take the time to get your character chronologies into shape before diving into the past. A list of dates is like a ladder with easy steps connecting the past of each of your characters to the time when they enter your story. To find the birth date, you subtract the character's age from the time of your story. With the birth date to anchor your chronology, you jot down a list of dates and events from your character's life. First day of school, first kiss, first crush, parents' divorce, death of a parent, first job interview, first job, first traumatic experience, death of a friend, high school graduation, military service, wedding night. Allow the images to roll as you probe the past.

2. *Writing the Back Story*.
Working from one key date in the chronology, write back stories for each of your main characters. You begin with an overview, and then move more deeply into the scene that becomes a turning point in your character's past. My suggestion is to time yourself, writing in the notebook for ten to fifteen minutes on each charac-

ter. Practice locking your writing down with one or more of the five senses: hearing, taste, touch, smell, sight.

Take a short break. Close your eyes. Breathe deeply. Then enter the material from your notebook into the word processor. Writing on the keyboard changes the rhythm and often produces new insights to add to the ones from the notebook.

3. *Wants List.*
Print out what you have written. As you read it over, start a wants list. What does Character A want? What does Character B want? How do their wants clash? Where in the story do their wants clash? Keep adding to your wants list as more characters emerge.

4. *Stay Organized.*
Complete back-story work for all the characters that you sketched on Weekend 1 and place them in their appropriate folders. Have fun. Make their lives interesting and dynamic.

Learning from Other Writers

Take a moment to see what you can learn by studying Tyler's handling of the past in *The Accidental Tourist*. The traumatic problem that begins the book is the death of Ethan, the only son of Macon and Sarah Leary. He's been dead a year or so, but the first references to Ethan's death appear briefly in a dialogue line in Chapter One: "Macon, now that Ethan's dead I sometimes wonder if there's any point to life."

What can you learn from this? First, by referring to the past in dialogue, Tyler maintains the pace of this efficient first chapter. The conflict builds; there is no slackening of drama. Second, Sarah's tone informs us she's weary, on the edge. Part of Tyler's strategy is to set up Macon, a victim of many blindnesses, to not see Sarah's mood. Third, as the subtext of grief bunches beneath the dialogue, the back story pokes up through the fabric of the scene like sharp-pointed sticks, pinpricks in the skin that torture the characters. Their separate reactions to

Ethan's death (she wants Macon to open up; he wants to stay isolated) provides early conflict, forcing her out of the house, which makes his problem worse. With her subtle reference to the back story, Tyler reveals Macon's and Sarah's motives.

In your own life, you probably know people like this. The wife wants to share. The husband doesn't. He hides inside himself. He likes it inside here, inside this glass bubble from which, safe, he can look out.

Think about Tyler's use of back story. Later in the novel, we learn that Macon is motivated to get revenge on his mother, flaky Alicia, because she married an engineer, thereby sending the Leary children off to live with their grandparents in Baltimore: "He [Macon] recalled his childhood as a glassed-in place with grown-ups rushing past, talking at him, making changes, while he himself stayed mute." Macon's revenge, against Mom, against Sarah, against Miriam, is his glass cage. Holing up inside here, afraid of connecting with the pain of losing his son, Macon gets even with his past.

Think about this motive for one of your characters: getting even with the past keeps them going in the present.

DURING THE WEEK

Looking Ahead to Dream

The earliest *dramas* were sacred/magical, performed in honor of each of the seasons (spring, summer, autumn, winter), with the same pattern of progression to each story: challenge of the hero, trial, marriage, sacrifice, and resurrection.

According to Barbara Walker, in her *Woman's Encyclopedia of Myths and Secrets,* one object of this early hero-drama was "attainment of religious ecstasy: entering into the 'dream.' "

One of the joys of fiction writing is discovering links, in plot and character, in word and concept and metaphor and task. When you succeed in making drama (using the trauma of your characters to help your audience/reader escape through the fictional dream you have created), your words reach back to those first dramas—torchlight, a primitive stage, costumes made from animal skins—where masked actors sweat to get their lines right.

As a writer, you sweat the same way: to get your lines right.

· **WEEKEND 3** ·
DREAM

Writing a dream, because it empowers you to begin digging deep into your character's mind, is a nice balance for the character sketch, which gives you the exterior and interior surfaces (the possessions and behavior that define your character's life-style).

Your write dreams for your characters for at least three reasons:

First, it's a shortcut inside, a window to the soul, that helps you learn more about your characters. It brings you close to the players in your novel. If F. Scott Fitzgerald had written a dream for Jay Gatsby, he might never have thought of replacing him with Tom Buchanan.

Second, dream writing enables you to work with images and symbols, where much of the power of writing is stored. If this is your first contact with symbolism, get ready to be rewired. My writing classes are packed with people who live in a world of symbols without seeing them. When they write dreams, using the start line that we will discuss shortly, "In the dream, I . . ." and they write for ten minutes without ending the sentence, they are surprised by the energy that pours out. They are surprised that the writing is so vibrant, so expressive, and so coherent. Writing dreams gives you an opportunity to explore the symbols that will take your readers into other worlds.

Third, writing dreams helps you to let go, to fly free without inhibition, to soar for a few moments on the wings of language. When you begin with the start line "In the dream, I . . ." your internal editor should be far away. This is Weekend 3 and you've been working hard, chipping away at the novel. It's time you had a little fun.

In the dream that follows, Susie gets revenge on Uncle Gabe.

Example: Susie's Dream

In the dream, she walked on air. In the dream, she walked on a cloud, fleecy and white with soft pink edges, into the kitchen. In the dream, she commanded the door of the fridge to open. "Open sesame," she said. The door swung open. In the dream, she saw the brand of the fridge. Borg something. In the fridge, she saw an egg with a yellow shell. It filled the top shelf, weighing it down, bending the metal. On the yellow egg were these words: *Eat me.* She got a hammer from the middle drawer by the stove. She raised the hammer and smashed down. She smashed the egg and a hole appeared. She kept smashing and smashing, tears in her eyes, the muscles quivering in her arms. Salt tears fell back into her throat, choking her. She grunted with each swing. The egg cracked open along the side. An arm reached for her. A voice called her name. It was Uncle Gabe's voice. She backed away from the egg, holding the hammer high, until she felt the edge of the sink cold against her back and by then Uncle Gabe was climbing out of the egg, the yellow shell fallen in crusty pieces and his body dripping with white goo, that stringy stuff that you get when the egg isn't cooked all the way and she wanted to run but her feet were stuck to the floor with egg yolk tough as yellow glue. Uncle Gabe climbed out of the egg and she saw that he didn't have any clothes on, just this goo dripping down off his chin and shoulders and chest, the dark hair matted, down to his belly button, and one slimy goo string drifting down his leg to his knee, and she raised the hammer as he came toward her grinning, big hands out, reaching for her, Uncle Gabe with the round eyes and the round face and the thick black hair on his head, the hair that Aunt Rosa liked, saying, "Hey, little dollie, hey," and she heard herself yelling, her voice like Mama's voice, Mama who was dead, "Damn you, Gabe. You stay away from me or I'll kill you, I swear it," and then he reached for her, his big arms roped with muscle, rubber arms like white tentacles, and she dodged and her feet popped loose from the yellow goo, her skin tight and screaming, and she ran for the door and almost made it but he caught her, his hand like a meat hook on her shoulder, his breath like old garbage, and she whirled, gripping the hammer, driving it into his face, smashing and smashing, the forehead cracking, a zigzag line, that pop like an eggshell cracking, and Uncle Gabe, eyes popping open in surprise, his chest circled by white rubber bands, and being jerked backwards yelling, "You bitch!" and Susie, laughing and hysterical, clutching the hammer, laughing and laughing, as the rubber bands contract, slamming him into the door frame, and then out the door.

Guidelines for Writing the Dream

Your goal is to write a dream that lets you explore inside the mind of your character, her wants and desires. Unlike the goals of the back story (from expansive narration to a focused trauma episode), the written dream can wheel across time and space—trip out to Xanadu, to Samarkand; visit a chocolate factory you've always wanted to explore. Broad narration affords you the opportunity to find hidden fantasies and to discover many different dimensions of your character.

You can also develop your dream like the back-story trauma sequence, where you narrow your focus to a single scene. Working in a single scene (Susie's dream takes place in the kitchen of her aunt's ratty little apartment) enables you to explore new levels of language while it leads you deep inside a specific element of your character. The best advice is to follow the words, keeping your internal editor at bay. If the dream wants to soar, go with it. If the dream wants to focus in tight on images and symbols, go with that.

Take ten minutes to speed-write the dream in your notebook, timing yourself, practicing letting go. Allow your creativity to take over.

Let's look at Susie's dream closely to see what kinds of patterns emerged:

The *beginning* of Susie's dream (as yours should) opens with parallel structure. Start each sentence with the phrase *In the dream*. Parallel structure is simple written repetition that makes it easy for you to start writing. Repetition of the key phrase keeps you focused on the dream task and helps you build momentum:

"In the dream, she. . . ."
"In the dream, she. . . ."

"In the dream, she. . . ."
"In the fridge, she. . . ."

The easy shift from dream to fridge, linked by parallels, brings on the egg, the first symbol. The words on the egg, *Eat me*, enrage Susie. Though she's only twelve, she understands the sexual message. Angry now, Susie hammers on the egg.

The *middle* of the dream, the central image, is the birth of the monster, Uncle Gabe coming out of the egg, then moving toward Susie in the slow-motion walk of nightmare.

In the *end* of the dream Susie calls out, using her mother's name, a child grasping for the power of the adult. The dream *climaxes* with an *action*—Uncle Gabe grabs her—and Susie's *reaction:* she tries to evade him. Since she can't evade, the dream whirls us into the final image: the hammer falling, Uncle Gabe's head cracking like an eggshell, the stringy white goo transformed into rubber bands that jerk him away. In the dream, at least, Susie has her revenge.

When you input your dream into your computer, you might discover the outlines of the three-part structure we see in Susie's dream—the classical *beginning, middle,* and *end*. Susie's dream also showcases three other writing strategies for you to borrow for your own work: *Repetition, logical sequence,* and *letting go*.

Repetition. When you repeat words in a passage, you form an echo effect. You let the words drift down through the writing like the recurring notes that make chords in a piece of music. If the repeated words are strung out, the echoes trailing like threads through a piece of cloth, repetition weaves a support fabric for the events in your story. When repetition bunches up to form word clusters, it hauls your images into the foreground, where they attract the attention of the reader. When you repeat a word, you're tagging it as important. When you fail to repeat a word, you take the risk of losing it in the jungle of words. If you use too much repetition, don't worry; you can trim the excess away when you rewrite.

The echo words in Susie's dream—*dream, fridge, hammer, egg, goo, white*—are everyday words angled in a kind of dream warp that works like boxes within boxes. The dream contains the fridge; the fridge contains the egg; the egg, a possible refuge or sanctuary for Susie, who desperately needs some kind of rebirth out of her situation (rebirth is one of the symbolic functions of the egg), contains her nemesis, Uncle Gabe. As she uses the hammer to hit the egg, we realize that the words *Eat me* were probably spoken by Uncle Gabe, before she had the dream. *White* is the color of egg-white, and also of Uncle Gabe's sickly flesh.

Logical Sequence. The rhythms of cause-and-effect stabilize the world as we know it. You turn the key; the lock opens. You feel cold air on your neck; the cold air makes you hunch down, pulling your coat collar tight.

Cause-and-effect, altered by dream magic, allows Susie to command the fridge door to open to reveal the egg. All is well: this universe works like a machine, with Susie at the controls. But problems appear at the command *Eat me,* which motivates Susie to grab the hammer to use on the egg. Rage blankets any surprise she might have exhibited. The action picks up when she smashes the egg with the hammer, with cause-and-effect still working as a hole appears in the shell. Susie has opened her own Pandora's box and logical sequence turns grim as Uncle Gabe climbs out of the egg. Inevitability rules now, the logic of cause-and-effect hurtling out of control: it's too late for the dreamer to reverse her actions. And because Susie, like all the king's men in the Humpty-Dumpty nursery rhyme, cannot put the egg back together again, she is forced to use the hammer on Uncle Gabe. Dream logic, built on a chain of images woven together by repetition, leads Susie to her terrible revenge.

Letting Go. The last sentence in the dream (beginning with "Uncle Gabe climbed out of the egg and . . .") is over a hundred words long. As the sentence expands, it gains momentum, building to the final image, Uncle Gabe grinning as he grabs Susie, and the climax, Susie smashing his forehead like an eggshell. As the sentence expands, moving past the hundred-word barrier, the central image expands, growing until it fills the screen: Uncle Gabe comes closer, grabbing Susie, his breath sickening. The message in this close-up is clear. He intends to rape her, giving her a reason to hit him with the hammer. This revenge fits. We want Susie to get even.

To help yourself let go when you're writing, you can use simple connectors—*and, then, and then, when, so, but*—and you can reincorporate key words and key actions, to create that sense of transformation that we understand as dreamlike. Near the climax of the dream, when Susie *smashes* Uncle Gabe with the *hammer,* his forehead cracks like an *egg*shell, reintroducing the egg. The stringy *white* goo is transformed into *white* rubber bands that jerk Susie's enemy out the door of her dream.

Practice these techniques as you write your characters' dreams.

WORKING THE NOVEL

Exercises

1. *Writing a Dream.*
Close your eyes and take a few deep breaths and let your mind roam free as it plays across images and symbols. Concentrate on your breathing, the rise and fall of your chest, that point on your nose where the air goes out. Examine the process of your breathing (this takes your mind off the real world). When you feel relaxed, open your eyes and make a list of symbols and images. For easy reference, keep a separate file of your symbols and images. When you can't think of any more, start a new dream. Take a couple of minutes to do the list. Use one of these three start-lines to write a dream for one of your characters:

> "In the dream, I . . ."
> "In the dream, he . . ."
> "In the dream, she . . ."

Write for ten or fifteen minutes, timing yourself to distract the internal editor. If you get stuck, repeat the start line, looping back, a kind of whipstitch with language. After you get rolling, allow your sentence to lengthen, expanding as it builds momentum.

When the timer rings, take a short break. Walk around. Breathe deeply. Don't talk to anyone. Don't read. Don't watch TV.

2. *Getting Close to Words.*
When you return from your break, circle the key words in your dream, using a colored pencil. Circling key words—the words that repeat—pulls you close to your language. When you have your key words circled, jot them down on a page in your notebook. At the top of the page, print "Symbols" and "Images." When a symbol or an image appears in your writing, add it to your list.

3. *Writing More Dreams.*
Write a dream for each of your main characters. Practice your deep breathing. If you didn't try a long sentence in your first dream, now is the time to do that. If you find that you need more direction, you can devise a list of symbols before you write the dream, adding associations to complete the loop of meaning. Here's an example from Susie's dream:

> *fridge:* cold, chilly, cage, suffocation
> *egg:* birth, embryo, yolk
> *hammer:* steel, heavy, strike
> *goo:* icky, white, glue, rubbery
> *yellow glue:* sticky, icky
> *shell:* cracked, thin, eggshell color

Learning from Other Writers

In *The Accidental Tourist*, Anne Tyler uses dreams to pull Macon Leary back to the past. He relives remembered scenes with himself and Ethan. He talks to his dead grandfather. Take a moment to check out these dreams:

Chapter Three: "He [Macon] saw behind his eyelids the soap dish on the kitchen sink. . . ." (Tyler follows this with a remembered scene when Macon and Ethan flew together on the plane.)

Chapter Four: "When the phone rang, Macon dreamed it was Ethan." (In the dream, Ethan talks to Macon. Then the phone wakes Macon up, dragging him out of the dream.)

Chapter Nine: "Early Wednesday morning, Macon dreamed Grandfather Leary woke him and asked . . ." (In this dream, Grandfather Leary tells Macon he's lost the center of his life.)

DURING THE WEEK

Looking Ahead to Dressing Your Character

Weekend 4 is Dressing Your Character. To do that, you'll assemble a wardrobe, garments from drawers, garments hanging in a closet.

Take ten minutes during the week to list the contents of your closet.

Here's a list from Susie's closet from the master bedroom of her home on a hill overlooking the water:

champagne carpet
beige walls
French doors
rows of drawers/underwear, stockings, bedroom slippers
costume jewelry
emerald from Colombia (wall safe downstairs)
middle drawers: labeled TENNIS, JOGGING, SWIMMING, GYM
     WORKOUT, et cetera
Bain de Soleil
skirts, Neiman Marcus
dresses in bags
dresses on hangers
silk, rayon, nylon, cotton, wool jersey
six robes

shoes, 120 pair
Jogbra
tennis panties
tennis skirt
socklets
new tennis shoes

• WEEKEND 4 •
WARDROBE: DRESSING
YOUR CHARACTER

Dressing your character brings her back from the recesses of dream and back story to the universe of exteriors. Now that you have a sense of each of your characters' back story and dreams, dress them to reflect their personal histories. While your character dresses, preparing for her entrance onto the stage of your novel, she goes through a ritual, or perhaps a series of rituals, that help to define her personality, age generation, life-style, and income status. Define these rituals by asking questions. How long does she take with her hair? What runs through her mind as she leans close to scrutinize her face in the mirror? Are those laugh lines deeper? Is there a wrinkle that wasn't there last week? Has it deepened overnight? Is that a gray hair?

Does she dress quickly, with supreme efficiency? Or does she fuss over her wardrobe, shoving clothes aside, the hangers clicking against one another, while she fingers the cloth of two different blouses? Does a maid arrive when she presses a call button? Or does she have to traipse downstairs to the laundry room, where she unfolds an ironing board to press the blouse that she forgot to press on the weekend?

If she dresses with efficiency, does this mean she's a cool one? Or does it mean she's in control for now, and will lose it later? If there's a loose step on the way to the laundry room, does it mean her husband forgot to fix it? Or does it mean he's not a Mr. Fixit kind of guy? Or does it mean there is no husband?

Exteriors are dangerous only if they don't do any work for your story. As we found in the guidelines to dream writing, repetition builds meaning, whether you're working with symbols from the interior or costume jewelry from the vast universe of the exterior. You get meaning by repeating *tiara, tiara, tiara*. You get meaning from repeating *black, eye*, and *black eye*.

You are the writer. It's your story driven by your character. You choose what to repeat and the repetition signals the reader what's important.

This is Weekend 4. You've built characters for your novel. You've done sketches and you've written dreams and back stories and now it's time to gird them in costumes and uniforms and proper makeup so they can come onstage and get to work in your story. The outfits they select offer clues, not only about where they're going (the office, the club, the street, the neighbor's, away on vacation, prison, school), but also what they expect when they arrive on the scene.

Here's Susie at thirty-four, dressing for tennis.

Example: Susie Dressing

The closet is L shaped, with champagne carpet and beige walls. Drawers to the right as you walk in, clothes hanging along the left. Between the drawers and the hanging clothes is room to park a Jaguar. You enter from the dressing room through French doors with glass panes framed in white wood. The French doors open out into the bedroom and have brass handles. The carpet is continuous from bedroom to dressing room to closet. It demands vacuuming once a day, shampooing each Friday. There are dust balls in one corner of the closet.

Drawers on the bottom row contain underwear, stockings, bedroom slippers. The drawers on the top row hold costume jewelry. The real stuff—diamonds and pearls and the emerald from Colombia—is in the safe in the library downstairs. The middle drawers are labeled according to activity: TENNIS, JOGGING, SWIMMING, GYM WORKOUT, COCKTAIL HOUR, MORNING, NOON, AFTERNOON, TWILIGHT, NIGHT, SUNNING. The drawer marked SUNNING is empty except for an ice cube tray and three bottles of Bain de Soleil. The labels on the drawers were her husband's idea, his invention to bring order into chaos. He died last year, leaving her in a mess.

She runs her hand over silky dresses, jazzy sport-coats, a row of skirts from Neiman Marcus on Fashion Island. Slacks on racks, a row of hooks where robes hang, three terry cloth, one wool, three silky sexy, seven robes, one for each day of the week. Shoes, a hundred and twenty pair, are tucked away in cubbyholes above the labeled drawers.

She opens the tennis drawer and pulls out a Jogbra and a pair of tennis panties. She steps into the panties and observes an extra fold of tummy as she bends. She's been skipping her workouts. Last week she jogged only once. She carries the clothes into the bedroom, where she sits on the bed. The phone rings; she lets the machine answer. Today is Friday. Two weeks ago today the maid shampooed the champagne carpet. The maid no longer works here. It's Antonio's day off. Antonio is the gardener, houseman, and chauffeur. Six weeks ago there were three gardeners.

Sitting on the edge of the bed to pull on her socklets she runs a hand down her right calf. Light stubble there where the razor missed a patch. The men she has known these last twenty years see her legs as her best feature. She likes her mind best, her legs next best. She laces up her tennis shoes, adjusting the tension over her instep. She has a doubles match today with three men on Court Six at Le Club. She is better than two of the men. She's beaten the third at singles. Her mind as she studies her reflection in the mirror is on money, how to borrow some when you have assets but no income. Her house is in jeopardy. Two of the players are bankers. She runs a hand through her hair. It is thick hair, ash-blond, heavy. In her college days, the hair was platinum blond. She likes her hair short, like a boy's. Men like it long. She wears it long. She is thirty-four years old. She likes playing games as long as she wins.

Guidelines for Dressing Your Character

Dressing your characters gives you an excuse to play.

You play with colors, fabrics, textures, thicknesses, brand names, precious stones, famous labels, the feel of cloth against skin, the rustle of cloth against cloth. As your character dresses, costuming herself in the manner of actors since the dawn of drama, you can work with reflections: mirrors, reverse images, close-ups as she tweezers an errant eyebrow, the play of light on her cheekbones. If she's dressing in a cheap motel, you can make good use of those ubiquitous green lights over the bathroom lavatory.

In Susie's scene, she dresses for tennis at Le Club of Newport Beach. There is motive to her dressing. She's broke, behind in her house payments. At this point, all we know, a feeling really, is that the house payment will be crippling, an irony if you consider her lavish life-style. This burden is her immediate problem, leading to her thoughts about money and men. To Susie, men are the source of money. Uncles, boyfriends, dates, husbands, bankers. The play of her thoughts adds resolve to her dressing. She's going out there today, not only to play great tennis, but also to knock them dead, to bowl them over. Purpose in a character lends energy to your writing.

To write the dressing scene, you bring in the list you made last week in your notebook, notations about layout, carpet, clothes. Focus on the closet as container, a metaphor for your character's life-style. French doors with brass handles plus wall-to-wall champagne carpet suggest upscale living. Labels on the drawers, while they provide a quick once-over of Susie's busy life (sports, exercise, cocktails, dancing), also recall the memory of Susie's husband, an orderly man whom she misses.

Cinderella put on a party dress so she could attend the ball. Susie dons tennis clothes to make a showing for the bankers, the men with money. Dressing your character puts you in touch with costuming, the ancient art of masking. Makeup is a mask, a preparation of the face to present to the world. Dressing is a ritual, getting into harness, donning armor for the battlefield.

As your character dresses, and as your writing digs deeper into the ritual, you can add details that reveal the flip side of a lavish life-style. Dust balls, clumped in a corner of the closet, symbolize the absence of the maid. Details from the setting merge with details about Susie's physical appearance—an extra tummy fold; stubble on her right calf— to make her seem human. Details build toward the telling insight: even though Susie likes her hair short, she wears it long because men like it that way. It is a game the character plays to get what she wants. What games do your characters play?

When you write, you work with sense perception because the five senses give you the best lock on establishing a solid point of view. Here's Susie: "Sitting on the edge of the bed to pull on her socklets she runs a hand down her right calf. Light stubble there where the razor missed a patch." Then, in a one-two rhythm, you deepen that sensation (explaining quickly why Susie does what she does) that reveals character: "The men she has known these last twenty years see her legs as her best feature. She likes her mind best, her legs next best."

Susie is no fool.

As you dress your character, keep these questions in mind: What does the character want? Will she get it? Is that why she plays the game? Whose story is this? Who will Susie meet when she leaves her house?

WORKING THE NOVEL

Exercises

1. *Describe a Closet*.
Sit on the floor of your closet. List what you can see. Clothes, shoes, belts, boxes, dust balls. In ten minutes, describe what's in the closet.

2. *Dressing*.
Dress your character to prepare her to move onstage into your story. For details, you can start with your own clothes, the reality of textures and colors and smells that you know so well. Or you can invent a fantasy wardrobe, using garments (and labels and prices) from fashion magazines (*Vogue, Elle, Cosmopolitan*) and also from direct mail catalogues (Spiegel, Neiman Marcus, Land's End, Victoria's Secret). Use the wardrobe to define your character, to present her to the reader.

3. *Dress Your Other Characters.*
In timed writings, five minutes apiece, dress your other characters. These wardrobes don't have to be complete, just enough to define the character. With practice, you'll complete these wardrobe activities a lot faster. Add your completed work to each character's folder.

4. *Start a Ritual Activity List for Each Character.*
Ritual activity—small connected actions that we do over and over—defines your characters while at the same time informing the reader about process. Dressing is important because it's part of the image we present to the world, what T. S. Eliot called "to prepare a face to meet the faces that we meet." Start a list of other rituals—bathing, shaving, slicing an onion, loading a gun, sharpening a harpoon, building a box—that help to define your characters. Add to this list as ritual activities appear in your writing: "X bathes again. Y watches." Put your lists into their appropriate folders.

5. *Try a Scene Change.*
If you have a couple of minutes, try a scene change. Move your character from the closet/bedroom (safety of the private world) to another setting (public world, danger, adventure). For stability, keep her in the same costume. For practice, write about your character from the point of view of another character.

Learning from Other Writers

You'll take more time dressing your characters now because you're in the learning stage. Dressing takes you into closets, into bedrooms and bathrooms. Dressing lets you feel fabrics and smell cologne and work the lipstick brush. You can learn from reading other writers. Here's Freddy Bascomb, the artist/mom protagonist from *Bones*, by Joyce Thompson:

Freddy Bascomb, playing herself. What would she normally put on today? On a normal day, she'd just be getting ready to paint, pulling on her sweats with the soft old matted-fleece insides and the thighs colorful, paint-caked from where she wipes her hands, no underwear, maybe some heavy cotton socks if the studio floor was cold. She upgrades it to jeans, the acid-washed ones, and a sweatshirt with no paint on it over a T-shirt with just a little, heavy silver earrings, and her running shoes.

With *normally* and *normal*, Thompson establishes the ritual. With *upgrades*, she indicates that today is different. The routine is broken. Her protagonist is headed outside, away from the house, headed for adventure.

Buying habits are a clue to character. You can mix a dressing scene with buying habits, as Elizabeth Tallent does in her novel *Museum Pieces:* "She straightens, takes her hairbrush from the dresser, and begins brushing her hair in rapid, fierce strokes, a ripping sound, the hair falling to her shoulders; then she chooses one of her new linen shirts and puts it on. She has two of these, pale yellow. Lately, whenever she finds something she likes, she buys two of it, in case one gets ruined: she has learned that much, at least."

Hot modifiers—*rapid, fierce, ripping*—add snap to a normal ritual of brushing the hair. The word *ruined* reaches beyond the two yellow shirts and behind the world of exteriors to suggest that much of her life lies behind her in ruins.

When you move your characters into the book, you won't always show the reader their dressing scenes. Instead, you'll bring them on-stage already dressed, the way Anne Tyler does in *The Accidental Tourist*. Here's Muriel Pritchett—Macon refers to her as the "frizzy" one—from Chapter Three of *Tourist:* "This evening she wore a V-neck black dress splashed with big pink flowers, its shoulders padded and its skirt too skimpy; and preposterously high-heeled sandals."

Muriel's zany clothes mirror her personality. In contrast, two chapters later, Tyler paints a picture of Macon's sister, Rose: "She was pretty in a sober, prim way, with beige hair folded unobtrusively at the back of her neck where it wouldn't be a bother. Her figure was a very young girl's, but her clothes were spinsterly and concealing."

If you focus your attention on the words (circling them with your colored pencil), you can learn technique from Tyler. For example, *splashed*, a verb turned into a participle, contains Muriel's verve; while *folded*, the same part of speech, contains Sarah's prim control. Muriel's key adverb is *preposterously;* Sarah's are *unobtrusively* and *spinsterly*.

The adverbs underline character traits: Muriel is explosive. Rose, like Macon, is contained.

You dress your character to prepare her for her first entrance onto the stage set of your novel. You send her out from her hut or castle into the world, where she encounters mystery, adventure, and romance.

Closing Thoughts

Watching Your Characters Grow

When I sketched my Stranger in the Room, I was writing a novel called *The Hit Man Cometh* (1988). The protagonist was a policeman, a Newport Beach homicide sergeant named Frank Branko. The antagonist of the book was a ruthless ex-mercenary who wanted to gain power by meddling in national politics. With these two roles filled, I cast my Stranger as Susannah Maxwell, a helper character. The minute she stepped onstage, however, Susie tried to break out of her helper role and take over as protagonist.

Her energy created a problem. In fiction, your reader can only identify with one protagonist; with two, you risk dividing the reader's attention. As I kept writing, I watched Susie grow. By midpoint, Susie had worked out a plan to help the policeman neutralize her enemy, the ruthless mercenary.

Susie's need to hold on to her hard-won upscale life-style, developed from deep character-work, became the force that drove *Hit Man*. The energy provided by her character was responsible for some great reviews for the novel, like the one from *The Miami Herald*, which called *The Hit Man Cometh* "a minor masterpiece."

Casting Director

Congratulations. You've made it through four weekends (and four weeks). You've survived. You've done some writing and learned some tricks of the novelist's trade. You've circled words, tracking repetition on the page, to discover pattern and rhythm in the language you just wrote. You've worked hard and your characters are ready to step onstage.

Even if you don't have a full cast of characters, cast the ones you do have now. If holes appear in your slate (great protagonist, great helper, no antagonist), you know what you need to do to fill them. Do more character work.

Cast one protagonist and one main antagonist. Cast one helper/guide/catalyst. Write their parts out in your notebook, the characters' names, age, sex, cultural type, followed by their role. True, characters can get capricious; the roles you assign now might not stick. But taking the time to cast them now gets you started and gives them an assignment in your first scene.

Good characters, like Susie and Cinderella, survive.

PART · III

Weekends 5–10
Scene Building

Your characters, dressed and expectant, wait in the wings for the cue that brings them onto the stage of your novel. In four weekends, you've created a dynamic cast of characters. They're multidimensional; shrewd, driven, directed, with hidden vulnerabilities known only to you. The have parents, siblings, friends, jobs, back stories. Like us, they dream. They're human.

This is the fifth week. You've worked hard. You've got a lot to show for it. Your notebook bristles with material. Your portrait-gallery file folder has a pleasant little bulge. In your notebook, you have lists, notes, snippets of dialogue, ideas for scenes. The next step is to move your characters onstage, into one of those scenes.

A scene is a single action or a series of connected actions taking place in a single setting in a finite period of time. If you alter the setting, from the living room to the backyard, consider that a scene change. If you change the time from present to the past, letting your character fall backward into a flashback, consider that a scene change. If you're careful about changing scenes, you'll bring the reader along to the next scene with a new stage setup, smoothly, without his or her knowing. As a way of illustrating smooth scene transition technique for the novel, let's take a page from the film industry and look at what film people call an "establishing shot."

You've probably seen establishing shots in film scripts. They're written entirely in caps—EXT: NIGHT—ON THE PATIO—and they tell the director and crew which scene this is so that the camera can inform the viewer. As moviegoers, we're accustomed to establishing shots that take only a few seconds onscreen. Behind those few seconds, however, might be days of set preparation and lots of film shot to get the right lighting, the right angle.

In a novel, the establishing shot is made with word pictures. As readers with attention spans shaped by movie watching, we might read over these passages of description because we're in a hurry to see what happens. But as writers, our role is reversed. We have an obligation to let the reader know the setting for each scene, the time, who's onstage, what they're doing, and who's coming on. One of the tricks of novel writing is to make these stage setups do double work. Not only do you set the stage, you also establish a mood with your descriptive detail.

During the next six weekends, we'll explore scenes, the word patterns you use to build them, and how to connect the scenes to form chapters in your novel.

Reasons to Write Scenes

You write scenes because they are the elements of drama, which is what propels the novel. You write scenes to make your characters act. Action drives drama. There is surface action: for instance, Character A says to Character B, "I'm going to kill you." She shoots Character B. Surface action is straightforward. There is also action beneath the surface, subtext. Subtext is the tension between what is said and what the character is really doing: Character A says to Character B, "What a lovely morning," while sizing up the firing distance between them. It's called subtext because that's where it is located—a layer under the text.

You write scenes because they impose limits on themselves and have an inherent structure that helps you write with efficiency. When a scene is over, you close it off with an exit line and write another scene. If you're not sure it's over, ask a couple of friends to read it aloud. If your ear doesn't tell you when it's over, your friends will.

You write scenes because, in their rhythms, they serve as structural building blocks for your novel. When you read a carefully constructed novel, present scenes echo their predecessors and foreshadow the scenes to come. Readers can't see the echoes but can sense them. If your novel has a compelling rhythm, your reader will not put it down. You should consciously write and structure your scenes to establish a rhythm to your novel.

Rhythm in Your Novel

In the section on character work, we explored ways you can use repetition: repeating *echo words* that drift down like threads through fabric, to link the patchwork pieces of your story; repetition of *words in clusters* that bunch up to bring images into the foreground of your book, where they take on high visibility for the reader. I introduced repetition early so that you could experiment with it in your own writing. You have to feel when to repeat, when not to. Repetition is part skill, part intuition—sometimes you just *know* when to use it—and one concept that helps you know when to know is rhythm.

Rhythm is patterned alternation. It's as simple as your heart beating, two feet marching, the one-two motion of the tides. If you're in tune with the cosmos, you notice the patterned alternation of night and day, night and day, where the ones and twos are spaced farther apart to make a larger rhythm. As you expand time, stretching days into weeks, you tap into the rhythm of the year—the patterned flow of spring, summer, autumn, winter—with all its inherent symbolism. Spring suggests rebirth after the graveyard of winter; summer suggests the heat of life before the colorful death of autumn. To sense the rhythm of the seasons, it helps to step back. Then you see, on a wide canvas, the slow one-two of spring rolling into summer. You see the faster one-two of a cold morning in June that feels so crisp that you expect to see autumn leaves falling. Rhythm is there. We don't think about it. But when someone says, "Life is a fast-track movement from womb to tomb," squeezing sixty or seventy years into a single sentence, we sense that one-two movement—one: womb; two: tomb—which is enhanced here by rhyme.

How do you establish the rhythms of your novel? At the largest level is structure, a movement of large actions through key scenes that rise to a high point we call the catharsis. (We will explore overall structure in more depth in the plotting section.) To begin, open and close your novel with key scenes that echo one another. In *The Art of Fiction*, John Gardner compares the overall structure of a novel to a symphony, with the end of the work echoing the key images introduced at the beginning. *The Great Gatsby* illustrates Gardner's idea. In Chapter One, narrator Nick Carraway sees his neighbor Gatsby stretching out his arms, a hieratic gesture packed with worship, toward the green light at the end of Daisy Buchanan's dock in East Egg. As the book closes, Nick tells us: "Gatsby believed in the green light, the orgiastic future that year by year recedes before us." The opening and closing images work like bookends, framing the scenes that tell Fitzgerald's story.

Strong scenes control turning points in your book, the twists and hot spots and pinnacles of power in your prose that keep the story line moving. Cooler, calmer scenes deepen character and function as transitional links between the strong scenes packed with power. Establish the rhythms of your novel by alternating strong active scenes with cooler, calmer scenes to produce a rhythm in words that is close to Gardner's metaphor of the novel as a symphony: strong movements, crammed with power and symbolic thrust, alternating with weaker movements that are subtler, smoother, and sometimes sweeter.

As we'll discover in the next six weekends, a scene has its own rhythm, similar to Gardner's symphony metaphor, but on a much smaller scale. Rhythm inside the scene comes when you alternate patterns of language: a passage of high action, for example, might alternate with description and dialogue followed by a passage of explanation. On an even smaller scale, you can also develop rhythm in a scene by alternating speakers in a dialogue:

> *Voice A:* I hope it doesn't rain. (One)
> *Voice B:* I don't mind a little rain. (Two)

If Character B doesn't answer, and if Character A keeps talking, the rhythm changes because now you're writing, not a *dia*logue, but a *mono*logue. (Monologue, which has its own rhythms, will come up again in Weekend 10.)

In fiction the simplest rhythm is the one-two. If you have an action, you follow it with a *re*action. If Voice A speaks, Voice B responds. If your character looks at something, show the reader what she sees, because beginners leave it hanging, often like this: "Maria scanned the chalkboard. She thought of yesterday with Brick, watching him eat. She wondered where . . ."

The rhythm is gone, and with it the chance to echo the larger structures of your novel. So on the rewrite, you try again:

> Maria scanned the chalkboard. Black Bean Soup, Corn Bread, Gram's Rhubarb Pie. Yum. She was starved.
> "What looks good, Mom?"
> "Nothing."

When you *show* the reader what the character sees, actually writing down the detail, you pick up the stitch that you could have dropped. You don't know how important a single detail can be until you write it into your scenes. Until you write Mom's dialogue line, "Nothing," you don't know what a lousy mood she's in. You could *tell* the reader in an explanatory line, something like this: "Maria's mom sure was in a bad mood today, she thought." But it is much more efficient to *reveal* it in dramatic dialogue, and not break your one-two rhythm. As Mom speaks, Maria gets a problem. And when Maria gets a problem, she must make a choice, must take action. Action and reaction propel the scene.

A novel's rhythm is determined by the choices the writer makes when constructing individual scenes and when placing those specific scenes along the larger storyboard. What I'm suggesting is that you write your novel as a series of rhythms (word, sentence, scene, scene-sequence, chapter) that echo each other at different levels of the work. Rhythm begins with sentences, but don't let that make you uptight when you write. When you write a sentence in writing practice, you let the rhythm happen. If it doesn't, no problem; you can always rewrite later, after you've pulled back for a look at the overall structure.

The Next Six Weekends

In Weekend 5, we'll begin with a close look at Tyler's opening scene in *The Accidental Tourist,* how it's built, its function in the novel. We'll move on to sketching out your scene using a constructive technique for novelists, a storyboard. Then, in quick fashion, we'll jot notes for a scene, using the storyboard as a base.

In Weekend 6, we'll use Tyler's stage setup scene as a model for building a stage setup of your own. It might help to view this process in three-dimensional terms, like building a set for a film or theatrical production. The great thing about being a novelist is power: you have control over everything, including the weather.

Dialogue, the subject of Weekend 7, is your shortcut to active conflict. Conflict is the heart of drama. Once again, we'll use Tyler's opening scene to illustrate the advantage of thoughtful use of dialogue. Once you understand that dialogue forms half of Tyler's captivating opening scene, you'll realize that good drama is all about active conflict. Beginning writers who open their books with weighty passages that explain things to the reader can use Tyler's dialogue-dominant opening as a model to follow in their own work.

In Weekend 8, you'll learn how to wrap a scene around large actions by studying Tyler. Two characters often means two large actions in conflict. When you line up your actions in a list, you'll get your first view of story line (in the plotting section). Each large action is supported by lesser actions. For example, flicking on the windshield wipers, a lesser action, contributes to the larger action of driving the car down the road into the rain.

In Weekend 9, you'll choose a point of view. You'll also learn how simple it is to control. Point of view is a magical lens created by the writer. Peering through this lens, the reader not only sees but also smells, hears, touches, and tastes from one specific frame of reference.

Weekend 10. After you write scenes, you connect them in scene sequences to make chapters. Weekend 10 helps you make chapters that make books.

• WEEKEND 5 •
SCENE ANALYSIS/SCENE SKETCH

Beginners with the dream of writing fiction often read a lot. They read fast, zooming over the words, skimming the pages. They read for fun and escape and relaxation. As a professional writer, reading is part of your business. In order to learn from other writers, you need to read more slowly now, listening for echoes, feeling for rhythm. Look deeply into the work to see what's there. You'll develop your eye for fiction, the same way you would if you were studying art or architecture.

If you were studying art, for example, you'd examine the work of other artists, their underlying forms (wedge, box, circle, et cetera), their layers of paint, the stylistic imprint left by their brushstrokes. Learning from others could save you years of trial and error. If you were building a house, would you plunge in without a blueprint and some training in carpentry?

I'm not saying it's impossible to teach yourself to write or paint or build a house by combining good intuition with years of trial and error. I'm saying that, for your first novel, you don't need to reinvent the wheel. Scene builders have come before you. You can learn from them.

As a professional writer, you study a scene, taking it apart to find out how it's built. By tracking the components of structure, you'll gain a sense of the built-in rhythm of a scene. You can then apply what you learn from other writers to your own work.

There's a big payoff in writing scenes: what you learn from building Scene A will transfer to the construction of Scene B, which will teach you something about building Scene C, which will help you make the drama of Scene A better when you rewrite. A scene is a bucket that contains drama. It occupies its own space for a finite amount of time. When time is up, the setup stays while we cut to a new scene. Scenes are great because they talk to you. They'll tell you the highway scene is finished. They'll tell you it's time to cut to the empty house.

Example

The scene that follows is the opening to Anne Tyler's book *The Accidental Tourist*. It's a great model for you to follow. The language is clean and efficient. The actions are subtle and familiar. The dialogue lines are genuine and rhythmic. The strength of these elements builds the scene to a compelling climax. Like the structure of the trauma episode you did for back story (Weekend 2) and the dream exercises (Weekend 3), this scene has a beginning, middle, and end.

After you have read over the scene, identify the elements of Tyler's construction: the beginning (setup and the introduction of her characters); the middle (a conflict between the characters); and the end (a climactic moment where each character makes an emotional choice).

SCENE

They were supposed to stay at the beach a week, but neither of them had the heart for it and they decided to come back early. Macon drove. Sarah sat next to him, leaning her head against the side window. Chips of cloudy sky showed through her tangled brown curls.

Macon wore a formal summer suit, his traveling suit—much more logical for traveling than jeans, he always said. Jeans had those stiff, hard seams and those rivets. Sarah wore a strapless terry beach dress. They might have been returning from two entirely different trips. Sarah had a tan but Macon didn't. He was a tall, pale, gray-eyed man, with straight fair hair cut close to his head, and his skin was that thin kind that easily burns. He'd kept away from the sun during the middle part of every day.

Just past the start of the divided highway, the sky grew almost black and several enormous drops spattered the windshield. Sarah sat up straight. "Let's hope it doesn't rain," she said.

"I don't mind a little rain," Macon said.

Sarah sat back again, but she kept her eyes on the road.

It was a Thursday morning. There wasn't much traffic. They passed a pickup truck, then a van all covered with stickers from a hundred scenic attractions. The drops on the windshield grew closer together. Macon switched his wipers on. Tick-*swoosh*, they went—a lulling sound; and there was a gentle patter on the roof. Every now and then a gust of wind blew up. Rain flattened the long, pale grass at the sides of the road. It slanted across the boat lots, lumberyards, and

discount furniture outlets, which already had a darkened look as if
here it might have been raining for some time.

"Can you see all right?" Sarah asked.

"Of course," Macon said. "This is nothing."

They arrived behind a trailer truck whose rear wheels sent out
arcs of spray. Macon swung to the left and passed. There was a
moment of watery blindness till the truck had dropped behind. Sarah
gripped the dashboard with one hand.

"I don't know how you can see to drive," she said.

"Maybe you should put on your glasses."

"Putting on my glasses would help you to see?"

"Not me; you," Macon said. "You're focused on the windshield
instead of the road."

Sarah continued to grip the dashboard. She had a broad, smooth
face that gave an impression of calm, but if you looked closely you'd
notice the tension at the corners of her eyes.

The car drew in around them like a room. Their breaths fogged
the windows. Earlier the air conditioner had been running and now
some artificial chill remained, quickly turning dank, carrying with it
the smell of mildew. They shot through an underpass. The rain
stopped completely for one blank, startling second. Sarah gave a little
gasp of relief, but even before it was uttered, the hammering on the
roof resumed. She turned and gazed back longingly at the underpass.
Macon sped ahead, with his hands relaxed on the wheel.

"Did you notice that boy with the motorcycle?" Sarah asked. She
had to raise her voice; a steady, insistent roaring sound engulfed
them.

"What boy?"

"He was parked beneath the underpass."

"It's crazy to ride a motorcycle on a day like today," Macon said.
"Crazy to ride one any day. You're so exposed to the elements."

"We could do that," Sarah said. "Stop and wait it out."

"Sarah, if I felt we were in the slightest danger I'd have pulled
over long ago."

"Well, I don't know that you would have," Sarah said.

They passed a field where the rain seemed to fall in sheets, layers
and layers of rain beating down the cornstalks, flooding the rutted
soil. Great lashings of water flung themselves at the windshield.
Macon switched his wiper blades to high.

"I don't know that you really care that much," Sarah said. "Do
you."

Macon said, "Care?"

"I said to you the other day, I said, 'Macon, now that Ethan's dead I sometimes wonder if there's any point to life.' Do you remember what you answered?"

"Well, not offhand," Macon said.

"You said, 'Honey, to tell the truth, it never seemed to me there was all that much point to begin with.' Those were your exact words."

"Um . . ."

"And you don't even know what was wrong with that."

"No, I guess I don't," Macon said.

He passed a line of cars that had parked at the side of the road, their windows opaque, their gleaming surfaces bouncing back the rain in shallow explosions. One car was slightly tipped, as if about to fall into the muddy torrent that churned and raced in the gully. Macon kept a steady speed.

"You're not a comfort, Macon," Sarah said.

"Honey, I'm trying to be."

"You just go on your same old way like before. Your little routines and rituals, depressing habits, day after day. No comfort at all."

"Shouldn't I need comfort too?" Macon asked. "You're not the only one, Sarah. I don't know why you feel it's your loss alone."

"Well, I just do, sometimes," Sarah said.

They were quiet a moment. A wide lake, it seemed, in the center of the highway crashed against the underside of the car and slammed it to the right. Macon pumped his brakes and drove on.

"This rain, for instance," Sarah said. "You know it makes me nervous. What harm would it do to wait it out? You'd be showing some concern. You'd be telling me we're in this together."

Macon peered through the windshield, which was streaming so that it seemed marbled. He said, "I've got a system, Sarah. You know I drive according to a system."

"You and your systems!"

"Also," he said, "if you don't see any point to life, I can't figure why a rainstorm would make you nervous."

Sarah slumped in her seat.

"Will you look at that!" he said. "A mobile home's washed clear across that trailer park."

"Macon, I want a divorce," Sarah told him.

Macon braked and glanced over at her. "What?" he said. The car swerved. He had to face forward again. "What did I say?" he asked. "What did it mean?"

"I just can't live with you anymore," Sarah said.

Macon went on watching the road, but his nose seemed sharper and whiter, as if the skin of his face had been pulled tight. He cleared his throat. He said, "Honey. Listen. It's been a hard year. We've had a hard time. People who lose a child often feel this way; everybody says so; everybody says it's a terrible strain on a marriage—"

"I'd like to find a place of my own as soon as we get back," Sarah told him.

"Place of your own," Macon echoed, but he spoke so softly, and the rain beat so loudly on the roof, it looked as if he were only moving his lips. "Well," he said. "All right. If that's what you really want."

"You can keep the house," Sarah said. "You never did like moving."

For some reason, it was this that made her finally break down. She turned away sharply. Macon switched his right blinker on. He pulled into a Texaco station, parked beneath the overhang, and cut off the engine. Then he started rubbing his knees with his palms. Sarah huddled in her corner. The only sound was the drumming of rain on the overhang far above them.

Beginning. The beginning is the setup. It introduces the characters, their connections, their behavior. For example, Tyler uses the repetition of *sight* words (*see, glasses, blindness, focused*) to show us how the Learys are really not communicating. The beginning of this scene runs from the opening passage ("They were supposed to stay at the beach a week. . . .) to Tyler's close-up of Sarah's tension (". . . if you looked closely, you'd notice the tension at the corners of her eyes"). The shift in distance forces us to pause as we zoom in on Sarah. The pause, this slowing down for a close-up, signals a subtle shift marking the end of the scene's setup. We know the setting, the characters, the connections; we are now ready to move on to their conflicts.

Middle. The middle section of this opening scene develops the conflict—a tight-lipped battle of the sexes over the death of their son. As you read, mark the middle at Tyler's description of the car closing in—"The car drew in around them like a room." She deepens the middle section with sensory detail (*chill, dank, smell of mildew, hammering on the roof*) that connects the characters to the stage setup (the car). Tyler also uses back story to alert the reader that the conflict which has been going on for a while—"I said to you the other day, I said, 'Macon, now that Ethan's dead . . .' "—has now reached an impasse.

Rain, the key symbol (or central image), punctuates the tension between the Learys, coming to a head with the verb *crashed* to send us on to the end of the scene. As Tyler skillfully demonstrates, conflict develops, getting deeper, in the middle section of a scene.

End: The end of a scene is where the characters make choices to resolve the conflict for that moment. Those choices create problems that push the characters into the next part of the novel. For example, the end section of Tyler's opening scene begins with more rain ("This rain, for instance . . .") and ends with rain drumming on the roof. It contains the climax, Sarah's request for a divorce, and Macon's befuddled reaction. The characters choose their respective fates: Sarah chooses to leave Macon, heading for a place of her own; Macon, who hates to move, chooses to remain in their empty house. A scene's end contains a climactic action that forces the characters to make a choice.

Storyboarding

Before you write a scene, use a storyboard to sketch out its parts, to focus your mind on the work you need to do. Since the heart of a scene is conflict, you use a storyboard to locate the points of conflict—the agenda of character A, for example, clashing with the agenda of character B—and then to itemize the parts of a scene you'll be using to develop the conflict: stage setup, character motives and relationships, dialogue, action, point of view, climax, and exit line.

Rein in your impulse to begin writing until you have at least a barebones storyboard, which frontloads your unconscious about the shape and promise of the scene. As you work out your ideas, don't fret over the language you use to express them. A simple phrase or a key word will suffice.

This movement from analysis to sketch to writing is one you'll make often as a writer. Sometimes the scene will build quickly from a detail in the stage setup. At other times, a key action (sneezing, laughing, ordering lunch, sipping coffee) will trigger an all-important insight about a ritual that defines a character. Sometimes a dialogue line will reveal secrets about a character's motives that unlock the entire book.

Storyboarding allows you to write the scene in pieces—timed writings on dialogue, action, stage setup—because it keeps you in mind of the scene as a unit, a container for drama. Once you have the storyboard, you can start in the middle, at the end, or at the beginning of the scene. Because it frontloads your unconscious, guiding it to the climax, storyboarding frees up your creativity. Because it gives you time to think, a breathing space before writing, storyboarding connects the pulse of your scene to the larger rhythm of your novel.

Here's a sample storyboard for Tyler's opening scene:

Stage Setup: inside the Learys' car; no specific make

> *time/place:* Thursday morning, on the road
> *temperature/season:* muggy heat, late summer
> *lighting/sounds/smells:* sky darkens as rain approaches; rain hammers roof; mildew, dank smell
> *symbols/images:* rain (water images), car, road, sight/blindness

Characters/relationships: Macon and Sarah Leary, a married couple in their mid-thirties, have lost a child

Dialogue

> *subjects:* rain, comfort, systems, the past
> *subtext:* anger that their child is dead

Action

> *Large:* Macon driving the car; Sarah asking for a divorce
> *Supporting:* passing, gripping dashboard, sitting up straight; turning on windshield wipers

Point of View: third-person omniscient

Climax: Sarah's line, "I want a divorce."

Exit line: rain drumming on the roof.

Then you do the same thing for your scene. Fill out a storyboard.

Deepening the Storyboard—
Notes to Yourself

If you're writing hot, you can move directly from storyboard to writing the scene. If you need an intermediate step, deepen your storyboard by making "notes to yourself" on content and direction for your scene. You keep your notes in sections, stage setup, for example, moving on to character, dialogue, action, and point of view.

Stage Setup. In Tyler's scene, this is a closed space, a bubble rolling down the road in the increasing rain. The car never stops. It's tight in here, confined, like a cage. Do you state that in a metaphor—"the car felt like a cage"—or do you leave the cage implicit in the language? As you write, you ask questions that can link you to the scene and get you started writing. For Tyler, Macon controls the action because he's driving. He's connected to the car parts (wheel, brakes, wipers) of the stage setup. Sarah's actions are reactions to the rain, the key symbol in the stage setup, and to Macon's driving. The air-conditioner is not running now, but it was. How does it *smell* now inside the car? You can use smell to sharpen the point of view. *Sound:* how loudly does rain hammer on the roof? Expand the rain symbol with water images: torrent, mud, lake, drops, flood, cloudy sky. Connect watery blindness to *sight* images: "Can you see all right?" Use in dialogue.

Characters. Motive: Sarah *wants* Macon to care. Sarah defines caring as sharing. To her, sharing means opening up. Macon's locked in his systems. Motive: he *wants* to keep a steady course, make tomorrow just like today. Opening this guy up will take a while. The Learys' problem: Ethan is dead. Use in dialogue line, evoking the past: "Now that Ethan's dead, I . . ." Clothes indicate character: Macon's suit, buttoned up, covered up, no tan. Sarah's dress, a strapless terry, shows her tan. Symbolism of tan/no-tan: two different trips, separation inside the cage of a car. Tension. Who are we with in this scene? Who do we root for?

Dialogue. Since it's raining in the stage setup, connect characters to the rain with dialogue lines. Sarah: Hope it doesn't rain. Macon: Not me, I like rain. Keep working the stage setup through dialogue and the one-two rhythm:

One: Look out the window.
Two: There's a boy on a motorcycle.

Good rhythm. Evoke the past: Ethan's dead. If they talk it out now, then Sarah doesn't split, then there's no story. They could fight because she's a fighter; he's not. She attacks through dialogue: "I don't know that you really care that much." Subject of argument: Macon's driving; Sarah, attacking, wants to stop. Good conflict. Build from their separate *wants*.

Action. Large Action: driving the car through the rain supported by lesser actions. Macon's actions: swerving, braking, pumping pedals, turning on windshield wipers. Sarah's large action, to ask for a divorce, builds through a series of lesser actions: sitting up straight, gripping the dashboard, raising her voice, slumping in her seat. Query: What does Macon *do* when Sarah asks for a divorce? What's his reaction?

Point of View. Because of the closed set inside the car, a result of stage setup plus sense perception, this feels like a third-person camera eye equipped with a remote sensor device that captures temperature and dampness as well as heat and sound. Because of the detail from the stage setup, the view feels objective. Question: Do we choose sides here? Or do we wait? Sense perception: chips of sky (sight); chill (feel); mildew (smell); hammering (sound).

After you create your storyboard, you're ready to write the scene.

WORKING THE NOVEL

Exercises

1. *Storyboarding*.
Sketch a scene for your novel. Use these slots.

> *Stage Setup:*
>> *time/place*
>> *temperature/season*
>> *lighting/sounds/smells*
>> *symbols/images*

Characters/relationships:

Dialogue

   subjects

   subtext

Action

   large

   small

Point of View:

Climax

Exit line

2. *Notes to Yourself.*

Deepen the storyboard by writing some notes to yourself on the content and direction of your scene. If you keep your notes in categories—Stage Setup, Character, Dialogue, Action, Point of View—you'll be prepared to move from the notes right into a part of the scene.

Practice Your Storyboarding

Page through your copy of *Tourist* until you find a scene that looks promising—lots of dialogue to provide conflict, terse description, two characters at center stage—and storyboard the scene as you read it. Framing scenes from novels will help you frame scenes from real life. Use the categories we've been working with: Stage Setup (time/place; temperature/season; lighting/sounds/smells; symbols/images); Characters/Relationships; Dialogue (subjects, subtext); Action (large, small); Point of View (who narrates this scene?); Climax; and Exit Line.

Here are suggestions for scenes you might use to practice your storyboarding: First Encounter, Macon and Muriel, Chapter Three, pp. 27–29; Macon Okays Muriel, Chapter Six, pp. 91–93; Macon Confesses, Chapter Eleven, pp. 188–191; Macon Visits Home and Family, Rose's Wedding, Chapter Sixteen, 256–261.

Learning from Other Forms

Watch TV with your notebook in hand. Time the scenes in a couple of sitcoms. How many minutes do they run? Where do they take a turn or wind into climax? Is there an exit line or does a visual shot take its place?

Time the scenes in a movie of the week or a one-hour drama series. Do these scenes run for the same time? Are they shorter? Longer? Where do the station breaks occur?

DURING THE WEEK

Looking Ahead to Stage Setup

Study the first two pages of Chapter Two in *Tourist*—the passages describing Sarah's belongings and the house—and make a list of details that develop the stage setup. Use this list to help you search:

Time:

Props (photos, heirlooms, machinery, equipment, books, diaries, signs, containers):

Temperature:

Place:

Season:

Lighting:

Five senses (sight, sound, smell, taste, touch):

For contrast, look at a stage setup from another author, perhaps from another era. You might try the opening of Chapter II of *The Great Gatsby,* where Fitzgerald lavishes three hundred words of description on the valley of ashes and the advertisement for the services of Dr. T. J. Eckleburg, the oculist who sinks into "eternal blindness."

Or you might look at the opening of Chapter X from *The Sun Also*

Rises, where Hemingway describes the landscape outside the moving car:

> In the Basque country the land all looks very rich and green and the houses and villages look well-off and clean. Every village had a pelota court and on some of them kids were playing in the hot sun. There were signs on the walls of the churches saying it was forbidden to play pelota against them, and the houses in the villages had red tiled roofs, and then the road turned off and commenced to climb and we were going way up close along a hillside, with a valley below and hills stretched off back toward the sea.

The characters are just passing through, but the writer takes infinite care with the detail. As a writer you never know when your hand will produce something on paper that you can use later. The innocent-seeming sentences of landscape description enabled Hemingway to write the prose—heavy on nouns (*country, land, houses, villages, village, roofs*) and light on the modifiers (*rich, green, well-off, clean*)—that made him famous.

Work pays off, even in stage setup.

· WEEKEND 6 ·
STAGE SETUP

Stage setup is the term we use to cover the description of the settings of scenes in your novel. This term covers time, place, temperature, lighting, season, and props. In Tyler's opening scene, the rain starts out as a prop, then builds into a major symbol. As we discovered in Weekend 3, much of the power of writing is conveyed with a subtle use of symbol. You can achieve that subtlety by consciously using your stage setup to introduce and develop your novel's symbols. A writer friend of mine who teaches lots of fiction workshops says it helps her to think of setting as a character. If thinking about stage setup as an independent character helps you to come up with more memorable detail and symbol, please feel free.

Stage setup, because it holds your scene in place, gives you a framework to write in. Sometimes when you're having trouble with a scene, you can ground yourself by taking ten minutes to rebuild your stage. In the rebuilding, you'll discover a detail that unlocks the scene.

You build a stage in your reader's mind to give the reader a familiar place to come back to. In *The Accidental Tourist*, Anne Tyler moves Macon Leary out of his lonely home to recuperate from a broken leg. Later in the novel, he returns to his home—a place detailed earlier in the work—changed. Tyler clues the reader into noticing changes in Macon by changing the description of his house: "The upstairs windows were softly glowing."

Stage setup gives your characters a place to act out their agendas, a season to dress for, a time of day to establish mood and lighting. If you build a stage in Detroit in January, there's a good chance it's snowing, with a wind chill well below zero. Your characters, dressing in response to the weather, decide what to wear, and that helps you write detail: parka, long underwear, snow boots, mittens. If you're building a stage in Sarasota in the winter home of a snowbird from Detroit, use contrasting details from the stage setups of the two homes, Sarasota and Detroit, to convey a sense of life-style for your characters.

Stage setup helps you, as a writer and as a narrator, to stay objective by using detail to convey information. Instead of telling and explaining, you're *showing* with careful detail. Showing is more professional and far more interesting to the reader. It's also hard work. As you train your eye, however, you'll grab on to better details faster. The payoff from writing stage setups comes when images cluster on the page to form symbols. Symbols add an extra layer of meaning to your story. That extra layer adds more dimension to your novel.

In Tyler's opening scene, rain, the key symbol in the stage setup, starts with *cloudy sky* and mere *drops* on the windshield. In five efficient pages she builds the rain into a force in the Learys' marriage.

Writing stage setup helps you to discover symbols. You can wrap a scene, or a fold of a scene, around the symbols.

Before reading guidelines, you might go back to the printed scene and circle the word *rain* and the water images. If you connect your circles with lines on the page, you'll see how the images tend to group together in clusters.

Example: The Symbols of the Stage Setup in *The Accidental Tourist*

The stage setup for the opening chapter of *The Accidental Tourist* combines weather with the road, the landscape that edges the road, and the car's interior. The make of the car is not given: it's a family sedan, we presume. It has windows and a steering wheel and an air-conditioner. The car functions as a cage, and is a symbolic extension not only of the Learys' marriage, but also of Macon's imprisonment. The car represents the cage of his own fears, feelings, and pain.

Macon's problem is that he keeps driving himself. He won't stop to face his own feelings or fears. So he keeps driving when the others stop. This action is symbolic of the state of his soul. It is a physical action that illustrates his own emotional desperation.

As the car moves down the road, and as the marriage grinds through time, the characters are stifling each other. The stage is set for change.

Weather metaphors frame the scene. Paragraph one shows us "chips of cloudy sky" viewed through Sarah's hair. The last paragraph closes the scene with the hammering sound of drumming rain. Weather dominates the day, a calm Thursday suddenly full of fore-boding as the sky grows black and random drops of water force Macon, the systems guy, to turn on the wipers. Weather brings that mildew smell to the inside of the car, dankness escaping from the bowels of the air-conditioner. Weather forces all the cars off the road except Macon's.

Tyler uses two techniques to work the symbolism that forms the stage setup. The first technique, a *repetitive echoing* of a single word, you have already seen in the dream analysis for Weekend 3. The word in this scene is *rain*, the key symbol of natural force, repeated nine times, with *raining* in paragraph five. As the rain increases in intensity, the danger to the travelers increases and the drama deepens.

The second technique is *expansion* of the rain *through water images* which enrich the visual pictures, thereby deepening the power of the symbol. To see how extensive the expansion is, let's list those water images, along with the paragraphs where they occur:

Paragraph 3:

enormous drops

Paragraph 6:

wipers/tick-*swoosh*
gentle patter
flattened, slanted

Paragraph 9:

arcs of spray
watery blindness

Paragraph 15:

hammering

Paragraph 16:

insistent roaring sound engulfed them

Paragraph 23:

sheets, layers, layers, beating, flooding, lashings, flung

Paragraph 32:

bouncing back the rain
muddy torrent
churned, raced, gully

Paragraph 38:

wide lake crashed against the car

Paragraph 40:

steaming, marbled

Paragraph 50:

rain beat so loudly

Paragraph 52:

drumming on the overhang

By stringing water images throughout the scene, Tyler deepens rain into a major symbol. To Macon, the rain is an obstacle, a visible force that he competes with, conflicts with. His weapon is the car, which he drives with his system. Macon, a tight guy, has a system for everything. To Sarah, who is more in tune with her emotions (and hence, we presume, the cosmos), the rain is an omen, a signal to get off the road, to wait until the storm passes. The drama in the scene comes from two conflicts:

Man (Macon) against Nature (Rain)
Man (Macon) against Man (Sarah)

On the surface, we read this as a linear progression building toward a dramatic climax: the car moves down the road, the rain worsens, Sarah asks for a divorce. The drama starts with the problem that has lurked between Macon and Sarah for some time—the memory of their dead child; Macon's inability to share his grief—but it builds in this scene because of the difference in their reactions to the symbols and images of the natural world.

The description is strong because the language is strong. In paragraph 6, the rain *flattens* and *slants*. In paragraph 23, the verbs slip into verbals—*beating, flooding*—and with a flick of her wand Tyler turns the next verbal into a plural noun, *lashings*. Strong verbs keep up the momentum in paragraph 32—*bouncing, churned, raced*—and in paragraph 38, with *crashed* and *slammed*. At rhythmic intervals, the weather reappears in prose passages laced with metaphor to separate the dialogue sections that build inexorably toward Sarah's demand for a divorce.

The lesson to learn from Tyler: Write your description strong; use the stage setup to convey mood and tone.

Guidelines for Writing Your Stage Setup

Before you write your stage setup, take the time to make a quick list of ingredients. Listing feeds the unconscious. Making lists before you write provides springboards for your imagination. Pretend for a moment that your mind is a diver. As you consciously create props and symbols, you're creating a diving board for your mind. With this diving board, you can soar higher, and then dive deeper into your unconscious. That's where the real treasures are—below the surface. Use the same categories we used for Tyler:

Time: Thursday

Temperature: muggy (warm enough for the AC)

Place: inside a car driving down the road

Season: summer (Sarah has a tan)

Lighting: cloudy to almost dark

Props: rain, pickup, van, trailer truck, pale grass, darkened look, dashboard, brakes, tunnel, motorcycle, field, wiper blades, parked cars, gully, marbled windshield, Texaco station

Five Senses: chips of sky (sight); chill (feel); mildew (smell); hammering (sound)

WORKING THE NOVEL

Exercises

1. *List of Ingredients.*
Make a list of the ingredients of your stage setup. Use the same slots we used for Tyler:

Time:

Temperature:

Place:

Season:

Lighting:

Props (photos, heirlooms, machinery, equipment, books, diaries, signs, containers):

Five senses (sight, sound, smell, taste, touch):

2. *Writing about Symbols and Images.*
Select a couple of props and write about them, five minutes for each one, to get a sense of depth. For example, your list of props might have included a clock. Clocks represent time. You record the sound of the clock. You zoom in for a close-up, reading the writing on the clock face. You spin off from the clock to write about time as a circle, time as a line. To get your hand moving, jot down word associations: clock, hands, face, human, time, lifetime, sands of time, hourglass, white sand, white sands, testing ground, desert, dunes, beach, white beach, palm trees, vacation.

3. *Writing Your Stage Setup.*
Working from your list in Exercise 1, with the energy from Exercise 2, write your stage setup. As you write, allow the images to wheel into each other. This is the discovery part of your work. You can always rewrite later.

4. *Moving Scene.*
The Learys' car moves through a stage setup that keeps changing. Hemingway does the same thing as he describes Paris at night from a taxicab moving along city streets. Before you leave stage setup, try writing a moving scene. Concentrate on the stage. Don't worry so much about the other elements of the scene. You can use a car, a bus, a train, a boat, a plane. Go with the flow.

Learning from Other Writers

If you were shooting a movie, someone else would build your stage. But this is your book. Here, you build your own stages, writing dozens of stage setups before you know how long they should be, how filled with detail. Looking at other writers helps. Here, for example, is the opening passage from Doris Lessing's *The Four-Gated City* (1969). Look at that detail:

> In front of Martha was grimed glass, its lower part covered with grimed muslin. The open door showed an oblong of browny-gray air swimming with globules of wet. The shop fronts opposite were no particular color. The lettering on the shops, once black, brown, gold, white, was now shades of dull brown. The lettering on the upper part of the glass of this room was *Joe's Fish and Chips* in reverse, and was flaking like stale chocolate. She sat by the rectangle of pinkish oilcloth where sugar had spilled, and onto it, orange tea, making a gritty smear in which someone had doodled part of a name: Daisy Flet . . . Her cup was thick whitey-gray, cracked. The teaspoon was a whitish plastic, so much used that the elastic brittleness natural to it had gone into an erosion of hair lines, so that it was like a kind of sponge. When she had drunk half the tea, a smear of grease appeared halfway down the inside of her cup: a thumb mark.

DURING THE WEEK

Looking Ahead to Dialogue

You can write better dialogue if your characters notice details in your stage setup. This is a simple technique, basic, part of the writer's craft, and often overlooked by beginners. If it's raining, you let your characters comment on the rain. If the room is smoky, you give your character a dialogue line: "Do you have any Kleenex?" And then he wipes his eyes.

Tyler follows this guideline with Sarah's first line. "I hope it doesn't rain." Hemingway, whose ear for dialogue made his dialogue the model for books and movies for half a century, is careful to weave details from the stage setup into his dialogue. The book is *The Sun Also Rises*. The scene is Jake's room in Paris in the mid-twenties. The characters doing the talking are Lady Brett and Count Mippipopolous:

> LADY BRETT: This is a hell of a dull talk. How about some of that champagne?
> THE COUNT: It isn't cold, yet.
> [Pause.]
> THE COUNT: Now, I think this is cool.
> LADY BRETT: I say, you might open it.
> THE COUNT: Yes, my dear. Now I'll open it.

As you write your stage setup, stay open. Let the details bubble to the surface and then use the details to work your story. If you write your stage setup first, you can attach dialogue lines to it. Sometimes, however, you'll automatically start with dialogue instead of stage setup. This is fine. Honor your creative impulses. Starting with dialogue can be a smart move because dialogue is a shortcut to conflict. Conflict is the essence of drama. When you have finished writing a passage of dialogue, use it as a starting point for your stage setup. With this kind of start, the energy from your dialogue, you can create a powerful setting for your story.

· WEEKEND 7 ·
DIALOGUE

In a novel, dialogue is two characters talking with purpose. You use it in your fiction writing because it is efficient. With a few lines of well-written dialogue, you can build character, advance the plot, convey information, and create tension lurking beneath the surface of the spoken language, which we call "subtext." Dialogue is the shortcut to conflict. Conflict makes drama.

At least half of Tyler's opening scene for *Tourist* is in dialogue mode. The seven dialogue sections grow longer—from two lines to twenty—as the tension deepens inside the car. Outside the car, in the stage setup, the rain gets heavier, weightier, more overwhelming.

It's sometimes helpful to step back from the actual dialogue lines to summarize what the characters are talking about. As a model, here are capsule summaries of Tyler's seven dialogue sections.

The Accidental Tourist, Opening Scene Dialogue Sections

Since we'll be looking carefully at Anne Tyler's dialogue in the opening scene, here are the seven sections I've identified. I have removed quotation marks and the attributions *he said, she said*, replacing them with proper names:

Section 1: In two quick lines, Sarah and Macon talk about their feelings for rain.

> SARAH: I hope it doesn't rain.
> MACON: I don't mind a little rain.

Section 2: Two more lines shift to question and answer as Sarah inquires about Macon's ability to see. Her tone suggests that she's asking more than her husband's perception of current road conditions.

> SARAH: Can you see all right?
> MACON: Of course, this is nothing.

Section 3: On the surface, the Learys bicker about seeing and glasses. Down below, emotions are heating up.

> SARAH: I don't know how you can see to drive.
> MACON: Maybe you should put on your glasses.
> SARAH: Putting on my glasses would help you to see?
> MACON: Not me; you. You're focused on the windshield instead of the road.

Section 4: Macon and Sarah bicker about road conditions. Sarah wants to stop and wait out the rain. Macon wants to push on ahead.

SARAH: Did you notice that boy with the motorcycle?
MACON: What boy?
SARAH: He was parked there beneath the underpass.
MACON: It's crazy to ride a motorcycle on a day like today. Crazy to ride one any day. You're so exposed to the elements.
SARAH: We could do that. Stop and wait it out.
MACON: Sarah, if I felt we were in the slightest danger I'd have pulled over long ago.
SARAH: Well, I don't know that you would have.

Section 5: The bickering expands from Macon's problems with seeing to his problems with caring.

SARAH: I don't know that you really care that much. Do you?
MACON: Care?
SARAH: I said to you the other day, I said, 'Macon, now that Ethan's dead I sometimes wonder if there's any point to life.' Do you remember what you answered?
MACON: Well, not offhand.
SARAH: You said, 'Honey, to tell the truth, it never seemed to me there was all that much point to begin with.' Those were your exact words.
MACON: Um . . .
SARAH: And you don't even know what was wrong with that?
MACON: No, I guess I don't.

Section 6: Lobbing key words (*comfort, system*) like live grenades, Sarah accuses Macon of not being a comfort. Macon, attempting to lob back, says he needs comfort too.

SARAH: You're not a comfort, Macon.
MACON: Honey, I'm trying to be.
SARAH: You just go on your same old way like before. Your little routines and rituals, depressing habits, day after day. No comfort at all.
MACON: Shouldn't I need comfort too? You're not the only one, Sarah. I don't know why you feel it's your loss alone.
SARAH: Well, I just do sometimes.

Section 7: Sarah, at the end of her patience, asks to stop the car. Macon, deep in his shell, evades her question, so Sarah asks for a divorce. Macon's reaction is to stutter. Sarah says she wants a place of her own. Macon says okay, if she wants.

> SARAH: This rain, for instance. You know it makes me nervous. What harm would it do to wait it out? You'd be showing some concern. You'd be telling me we're in this together.
> MACON: I've got a system, Sarah. You know I drive according to a system.
> SARAH: You and your systems!
> MACON: Also, if you don't see any point to life, I don't see why a rainstorm would make you nervous.
> MACON: Would you look at that? A mobile home's washed clear across that trailer park.
> SARAH: Macon, I want a divorce.
> MACON: What? What did I say? What did it mean?
> SARAH: I just can't live with you anymore.
> MACON: Honey, listen. It's been a hard year. We've had a hard time. People who lose a child often feel this way; everybody says so; everybody says it's a terrible strain on a marriage—
> SARAH: I'd like to find a place of my own as soon as we get back.
> MACON: Place of your own. Well. All right. If that's what you really want.
> SARAH: You can keep the house. You never did like moving.

Tyler's dialogue runs like an armature down the center of her opening scene. Now that we have a sense of the content, let's take a closer look at some of Tyler's techniques for writing dialogue. The first technique is one we spoke of last week—grounding your dialogue by attaching lines to the stage setup. Tyler's opening gambit has both characters reacting to the rain, a key element of the stage setup. Let's begin here, with the stage setup, and unearth the secrets of Tyler's dialogue:

Technique I: Stabilize your scene early by attaching dialogue lines to details in the stage setup.

Sarah's first line is "I hope it doesn't rain." In dialogue section 7, she comes at it again—"This rain, for instance . . ."—using the rain as a point of reference as she keeps digging at Macon to stop the car and wait out the storm. Sarah tries in section 4 to connect herself to the landscape and to Macon with the words "Did you notice that boy with the motorcycle? . . . He was parked there beneath the underpass." But Macon, who connects only by competing with the elements, asks, "What boy?" Sarah's and Macon's comments about the stage setup alert the reader to the subtext of the scene—the deep-rooted tension in their marriage.

Technique II: Foreshadow argument with evasive action.

In section 4, when Sarah connects to the boy on the motorcycle (part of the stage setup), Macon deflects by generalizing: "It's crazy to ride a motorcycle on a day like today. Crazy to ride one any day." With each level of abstraction, Macon pulls away from the car (the stage setup), from Sarah, from their grief, using a mode of deflection to change the emotional arena. While Macon spirals out, Sarah tries again, digging at him (section 4) to stop the car: "We could do that. Stop and wait it out."

Sarah digs at Macon, trying to wake him up from his dead sleep. Macon's reaction is to keep evading with his own system of verbal deflection. Sarah opens section 3 by saying, "I don't know how you can see to drive." Macon evades, hinting that her vanity is in the way: "Maybe you should put on your glasses." Then he directs her to focus on the road, not the windshield. Sarah says nothing. She retires to her side of the car to gather her strength for another run at Macon.

Technique III: Spark conflict with argument.

In section 6, when her comments about driving and rain don't work, Sarah hammers Macon with accusations, telling him what's wrong with him:

SARAH: You're not a comfort, Macon.

MACON: Honey, I'm trying to be.

SARAH: You just go on your same old way like before. Your little routines and rituals, depressing habits, day after day. No comfort at all.

MACON: Shouldn't I need comfort too? You're not the only one, Sarah. I don't know why you feel it's your loss alone.

SARAH: Well, I just do sometimes.

In this exchange, Sarah's getting tougher. Macon, a whiner, is in retreat.

Sarah has thirty-one lines of dialogue. Eight of those lines—roughly twenty-five percent—are questions. Sarah's questions are combative, adding a sharper edge to the conflict. In real life, we are always sparring. Carrying that element of combat into your dialogue is a great way to handle conflict in your story.

Technique IV: Broaden the canvas by evoking the past.

Sarah, digging into Macon's problem, brings up the death of their child (section 5): "I said to you the other day, I said, 'Macon, now that Ethan's dead . . .' " Evoking the past in dialogue is a shrewd way for you to handle back story. It sounds natural for the characters to bring up an event from the past. This is efficient: the characters use the past as a source of ammunition for their conflict in the present.

Technique V: Repeat key words—echo words—to stress key issues.

When one character echoes the words of another, you get unity between the lines, and sometimes irony, as the echoes ripple out. In the middle of the opening scene (section 5), Sarah's into full attack mode as she tries to force Macon to admit something about the way he's feeling: "I don't know that you really care that much. . . . Do you?" Macon, on the defensive, answers with a weak echo that stalls for time: "Care?" By echoing one of Sarah's key words, Macon avoids a straight answer. Without knowing it, he tightens the lid on his glass box.

Guidelines for Writing Your Dialogue

Tyler's seven dialogue sections get increasingly longer as we move through the scene, feeling the intensity build to a climax in section 7. The first section is two lines long. The last section, where Sarah asks for a divorce, runs to twenty lines. As a professional, Tyler knows that more dialogue lines, packed tightly together, will house a sharper climax.

When you write dialogue you go for rhythm, the one-two alternation of two voices talking, from your very first lines. Tyler keeps her opening lines short—Sarah opens with five words, Macon has six—as her characters talk about the weather:

> SARAH: I hope it doesn't rain.
> MACON: I don't mind a little rain.

Tyler's first two lines in this opening scene in the car create a model for you to follow in starting your dialogue. The talk is normal, average, everyday. The rhythm between the lines is easy, a one (Sarah's line) followed by a two (Macon's line). Both speakers use the pronoun *I;* both connect to rain, the symbol from the stage setup; both use soft verbs. Sarah's *hope* is a verb of the heart. Macon's *don't mind* is a negative verb of the head. The characters don't shout to produce conflict. They are speaking quietly, with maximum calm. Beneath the everyday talk, however, tension builds as Macon disagrees with Sarah just a tiny bit, hinting that he can handle the weather better than she can.

You build, in your own work, from an opening rhythm with its lovely simplicity to a larger section of dialogue. One way to build while you convey information about your characters is to work in an image cluster, a tight packet of images grouped closely together on the page. In dialogue sections 2 and 3 Tyler uses metaphors of sight and blindness to fire off the first muffled rounds in their war. Try circling the key words (in caps here), then linking them together with lines so that you can feel the connection:

> SARAH: Can you SEE all right?
> MACON: Of course, this is nothing.
> SARAH: I don't know how you can SEE to drive.
> MACON: Maybe you should put on your GLASSES.
> SARAH: Putting on my GLASSES would help you to SEE?
> MACON: Not me; you. You're FOCUSED on the windshield in-
> stead of the road.
> SARAH: Did you NOTICE that boy. . . .

Images and symbols in the dialogue add an extra layer of texture to your story. With her image cluster of sight and blindness, Tyler creates a deeper level of meaning: on the surface level, Sarah's saying Macon can't see the road; on the emotional level, she's crying out that he can't see into his own heart, much less into hers. To say it that way—"Macon, you're so blind, you can't see into your own dull old gray heart"—would ruin the tone, which would ruin the story. In fiction, less is more and the subtext cradles a deep reality. The lesson for you: Say it with metaphor.

To hold your dialogue sections together, you use *repetition*, which we first saw working in the guidelines to dream, on Weekend 3. By repeating rain, the key symbol, Tyler intensifies the drama of the storm. *Drive all you want to,* she says. *You can't escape until the scene ends.*

That same intensity occurs across shorter spans when Tyler repeats other key words. In dialogue section 6, for example, she repeats the word *comfort*, tying those lines together as a unit so Macon can echo Sarah: "Shouldn't I need comfort too?" There is no sympathy for Macon now. He's all alone and Tyler seems to be asking why we should feel anything for a deflector-mode guy who steals a lousy word from his wife so he can twist it, using it against her. In section 7, Tyler repeats the word *system* in dialogue to lift higher the wall of separation between Macon and Sarah. When Sarah echoes Macon—"You and your systems!"—she's revving for the final assault.

When Tyler extends her dialogue repetition, from words into phrases, she uses *parallel structure* (repetition of a consistent form) to build frames that link sections of the scene. In dialogue section 2, for example, Sarah says, "I don't know how you can see to drive." In section 4, she echoes herself, using the same words, "Well, I don't know that you would have."

Here are Sarah's lines, repeating across the middle of the opening scene as Tyler uses parallel structure to link sections 3, 4, and 5:

I don't know how you can see to drive. [section 3]
I don't know that you would have. [section 4]
I don't know that you really care that much. [section 5]
And *you don't even know* what was wrong with that? [section 5]

The first line of Macon's reply ("No, I guess *I don't*") ends dialogue section 5, then links to section 6 as, unable to come up with a better answer, he echoes Sarah:

I don't know why you feel . . . [section 6]

As Macon echoes Sarah's I-don't-knows with his own, his voice is pitched in a low whine, using the intense emotional buildup in Sarah's linked parallels to tell the reader that she will win this battle, and soon.

Parallel structure is a powerful device. It gives you rhythm and order. It tightens and controls. Here Tyler uses it, not only to link three sections of dialogue, but also to build tension as Sarah hammers at Macon to open up and share his grief. In dialogue section 7, parallel structure gives us a sharp picture of Macon's confusion as he tries to deflect Sarah's request for a divorce by retreating into abstraction again:

"People who lose a child often feel this way;
everybody says so;
everybody says it's a terrible strain on a marriage. . . ."

But Sarah's not listening. She's out of here. She wants a place of her own.

"Place of your own," Macon echoes, in a dying fall.

This is a great dialogue to use as a model for your own work. There's multileveled conflict creating compelling drama. They're talking but not communicating and we have the feeling this has been going on a long time. The techniques—echo words, parallel structure, attaching to stage setup, evoking the past, et cetera—are easy to use.

WORKING THE NOTEBOOK

Exercises

1. *Recalling.*
Close your eyes. Take some deep breaths. Zip back in time to a remembered conversation. One you had. One you overheard. Let

the conversation play inside your head. Open your eyes and write it from memory for ten minutes.

2. *Operation Eavesdrop.*
Go to a public place and eavesdrop on a couple of conversations. Write down the dialogue, the key words. List items in the room. Colors, shapes, objects, shadows, lights, candles, people moving about. Do the dialogue speakers respond to the setting? What happens over and over in this place? What's the routine here? What's on the table in front of you? What can you smell? What can you touch? Ask questions.

At home rewrite the dialogue, working in echo words and image clusters (suggestions: sight/blindness; garden/growth; eating/desire; light/dark, and so on) to develop a rhythm.

3. *Exploring Character.*
Go back to the list of ingredients for a stage setup that you sketched last week and place two of your characters together in that setting. Let them talk. Begin by connecting character to some detail in the stage setup, using a line like Tyler's "I hope it doesn't rain," and then let your characters run with it. Do the same thing with a line from Hemingway: "How about some of that champagne [changing the detail to fit your list of ingredients: wine, booze, pot, goulash, bean dip, caviar]?" As you record what your characters say, use the different techniques to develop deeper levels of conversation. Notice what they're doing with their hands. Writing dialogue using solid technique (evoking the past, echoing, connecting to the stage setup, writing with rhythm) helps you get the subjective author out of the way of your story.

Tip: When you practice writing dialogue, leave out stage directions, quote marks, and attributions like "he said" and "she said." Let the dialogue run. See where it goes. From their first entrance onto the stage of your novel, give your characters freedom. They'll do the bulk of your work. You can patch the holes later.

Learning from Other Writers

In her book *You Just Don't Understand*, linguist Deborah Tannen explores the different ways men and women talk. In their talk, Tannen says, women strive to make connections along a network. When they talk, women negotiate for closeness. It's more comfortable for women to make decisions by consensus. "Life," Tannen says, "is a community, a struggle to preserve intimacy and avoid isolation."

A man, on the other hand, engages the world as a ladder, a hierarchy where the guy on top has more status than the guy lower down. When men talk, they negotiate to see who's where on the ladder. If you're on top, you want to stay on top. If you're down below, you want to climb higher. Life for a man, Tannen says, "is a contest, a struggle to preserve independence and avoid failure."

If you apply Tannen's observations to your own dialogue—one more key to producing drama—you'll probably write better stories. Look at the male-female talk in Tyler's Chapter One: Sarah, frustrated by Macon's refusal to match her grief with his own, talks to him about *comfort*; Macon, fighting to maintain control, refuses to stop, to give in to the weather and the road conditions, because to give in would force him to face his fears.

And then read this passage in Tannen: "If women are often frustrated because men do not respond to their troubles by offering matching troubles, men are often frustrated because women do. Some men not only take no *comfort* [italics mine] in such a response, they take offense."

Sound like a blueprint for good dialogue?

Ask two of your friends to read your dialogue aloud while you sit, relaxed, listening with your eyes closed. After a couple of read-throughs, have the friends switch parts before they read again. Take notes. Is it smooth? Are your echo words working? Do you have enough parallel structure? Do the voices ring true? Can you apply Tannen's ideas (women and community; men and independence) to your characters? Which character dominates? Which character recedes? Ask your friends for feedback. Take notes on their *reactions*.

DURING THE WEEK

Looking Ahead to Action

Chapter Sixteen of *Tourist* climaxes with Rose's wedding, a key scene, symbolizing unification, a significant coming together in this novel about separation and isolation. The actors are standing around. The actions are small. Try listing out the actions, one by one, to make a chain that gives you a feel for how much you can do with gestures and looks:

- June, Porter's ex, pecks Macon on the cheek.
- Porter's children eye Alexander.
- Alexander knots his fists.
- June speaks to Julia (Macon's mother).
- Julia answers.
- Macon watches Rose talk to the hardware man.
- Conversations overheard by Macon:
    Charles to the dentist
    Muriel and June
    Julia and Alicia
    Mrs. Barrett and the mailman
    Sarah and Macon (their topic, weather, recalls the
       rain from chapter one; it's sunny today)
- Macon looks at Sarah.
- Sarah looks past Macon to Muriel.
- Rose touches their arms.
- Macon and Sarah follow Rose to the makeshift altar.
- Macon fingers the wedding ring.
- Sarah stares into his face.

Once you have a feel for Tyler's actions, list actions for your scenes.

"A good writer," says Gardner in his *Art of Fiction*, "can get anything at all across in action and dialogue, and if he can think of no powerful reason to do otherwise, he should probably leave explanation to his reviewers and critics."

• WEEKEND 8 •
ACTION

Action in your novel is what characters do. What they do to each other, to objects, to the landscape, to animals, and to themselves. A man flicks on the windshield wipers. A woman, tense in the passenger seat of the same car, grips the dashboard. The rain makes her edgy as the car, driven by the man, hurtles down the highway. The man looks relaxed, but his knuckles turn white as he clutches the wheel.

When you write action, you are not only moving the plot along, you are also providing clues to character motivation. The flicking on of the wipers is a challenge, as the man responds to the rain. The woman's gripping of the dashboard shows anxiety about riding in the hurtling car in the storm.

You use action to *reveal* character. Action adds irony to your dialogue. As Character A utters this dialogue line, "I love you, darlin'," she blows Character B away with a Clint Eastwood .44 Magnum. Her action, shooting Character B, reveals her character and throws into question her definition of love. Before she pulled the trigger, love had a bittersweet taste. Now it tastes ugly.

When Character A kills Character B, that's a large action. It stands out from the other actions. It is made up, in the writing of your scene, by other smaller actions: loading the gun, finding the trigger, wiping a tear away from the cheek, watching the gun muzzle wobble and weave. A large action forms the core of your scene, which you can encapsulate into headlines for your unconscious: LOVER MURDERS LOVER.

The opening scene from Anne Tyler's *Tourist* has two large actions: Macon drives the car; Sarah asks for a divorce. When you're writing notes to prepare for a scene, jot down large actions and place them on your storyboard (see Weekend 5). Then work the scene around them. You build to the large actions with smaller actions. To keep the action from getting flat, add *re*actions. In the rhythm of your novel, action is the one, reaction is the two.

Guidelines for Writing Action

When structuring your scenes, work on rhythm, the patterned alternation of one-two. Follow each action with *re*action. This sequence occurs in paragraph 9 in Tyler's first scene.

Action: They arrived behind a trailer truck.
Reaction: Macon swung to the left and passed.
Reaction: Sarah gripped the dashboard with one hand.

Use reactions, their intensity, their number, to emphasize how important each action is. In the above sequence, if Sarah had yawned instead of gripping the dashboard, her reaction to Macon's driving would produce less tension.

In a longer action-reaction sequence, alternate action and reaction with breaks or pauses, little stopping places where your readers catch their breath. That's what Tyler does in paragraph 15, where the car hurtles into an underpass, linking action to stage setup: "They shot through an underpass. The rain stopped completely for one blank, startling second. Sarah gave a little gasp of relief, but even before it was uttered, the hammering on the roof resumed. She turned and gazed back longingly at the underpass. Macon sped ahead, with his hands relaxed on the wheel." Here's a breakdown showing action and reaction in the passage:

Action: They shot through an underpass.
Reaction: The rain stopped completely for one blank, startling second.
Reaction: Sarah gave a little gasp of relief
Break: but even before it was uttered

Action: the hammering on the roof resumed.

Reaction: She turned and gazed back longingly at the underpass.

Reaction: Macon sped ahead, with his hands relaxed on the wheel.

The actions and reactions pack the car with conflict. There's no dialogue, but the reader senses trouble because of the extended action-reaction sequence.

How important is this rhythmic sequence? One way to find out is to remove a reaction. If something happens in your story and your characters fail to react, a tiny hole appears in the fabric of your story. Let's rewrite that underpass sequence, leaving out Sarah's reactions to make a tiny hole: "They shot through an underpass. The rain stopped completely for one blank, startling second. The hammering on the roof resumed. Macon sped ahead, with his hands relaxed on the wheel."

Sarah is gone. The balance in the passage vanishes. There is no tension, no conflict. It's just a guy driving a car into an underpass and then back out into the rain. The hole in the fabric of your story, once no bigger than a pinprick, is now much bigger. The drama leaks out. If you wrote a whole scene this way—all action and no reaction from the characters—then the pinpricks would clump together, massing until the fabric ripped itself apart.

And there goes your story.

Writing in action-reaction sequences is one key to writing scenes that are strong, active, and fully realized. The other key is to use powerful verbs. A powerful verb is an active-voice verb that creates a word picture (*swung, gripped, fogged, pumped, cut, huddled*) or at the very least delivers concrete information about the physical world: *arrived, cleared, turned and gazed, passed, kept, parked.*

Tyler writes mostly in the active voice (subject-verb-object): "Macon switched his wiper blades to high." The action of the sentence runs in a straight line from *Macon* (the subject) through the verb *switched* to the object, *wiper blades*. If you rewrote that sentence in the passive voice, it would look like this:

The wiper blades were switched to high by Macon.

And if you rewrote other sentences in the passive—a pickup truck was passed (by them); the dashboard was gripped by Sarah; the brakes were pumped (by Macon)—the weak writing would crowd the strong writing out of the passage. If you're confused about the passive voice, remember that the passive voice reverses the flow of the sentence:

> *Active:* Macon switched his wipers on.
> *Passive:* The wipers were switched on by Macon.

If you look at the sentence as a movement of 1-2-3, the active voice looks this way:

>   1   2   3
> Macon switched his wipers on.

And the passive voice looks this way:

>   3   2   1
> The wipers were switched on by Macon.

The meaning is the same but your writing has suffered a power loss.

Passive voice is okay for dialogue when it echoes the rhythms of everyday speech. In paragraph 16, Sarah uses a passive-voice verb, *was parked*, to explain the presence of a boy on a motorcycle—"He was parked beneath the underpass"—and it sounds perfectly normal here. But when you write action, stick to active-voice verbs that create word pictures.

Word pictures build into large actions that build into scenes.

WORKING THE NOVEL

Exercises

1. *Writing to Discover Action.*
Using different start lines, write three or four action sequences. They should take ten minutes apiece. In at least two of the sequences, allow yourself to write in one long sentence, using simple

connectors like *and, then, so, and then, and so, when, and when,* which help you speed along, writing action and reaction without slowing down for reflection. You may use dashes but no periods or semicolons. Sample start lines:

"The car swerved and the driver . . .
"He swung the ax with a heavy chopping motion and . . ."
"She slid the needle into the fabric and . . ."
"Leaning into the mirror, she touched the lipstick to . . ."

2. *Rewriting with Strong Verbs.*
Make four lists of verbs. One list for meat cutting (*slice, chop, skin, flay, gut,* et cetera). One list for sewing (*knit, weave, pin,* et cetera). One list for playing a sport (*serve, return, volley, lob, smash, stroke,* et cetera). And one list for making love (*hug, dance, touch, kiss, squeeze, stroke,* et cetera).

Then select your least favorite action writing from exercise one and rewrite it, replacing weak verbs with strong verbs.

3. *Writing a Scene.*
Put your rewritten action from exercise 2 together with your characters from "Character Work" and write a scene. As you keep working, add dialogue and stage setup. Work on each piece in a separate timed writing, ten to fifteen minutes for each piece. Let them flow together. Make sure, before you bring characters onstage, that they have agendas.

4. *List of Large Actions.*
Make a list of large actions for several scenes in your book. Place each action in its appropriate position on the storyboard for each scene. To develop the large action, you add smaller actions (and reactions).

Remember: large actions start with powerful verbs. When you're working the storyboard, try some of these: *walked, sauntered, angled, forced, rammed, stuttered, coughed, prayed, stayed, slithered, connected, grunted, batted, battered, hammered, stared, leaned, turned, drew, licked, tilted, reached, touched, ran, swallowed, cocked, pointed, clutched . . .*

Learning from Other Writers

Ernest Hemingway (1899–1961), a hunter and a fisherman and an aficionado of the Spanish bullfight, made his reputation writing action sequences like the one below, from the climax of "The Short, Happy Life of Francis Macomber":

> Wilson, who was ahead, was kneeling shooting, and Macomber, as he fired, unhearing his shot in the roaring of Wilson's gun, saw fragments like slate burst from the huge boss of the horns, and the head jerked, he shot again at the wide nostrils and saw the horns jolt again and the fragments fly, and he did not see Wilson now and, aiming carefully, shot again with the buffalo's bulk almost on him and his rifle almost level with the on-coming head, nose out, and he could see the little wicked eyes and the head started to lower and he felt a sudden white-hot, blinding flash explode inside his head and that was all he ever felt.

Take a moment to study how Hemingway did it. Circle the verbs in this passage (*was, was kneeling/shooting, fired, etc.*) and then circle the verbals (verbs ending in *-ing*). Draw blocks around the parallel phrases (*almost, almost*). And then work out the sequences of action and reaction. Here's one:

Action: he shot again at the wide nostrils
Reaction: and saw the horns jolt again
Reaction: and the fragments fly

DURING THE WEEK

Looking Ahead to Point of View

Your main goal in choosing a point of view for your scenes is to find one that works for you. I like first person. It feels good to me. It feels right there and I can find my voice faster than I do with third. But first person does have limitations, which is why most writing teachers advise you to start out with third person. Here's John Gardner, writing about point of view in *The Art of Fiction*: "The traditional third-person-omniscient point of view, in which the story is told by an unnamed narrator (a persona of the author) who can dip into the minds and thoughts of any character, though he focuses primarily on no more than two or three, gives the writer greatest range and freedom." (p. 76)

In *The Art and Craft of Novel Writing*, Oakley Hall expands on this choice of third person omniscient: "As she gains expertise, the writer can shift this point of view camera from behind the viewpoint character's eyes, to over his shoulder, to a spot at some distance away and including the character within the viewed scene, moving in and out; these options give third person so much more flexibility than first."

· WEEKEND 9 ·
POINT OF VIEW

Point of view is the angle from which your story is told. It is the writer's narrative stance, the place where the narrator stands (Close to the story? Removed? Distant?) and it is also the attitude taken by the narrator (comic, tragic, ironic, objective, subjective) about the material. The material includes the action, dialogue, characters, events, and physical details of your novel. When you study fiction, hunting for keys to unlock your own writing, you can usually track down the point of view by hunting for pronouns: *I, we, he, she, they, you.*

First person is *I/we*; third person is *he/she/they*; second person, used mostly as change of pace, is *you*. A pronoun takes the place of a noun. It's an empty container, a pointer that points to the nearest noun of the same person and gender. Anne Tyler opens Chapter Two of *The Accidental Tourist* in third person omniscient: "After HIS wife left HIM, Macon had thought the house would seem larger. Instead, HE felt more crowded. The windows shrank. The ceilings lowered. There was something insistent about the furniture, as if it were pressing in on HIM."

In this example, Tyler's protagonist (Macon Leary) has the point of view, third person omniscient, made more emphatic by our capitalizing the third person pronouns, HE, HIS, and HIM. Anne Tyler's point-of-view technique, third person omniscient, is a good one for you to follow. It brings the reader close while still maintaining just the right distance.

Let's explore her technique for handling point of view. First, the writer locks in her protagonist's point of view with verbs of sense perception. The verb *felt* provides a sense of touch for the character; *were pressing* gives us a sense of his being crowded. The third person singular pronouns (*he, his, him*) let us be with Macon as the house closes in. Second, she increases the psychic distance, muting the closing in of the house while she narrates the events that have taken place since Sarah asked for a divorce in Chapter One. (Psychic distance is the distance the reader feels, or senses, between herself and the story.)

Sarah, a major force in the opening scene from Chapter One that we've already analyzed, has made her exit from the novel's stage. Now, in this house scene, through Macon's point of view, we experience the symbolism of emptiness following her departure: "Her shelf in the medicine cabinet, stripped, was splashed with drops of liquid rouge in a particular plummy shade that brought her instantly to Macon's mind." For the reader, who sees the careful detail of the stage setup filtered through Macon's eyes (*liquid rouge, plummy shade*), there is a deepening of the sadness from Sarah's departure.

Guidelines for Choosing Your Point of View

Following the combined advice of John Gardner and Oakley Hall (discussed last week)—and the example of Tyler—start writing scenes for your novel using third person omniscient. To lock in your point of view, to keep it consistent, stick tight to objective detail. Learn all you can from Tyler, starting with her opening scene, where the point of view is third person omniscient cinematic (an overall view instead of a view from the perspective of one single character).

Beginners often open their novels with several pages of thoughts from the character's interior, telling instead of showing. Tyler's opening scene is an excellent model for you to follow because she works with detail that is largely exterior—clothes, landscape, weather, actions, the car—enabling her to stay *out of the heads* of her characters, thereby letting the characters' actions speak for them.

Instead of invading the heads of her characters, Tyler stays objective by moving the camera: swinging the lens to the window for a wide view of the landscape; zooming in for a close-up on the faces of her characters; pulling back, changing the psychic distance, to pause for an explanation that guides the reader along.

In paragraph 1, for example, she pulls back to explain why the Learys are coming home early from the beach: "Neither of them had the heart for it. . . ." In paragraph 2, she pulls back *after* she gives us a hint about clothes—Macon's formal summer suit, Sarah's strapless terry beach dress—to explain what these different clothes mean: "They might have been returning from two entirely different trips."

This is the strength of third-person omniscient. You change the psychic distance, pulling the camera back or zooming in for a close-up. These changes, done right, produce a rhythm that catches the reader's attention. You can learn a lot from Tyler about handling point of view.

Follow Tyler's strategy. Present the detail first—the subtly clashing contrast in Sarah's and Macon's traveling clothes—and then you fill in, if necessary, with an efficient explanation. You guide the reader along, gently leading. The danger, of course, comes when you guide too much, allowing your prose to mushroom out of control, forming huge, lumpy paragraphs of explanation that slow the action of the novel.

To solve this problem, you return to rhythm, one-two, one-two. In paragraph 14 of the opening scene, for example, Tyler changes the psychic distance with a close-up on Sarah: "She had a broad, smooth face that gave the impression of calm, but if you looked closely you'd notice the tension at the corners of her eyes." The modifiers *broad*, *smooth*, and *calm* describe Sarah's seeming exterior. The closer look tells a different story: tension at the corners of Sarah's mouth. The rhythm is there, description, then a quick close up. One, then two.

The Safety of Sense Perception

If you can think of point of view as an interface between the reader and your story, you can strengthen the interface by linking it to the sense perceptions of your characters.

Experts tell us the bulk of our information about the world (eighty to ninety percent, they say) is visual. Since reading is a visual activity, it's only natural for you to write visual detail first. That's what Tyler does: "He was a tall, pale, gray-eyed man, with straight fair hair cut close to his head, and his skin was that thin kind that easily burns." And then, as she deepens the scene in the car, she adds details of sound, touch, and hearing:

Sound (paragraph 6): Macon switched his wipers on. Tick-*swoosh*, they went—a lulling *sound*; and there was a gentle *patter* on the roof.

Touch (paragraph 15): . . . some artificial *chill* remained, quickly turning *dank*. . . .

Smell (paragraph 15): . . . carrying with it the *smell of mildew*.

Sound (paragraph 15): . . . the *hammering* on the roof resumed.

Sound (paragraph 50): . . . and the rain beat so *loudly* on the roof . . .

Sound (paragraph 52): The only *sound* was the *drumming of rain* on the overhang far above them.

Point of view in fiction is a function of style and scene and character. It exists because they exist, not as an intellectual construct apart from them. If the characters perish and the story keeps going, the author has the point of view.

The best way to handle point of view is to let it grow from the writing as the characters react to the story. In *The Accidental Tourist*, the rain hammers down on the car. Inside the car, Sarah shrinks into the upholstery. In the driver's seat, hands relaxed on the wheel, Macon pumps the brakes and plows ahead. If you now write, "Sarah's ear felt hot, ready to explode," you give her the point of view as a function of *touch/feeling* (the verb *felt*). If you now write, "The brakes felt bruised, punished by the foot of the electro-humanoid," you give the point of view to the brakes. Point of view lives in words and sentences. What you call it, whether "third person omniscient" or "first person unreliable," is not as important as what it does to the story. If you give the point of view to the brakes on Macon's car, you wake the reader from the fictional dream. The reader identifies with characters, not inanimate objects.

Three Suggestions for Handling Point of View

1. *Close off your scene*—a room, a compartment, a blanket on the grass, a vehicle in motion—*and stay with one point of view until the scene is over.* For now, while you're learning the moves, play it safe. Write your first novel with the closed-set mentality, sticking tight to detail.

2. *Link your point of view to your characters*—*their bodies, their sense perceptions*—and not some disembodied authorish voice. When the Learys hear the hammering on the roof, we hear it too. Their point of view, tied to *sound*, holds us inside the scene inside the car. Point of view makes the scene seem real. They react. We react.

3. *Have a reason for choosing a point of view.* In her opening scene, for example, Tyler uses third person omniscient cinematic to give us a view of *both* characters. We might understand Macon; we might sympathize with Sarah; but we don't choose sides yet because Tyler does not. The point of view in the opening scene (Chapter One) holds us in suspense until the second scene (Chapter Two), where, at the first sentence, we know it's Macon's story.

WORKING THE NOVEL

Exercises

1. *Practicing with Third Person Omniscient.*
On a sheet of paper, write down four or five events from your own life where at least three people were present, including you. Select

an event and do three timed writings, ten minutes apiece, and change point of view with each writing. Use third person pronouns for all three. The shortcut to understanding point of view is to experience the process: What does it look like (feel like, sound like) when you perceive from someone else's point of view an event you experienced?

2. *Point of View and Stage Setup.*
Put two of your characters in a moving vehicle—car, train, plane, bus, space ship, yacht. Using your list from Weekend 6, write for ten minutes while you explore distance in a scene (Tyler's move from the opening line to the cloudy sky to Sarah's tan to Macon, the tall, pale, gray-eyed man). Let the point of view work by itself as it moves across your list of details. Don't force it.

3. *Rewriting.*
When exercise 2 has cooled, read it into a tape recorder. Listen to the tape and then rewrite, working quickly, trying to stay present with the words as you include details from the stage setup that you left out before: temperature and weather and their effect on the characters. If it's muggy and the air-conditioner isn't working, let them sweat. If it's snowing and the heat is off in the wagon-lit on its way from Paris to Vienna, let them shiver and reach for clothes and blankets.

4. *Point of View and Sense Perception.*
Write a scene setup with Character A coming onstage while Character B has the point of view, which is third person omniscient. For example, "When Eleanor entered the room, her eyes narrowed in a frown, Biff sat back in his chair, one hand massaging the crick in his neck, and . . ." The *crick* locks point of view with Biff. Write for ten minutes, timing yourself. Then switch the point of view to Character A and do the scene again. "Eleanor entered the room, her heels going tap-tap-tap on the hardwood floor, and frowned when she caught the odor of cigarette smoke. Biff didn't smoke.

The cigarette, still smoldering, rested on the ashtray on the edge of his desk. . . ." Because Eleanor *smells* the smoke, the point of view belongs to her.

Learning from Other Writers

Study this passage from *Ulysses* by James Joyce, then copy it into your notebook. Circle the verbs: *leaned, gazed, was, fretted,* and so on. List the verbs on a separate sheet of paper. Then circle the concrete nouns and list those: *elbow, granite, palm, brow, edge,* et cetera.

> Stephen, an elbow rested on the jagged granite, leaned his palm against his brow and gazed at the fraying edge of his shiny black coat-sleeve. Pain, that was not yet the pain of love, fretted his heart. Silently, in a dream she had come to him after her death, her wasted body within its loose brown grave-clothes giving off an odor of wax and rosewood, her breath, that had bent upon him, mute, reproachful, a faint odor of wetted ashes. Across the threadbare cuffedge he saw the sea hailed as a great sweet mother by the wellfed voice beside him. The ring of bay and skyline held a dull green mass of liquid. A bowl of white china had stood beside her deathbed holding the green sluggish bile which she had torn up from her rotting liver by fits of loud groaning vomiting.

The passage comes from the opening chapter of *Ulysses* (1922), by James Joyce. *Ulysses*—with its myth-based structure, its heavy symbolism, its deep analogy, its narration via the stream of consciousness—changed the face of modern literature.

As you make your lists, tracking Joyce's technique, you'll see the movement of his camera eye, changing the rhythm of the piece within the point of view as Stephen, his narrator, shifts:

- from cuff to dream (close-up to interior)
- from dream to smell (interior to sense perception)
- from smell to cuff (sense perception to close-up)
- from cuff to sea (close-up to long shot)
- from sea to bowl of vomit (long shot to memory)

The *smell* locks down the point of view: it's Stephen's. The symbolism punches home Stephen's guilt about the death of his mother. The dull green mass of liquid held by the bay is symbolized by the bowl of bile-green vomit from Stephen's mother. Joyce uses his point of view to build an analogy. He's having fun (rhyming *wetted*, an adjective, with *fretted*, a verb), not a bad idea for you to consider. He's making a point about life and death and Ireland and being young.

As you learn your writer's craft, you'll struggle a bit with point of view. You'll get a lot of advice about it, some from people who get their kicks by giving advice to writers, some from experts in the know. Novelist Henry James, for example, held that first person was "barbaric."

Maxwell Perkins, the Scribner's editor who helped Fitzgerald and Hemingway and Wolfe and James Jones, among others, advised Fitzgerald to change the point of view from first to third when he was revising *This Side of Paradise.* While Perkins liked the verve of Fitzgerald's writing, he felt the book was brash and self-indulgent. Changing to third person launched Fitzgerald as a big-time writer. As A. Scott Berg writes in *Max Perkins: Editor of Genius, "This Side of Paradise* unfurled like a banner over an entire age." Published in March, 1920, *Paradise* had sold 50,000 copies by the middle of 1923, not bad for a first novel in any era.

In *Writing Fiction: A Guide to Narrative Craft*, Janet Burroway explores point of view for writers, moving from third person omniscient (including both editorial and limited) to third person objective (her example is Hemingway's "Hills Like White Elephants"); then to second person ("you" as character and "you" as reader-turned-character); and on to first person central and first person peripheral. In Forms, which she links to point of view, she covers oratory; reportage; stream of consciousness; monologue; interior monologue; diary; and journal. She discusses eight kinds of narrative distance (spatial, temporal, et cetera), three types of irony (verbal; dramatic; cosmic), and tracks the unreliable narrator through Othello, Faust, Huck Finn, and Benjy Compson (Faulkner's idiot in *The Sound and the Fury*). If you want to learn more about point of view, you can save time by studying Burroway.

DURING THE WEEK

Looking Ahead to Making Chapters

The easy way to make a chapter is to write a scene and give it the right chapter number and connect it to your story line. Write another scene. Link it to the one before it. Keep going, one chapter/one scene, until you finish the book.

Anne Tyler's opening chapter to *The Accidental Tourist* functions as one single scene. At the exit line, Macon and Sarah sit in the car under the Texaco overhang with the rain drumming. Chapter Two, composed of three interlocked sections, changes the rhythm, slowing down to show the reader Macon alone in the house. Chapter One moves fast. Chapter Two slows the story down. Did Tyler plan this?

· WEEKEND 10 ·
BUILDING CHAPTERS

The scene is the basic building block of the novel, but beginning writers in my fiction classes often assign that role to the chapter. Their next step is to make an assumption that could mean trouble for the writer. The assumption goes something like this: "Okay. Since Tyler wrote twenty chapters and made a book, all I have to do to make a book is to write twenty chapters."

The assumption, from the beginner's perspective, is not illogical. When you open a book, there's Chapter One. You read on, there's Chapter Two. The chapters are numbered in sequence, Chapter One, Chapter Two, Chapter Three, to provide the reader with a sense of progression. In nineteenth-century novels, authors like Melville and Hawthorne and Dickens gave much careful thought to naming their chapters, and when I thumb my copy of *Moby Dick* to check a quote from Melville, I get a thrill just saying those chapter titles out loud, hearing them echo down through time: "Loomings"; "The Whiteness of the Whale"; "The Doubloon."

And while chapters can be fun, the chapter is not a basic building block for your novel. It's a unit of division, a handy way for the novelist to collect scenes, to group them together for a particular purpose in the story. Purpose, knowing what you're doing, is the key to building solid chapters.

You can see Tyler's purpose clearly by looking at the first two chapters of *The Accidental Tourist*. In Chapter One, for example, Tyler uses one scene as her chapter. She packs in dialogue, action, the symbolism of the slashing rain, to produce maximum drama for her opening. The chapter is short, five pages in the paperback, and the Learys never leave the car. We see them from the outside. We eavesdrop on their grief over the death of Ethan, their son, and we experience the same rainstorm. But we can only *guess* at what they are thinking.

In Chapter Two, however, we are alone with Macon in the house, which rattles with emptiness now that Sarah's gone. Tyler shows us the inside of Macon's house and the inside of Macon's mind. Chapter One is one single scene with three parts, which we explored in detail earlier. Chapter Two, in similar fashion, is built in *three* separate scenes: one phone call from Macon's sister Rose, sandwiched in between opening and closing scenes rich with detail describing Macon's isolation inside the house he once shared with Sarah.

While Chapter One moves quickly to an inexorable climax, the splitting up of Macon and Sarah, Chapter Two slows down. The climax of Chapter Two—Macon trying to place the blame for Ethan's death—occurs *inside* Macon's mind. In these first two chapters, Tyler establishes a rhythm for the book. One: fast. Two: slowing down.

From the work you've done already, you know how to build scenes. Because scenes contain drama, you know how important they are to the energy of your story. To build chapters, you have two choices: You can either use one scene as one chapter, the way Tyler does in Chapter One; or you can combine scenes, slowing down to explore and explain, the way Tyler does in Chapter Two.

You can view this mix as a recipe for cooking up a chapter. Like a recipe, you change the ingredients to match your purpose and your needs for the novel. For example, if your story needs more drama, you add more scenes. If you're coming off a dramatic moment, and there are some things left unexplained, things the reader really needs to know, then you slow down, changing the pace of your story while you take time to explain. Coming off her very dramatic Chapter One, where we know that a son is dead and the marriage is in trouble, Tyler is careful to slow down as we get to know Macon. From the dialogue in Chapter One, we remember he's a systems guy. In Chapter Two, we see his systems in all their glory as he tries to subdue the empty house.

But even in a chapter where you're slowing down, changing pace to explain things, you still want to build to a climax. Tyler's climax in Chapter Two is a good model for you to follow. After a short flashback about Ethan growing up, Tyler climaxes the chapter with a powerful passage where Macon, forever locked into working his systems, tries to sort out the blame for Ethan's sudden death: "Blame the camp for not supervising. Blame Burger Bonanza for poor security. Blame the cabin-mate for . . ." The passage, built on the repetition of the powerful imperative verb *blame*, shows us Macon still trying the rational approach to deal with his grief. Now that Sarah has left, Macon's problems (fear and "systematized" isolation) are getting worse.

If you're planning chapters of one single scene, you can skip ahead here and move on to plot. If you're planning on building some complex chapters—two or more scenes connected in a purposeful sequence—then you'll be interested in studying how Tyler builds a complex chapter.

Example: Tyler's Chapter Seven

The chapter we'll look at in some detail is Chapter Seven, which launches Act Two of *The Accidental Tourist*. Chapter Seven is made of nine scenes that build to an electric climax, when Muriel Pritchett, the helper character, chokes Macon's dog. To get from one scene to another, Tyler uses cuts, a technique borrowed from the world of film-making. Cutting, which saves transition time, speeds the story along. Tyler's cuts from one scene to another work because she prepares the way with key words and recurring themes.

To make it easier to look at the development of Chapter Seven, I've summarized the content of each scene, listed below.

Scene 1: Muriel, hired by Macon, breezes onstage to take over the obedience training of Edward, Macon's dog. Muriel is the last hope, Macon's buffer between himself and the Leary family, who want to get rid of the dog. Conflict deepens because Edward belonged to Ethan, Macon's dead son.

Scene 2: Macon, on crutches because of a broken leg, has trouble making Edward mind, highlighting his need for Muriel.

Scene 3: Muriel builds a relationship with Macon by telling him stories of what it was like for her during the teenage years.

Scene 4: On Dempsey Road, Macon sweats as he tries to train Edward on his own.

Scene 5: In a back-to-high-school dream, circa 1957, Macon dreams that a girl he doesn't know turns into Muriel.

Scene 6: Muriel, still busy building a relationship, tells Macon about her marriage.

Scene 7: On the phone to Meow-Bow, where Muriel works, Macon learns that she is a single mom. Her little boy (who will remind Macon of Ethan) is sick.

Scene 8: In the office of Julian English, Macon's publisher, the talk turns to romance when Julian shows interest in Macon's sister, Rose.

Scene 9: Enraged that Macon has discovered her secret (the existence of a child), Muriel chokes Edward when he threatens her with barks and a fanged attack. Furious, Macon fires Muriel.

Guidelines for Chapter Building

1. To build a complex chapter, you knit together *two or more scenes* that have a common thrust. The thrust in Tyler's Chapter Seven comes from Muriel Pritchett. She wants to get to know Macon, so she pushes inside the closed circle of his life, posing as a dog trainer. There is good fun here because, in her opening monologue, Muriel explains that she really doesn't like dogs. Macon, perplexed by the seemingly undisciplined confusion of her mind, does not get the message.

2. To build a complex chapter, you *explore the motives* of at least one major character. Tyler's Chapter Seven, for example, explores the motives of *two* major characters: Macon Leary, the protagonist with the problem, and Muriel Pritchett, the helper with the solution. The power and delight of the chapter comes from the clash between Muriel's furious energy and Macon's systematic withdrawal from life.

3. To build a complex chapter, you *focus on your climax*, making sure that when you reach the high point, everything is in place for a big change. When Muriel chokes Edward, venting her fury because Macon knows she has a son, she cuts short the training session and at the same time cuts off her connection, the relationship she has built so carefully, with Macon.

Since Chapter Seven belongs to Muriel, let's take a moment to explore how she got here. She first spots Macon in a first-encounter scene at the Meow-Bow in Chapter Three. In Chapter Four, she phones Macon up, wanting to talk. In Chapter Five, a neighbor alerts Macon that Muriel's been sniffing around his house while he convalesces at Leary House with his family. In Chapter Six, after Edward the dog bites his hand, Macon hires Muriel, setting the stage for her full-blown entrance in Chapter Seven as Edward's trainer.

When Muriel, the Lonely Huntress Disguised as Dog Trainer, comes onstage in Chapter Seven with a monologue about how she didn't like dogs as a little girl, the reader already knows she's after Macon. Macon, buried under the weight of Muriel's monologues, doesn't have a clue.

When you build a complex chapter, knitting scenes together, you open up some room for character development. That's what Tyler does in Chapter Seven, as she adds details about magic, mystery, secret animal lore, and the world of the unseen to expand Muriel's helper role, making her a Good Witch/Fairy Godmother. The detail is subtle, showing Tyler's excellent touch.

Talking to Macon in scene 3 (p. 101), Muriel explains breezily how she made good grades in high school: "There's a trick to everything." In scene 5 (p. 106), she invades Macon's dream, replacing the girl he doesn't know with one he does: "She took his keys from him and set them on the dashboard. Gazing steadily into his face, she unbuckled his belt and slipped a cool, knowing hand down inside his trousers." In scene 6 (p. 108), Muriel recalls how Norman, her ex-husband, made her feel as if she had *powers* (italics mine). In scene 9, just before the climax, Muriel asks Macon: "You think I'm *magical* or something?" (P. 115, italics mine.) And just before the climax, defending herself after Macon asks about Alexander, her little boy, she says: "You think I'm some kind of unnatural mother?" Here, she blocks any criticism, defending her position with a rhetorical question as she denies any assumed connection Macon might make between herself and witchery. Near the end of scene 9, after choking Edward to stop his charge, Muriel admits in a sly aside to Macon that her ability to control dogs could be due to her understanding of a *secret* language.

Cutting to the Next Scene

To move between scenes and sections in Chapter Seven, Tyler uses quick cuts, a film technique. In the first scene, for example, Macon can't control Edward, so Muriel hisses, showing her power, showing off for Macon. After the hiss dies, the scene ends with Edward attacking the front door, a preview of the next scene. Tyler cuts to scene 2, which shows Macon's increasing difficulty with the training of Edward, thereby underlining his growing need for Muriel, who bounces back onstage in the next scene to deliver another zesty Muriel monologue.

Her opening line of scene 3—dating, making nothing but A's—blossoms into the longest monologue in the chapter, about her sister and dating in high school and the nastiness of boys. Tyler then cuts to the next scene (4), showing Macon training Edward alone on Dempsey Road. His description of the people on Dempsey Road, "an old people's street," contrasts with Muriel's memories from scene 3 of youth and high school. The Dempsey Road scene ends with the realization that he and Rose and the boys are getting old. Thoughts of aging trigger thoughts about being young, and in scene 5, Tyler cuts to Macon's teenage past, picking up the high school thread from Muriel's high school woes in scene 3. In scene 5 the unknown girl in Macon's grandfather's 1957 Buick is transformed into Muriel. The message is clear: Even in his dreams, Macon can't escape Muriel, or her furious energy, which contains the magic to transform him.

Themes—age and youth, dating and sex, Macon's inability to handle Edward or anything else—unify the chapter and make the quick cuts not only possible, but also efficient.

Cutting is a good technique for you to learn. Try it when you start building chapters.

WORKING THE NOVEL

Exercises

1. *Identify the Climax of Your Chapter.*
Let's say you have three scenes about the same subject (first encounter, first date, first kiss) and you want to make a chapter. You comb through the scenes in search of a climax. It might be an action, Muriel choking Macon's dog. It might be a dialogue line: "I want a divorce." It might be a well-constructed passage, built with careful repetition of a hot verb like *blame*. After you find your climax, deepen it by writing for ten minutes as you let your mind dig in. Using a storyboard (dialogue, action, stage setup), rethink the scene containing your climax.

2. *Define Your Purpose.*
What do you want this chapter to do in the story? Do you want speed? Do you want to get deeper with character? Write for five minutes: "The purpose of this chapter is to . . ."

3. *Explore Motive as You Build to the Climax.*
Now that you know your purpose, use a quick list—actions, events, symbols, lines of dialogue—to explore the motives of the characters in this chapter. If your chapter climaxes with a woman saying, "I want a divorce," then you're obligated earlier in the chapter to load in information that dramatizes the problems with this mar-

riage. Try the information in dialogue first, evoking the past, echoing another character, et cetera. If one of your characters turns suddenly violent—Muriel choking the dog—then you're obligated to build to that moment of intense action, exploring character the way Tyler explores Muriel, her costumes, her exorbitant monologues, her "secret" powers.

4. *Tune Up Your Scenes.*
In timed writings of ten minutes each, tune up the original scenes that made you want to build this chapter in the first place. If, at the end of ten minutes, you find there's more to write, make a note about it and press on to the climax. Push yourself here to write to closure.

5. *Practice Cutting Between Scenes.*
Before you bridge your chapter, slowing down your story to explore and explain, try cutting from one scene to the next. Learning to cut now saves you time. It moves the story along. It tightens the book. Tip: Look again at the end of Tyler's section 8. Waiting for Rose on the curb outside Julian's office, Macon pictures Muriel inside his mind, feeling empathy for her broken arm because he himself is still on crutches: "Her arm hung lifeless; he knew the leaden look a broken limb takes on." Muriel's imagined broken arm makes an easy cut to scene 9, the following morning, as Macon's mental image from scene 8 becomes Muriel in the flesh, breezy, bouncy, dressed to kill: "She arrived the next morning with a gauzy bouffant scarf. . . ."

Muriel arrives onstage with an agenda; when you bring on your characters, make sure they have agendas too.

Learning from Other Writers

As you grow as a writer, you will discover new ways to build chapters. Two examples to consider:

The detective writer Raymond Chandler liked the ratio of one chapter/one scene. For example, the opening scene of *The Big Sleep* (1939), which takes place in the entryway of the Sternwood Mansion in the Los Angeles hills, is also Chapter One. Scene one/Chapter 1 ends as Marlowe, Chandler's detective, walks out with the butler. Chapter 2, which is also scene two, takes place in the greenhouse with General Sternwood. An envelope changes hands. Chandler uses dialogue to fill us in on the case. Marlowe exits into a quick narration that takes him to scene three, Chapter 3, his interrogation by Mrs. Regan, in another room of the Sternwood place.

In contrast, F. Scott Fitzgerald, who likes chapters made with a mix of scenes, opens chapter four of *The Great Gatsby* (1925) with a list of guests for Gatsby's parties. The mixture of names (animals, fish, party food, a French philosopher) are meant to be funny: Leech, Civet, Voltaire, Beaver, Endive, Flink, Hammerhead, Beluga, Duckweed, Ferret.

Scene 2 of the chapter is a buddy-pal scene between narrator Nick Carraway and Jay Gatsby, including a dazzling description of Gatsby's yellow car—"It was a rich cream color, bright with nickel, swollen here and there in its monstrous length with triumphant hat-boxes and supper-boxes and tool-boxes, and terraced with a labyrinth of windshields that mirrored a dozen suns"—a monologue by Gatsby (lies and half-truths) on his past, and a long-distance stage setup as Nick and Jay enter New York City.

Scene 3, lunch in the city, is where Nick discovers Urban Eastern Depravity as Gatsby tells him that their luncheon buddy, Meyer Wolfsheim, was the man who fixed the World Series.

Scene 4 is back story in the first-person voice of Jordan Baker, who tells Nick about Daisy and Gatsby in Louisville during World War I.

Scene 5 is a dialogue between Jordan and Nick, as Jordan sharply analyzes Gatsby's motives for buying the big house, for throwing the parties: "I think he half expected her to wander into one of his parties, some night. But she never did." Since that strategy failed, Gatsby gets Nick to invite Daisy to his house for tea. The plot thickens—Gatsby, Nick's next door neighbor, plans to happen by to "accidentally" run into Daisy—and the irony deepens because Gatsby's waited five years to reconnect with Daisy, his dream girl.

The chapter climaxes with this irony.

DURING THE WEEK

Looking Ahead by Sketching

If you were a painter, lost in minute bits of color and the textures made by your brush, you would step back so that you could see the larger shapes of your art. Some writers use diagrams—quick sketches on paper—to help them see the shape of their writing. A diagram allows you to step back from the pulsing beat of your words to get a wider view of your work. Stepping back enables you to see pattern now, instead of having to wait, putting the manuscript aside while the words cool down.

If you did a quick diagram of the structure of Tyler's Chapter Seven, for example, what would it look like? You might start by drawing a line across your page with a gradual ascent from left to right to simulate the *rising action* in her chapter. The climax for Chapter Seven occurs in section 9, so you draw an arrow to mark the spot and you print these words, "Edward Attacks Muriel, Muriel Chokes Edward," above the arrow.

To convey the overwhelming wordage of Muriel's monologues, you draw bubbles around sections 1, 3, and 6, labeling them "Muriel's Monologues." In sections 2 and 4, Macon trains Edward alone. Since Macon's submerged, a way-down-under guy, you place his sections *below* the line.

Macon's erotic dream, the car, the unknown girl, occurs in the middle of the chapter, to illustrate in dream language that Macon cannot get away from Muriel. Since she dominates the dream, you print "Muriel-Dream" above the line. Section 5, Tyler's *mid*point for the chapter, connects the flighty, airy world of Muriel with the submerged underworld of Macon. At midpoint, on your diagram, they are *joined* by the dream.

In section 7, Macon phones Meow-Bow, calling from his world below the line to penetrate the secret of Alexander. Section 8, Macon and Rose, Macon and Julian, is a thick section below the line that connects the main plot (Muriel Hunting Macon) with the Romance-Marriage subplot of Julian and Rose. You might draw a line connecting section 8 to section 9 to indicate the transfer of Macon's mental image of Muriel (with the broken arm) to her appearance onstage in section 9. Print "Mental Image" on the connecting line.

To get a feel for diagraming structure, you might do a quick pencil sketch of the diagram for Tyler's Chapter Seven from the following page. Print the words, taking your time, while you breathe deeply. Feel your mind slowing down as you try out the process for the first time. You start with a chapter diagram here so you can get ready for a plot diagram in the next section.

You learn to diagram by sketching the structure of a story section that's already written, Tyler's Chapter Seven (see Fig. 1) where the diagram might feel like a passive tool of analysis. After practicing on Tyler, you try out a diagram on your own work in progress, where it becomes an *active tool* for creating fiction. A diagram, because it cuts through the clutter in your mind, can help you at any stage of the writing process—before you write or during the writing—by plotting the paths of your mind.

Closing Thoughts

You want to write scenes for your novel because they contain drama. Drama—often called entertainment—is what audiences pay for and you can tell from a read-through by your writing friends whether you've captured drama or not. If your scene is too short, your drama feels choked off. If your scene runs too long, the drama sags and your audience wanders out to the fridge for an egg-salad sandwich. Writing scenes trains you to compress and crystallize, good discipline for a writer. If you write scenes, and if you test them out on your friends, you'll improve quickly.

The best way to write scenes—whether you're just starting out or whether you're an old pro—is to work in stages, from the sketch through the parts to make the whole. You start with a sketch of a scene, noting on a piece of paper the time and place, the temperature and season, the lighting, character, purpose, point of view, climax, and curtain line. The sketch gives you an outline of a scene, the bare bones.

Symbolism of the Diagram:
Muriel in Control,
Above the Line.

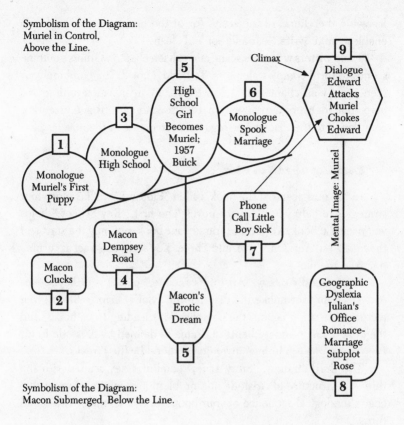

Symbolism of the Diagram:
Macon Submerged, Below the Line.

Fig. 1 Sketching a quick diagram of a part of your structure can help the writer step back for a wider view. After you have practiced on Tyler (or another novelist), try sketching one of your own chapters. You can use a rising line of action, like the sketch here, or you can devise your own shape: triangle, circle, vortex, web, maze, Bix X, labyrinth, cocoon. A diagram loads your unconscious so it can work while you sleep.

Knowing the climax of the scene (or of the chapter or of the book) enables you to write clear and hot and clean.

Some writers write one scene and call it a chapter. Others combine scenes to form complex chapters. To build a novel, you combine your scenes and your chapters into a structure, an organization of dramatic parts that delivers a moment of release and/or satisfaction and/or completion to the reader. The organizing structure of the novel is plot.

Looking Ahead to Plot

In the next scene of the book, called "Plotting," we'll explore four strategies to help you plot your novel. The first, "Key Scenes," helps you pace the book. Key scenes frame your book, not only the start and the finish, but Acts One, Two, and Three. Key scenes also act as turning points in the plot.

The second strategy, "Aristotle's Incline," places your key scenes on a diagram (not unlike the diagram for Tyler's Chapter Seven) that pictures the rising action, the complications leading to catharsis, and the denouement—ingredients of drama as defined by Aristotle in his *Poetics*. Drama is a human invention codified by the Greeks.

The third strategy, "Story Line," combines key scenes with the three-act structure of Aristotle in a problem-and-solution format that charts the logical sequence of your book through its major twists and turns.

The fourth strategy, "Scenario," puts your story into narrative form. In the simple language of the storyteller, you write down what happens in your novel. Writing the story down gives you an overview of the story as it has grown to this point, and also helps you make the transition into writing the novel.

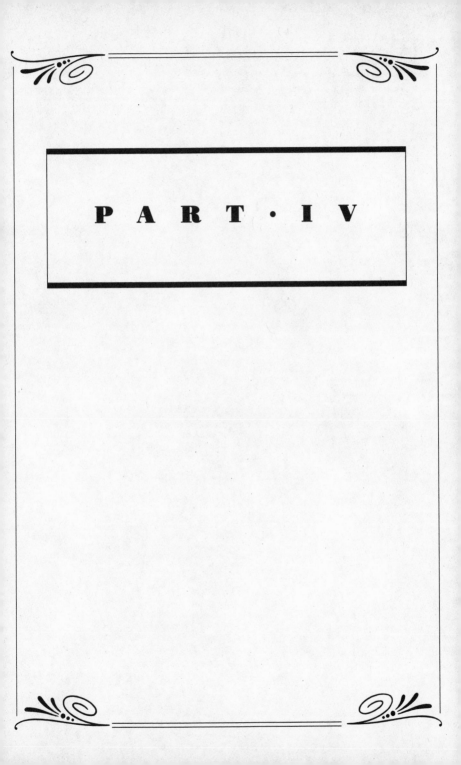

PART · IV

Weekends 11–14
Plotting

A plot is a plan, a design, an outline. In politics, when rebels scheme to overthrow the monarch, their plan is called a *plot*. In mathematics, a scholar *plots* a formula by drawing a curve that connects points on a graph. In literature, a *plot* is an arrangement of parts (acts, scenes, events, actions) that builds your story.

A plot of your novel can be the conception (your *idea* of the plot, the design inside your head) or an actual sketch (in which you map out the action and diagram the arrangement of parts) or both. Plotting a novel means thinking specifically about the best way to arrange the parts. Some writers plot before they begin writing. Others plot after they have some words down on paper.

A plot sketch is a blueprint for building your novel. It lets you test parts of your book in conceptual form before you invest time in the work of writing. A plot sketch that takes only minutes can save you weeks of work. A plot sketch keeps you on track. At the midpoint of your novel, when you hear the siren song of possibility wooing you off your story line, it's time to do another plot sketch.

Plotting helps you reach the end. Reaching the end, you have a better grasp of your beginning.

When you do your sketch, it helps to visualize your plot in a recognizable shape. You step back, pulling away from the words to get a wider view, and you see the shape of the action. The shape for F. Scott Fitzgerald's *Tender Is the Night*, for example, is a big X. The protagonist, psychiatrist Dr. Richard Diver, starts high, at the top of the X, on the left hand side, and ends way down low, low, low on the right. (Some scholars think his name, Diver, is symbolic of his fall.)

As Dr. Diver descends, sinking lower and lower, his wife, Nicole, rises, moving from low on the left to high on the right. Her story begins with Nicole as a mental patient—a victim of child molestation by her father—and ends with her nearing the top of the X on the right-hand side. Through a physical liaison with a muscleman, a virile man quite opposite to her husband (a doctor of the mind), Mrs. Diver has regained her mental balance.

As a novelist, you would make the X structure for your book by giving equal time to both characters: half the book to the character who descends; the other half to the character who rises. As the characters pass each other, somewhere near the middle of the book, your big-X structure produces wave after wave of irony.

The Best Plot for You

Plot shape can take several forms, big X, big W, figure 8, hero cycle (a loosely formed circle), maze, but the best one for you is a straight line plot divided into three acts. Aristotle called this linear plot the *energeia*. Like the structure for a scene, linear plot has a beginning, middle, and end. You turn these, in a novel, into three acts paced by turning points. The plot builds through rising action to a high point in the story, a moment of release that Aristotle called "catharsis," which means a purging of emotion. The linear plot with its three-act structure dominates products of the screen, both feature films and television, so it has wide audience acceptance. It's classical, with deep roots reaching back to Aristotle. It's a great structure to bring your novel to life.

For the next four weekends, we'll study the plot of *The Accidental Tourist*, with an occasional look, for contrast, at the classical structure of Cinderella.

The Next Four Weekends

On Weekend 11, we'll begin to look at plot structure by identifying key scenes from Tyler's *Tourist*. In the scene-building section, you explored one key scene in depth, Tyler's opening sequence in the car, which sets up Macon's problem of isolation. In Chapter Twenty, capping off the end of the book, there's a matching scene from the interior of a car, a Paris taxi, with Macon telling the driver to stop. These two car scenes frame the novel. Like twin bookends on a shelf, they act as containers for the events of your story. Other key scenes act as turning points, closing off larger sections of the novel much in the same way that curtains close off acts in a theatrical production.

On Weekend 12, we'll compress the key scenes from *The Accidental Tourist*, squeezing their drama into labels (Inside the Car, Macon Okays Muriel, Macon Confesses, et cetera) so we can place them on a helpful diagram called "Aristotle's incline." Using Aristotle's incline to straighten out your plot can save you hours and hours of writing.

On Weekend 13, we'll turn the plot insights gained from diagraming the key scenes into a story line (a bare-bones description of a novel's plot). We'll step back, away from the work, to trace a pattern of problem and solution that takes your story from beginning to end. The key to the story line is to find solutions that have problems buried in them. For example, *The Accidental Tourist* starts with Ethan's death, so you might explore the story line in the one-two of problem and solution, like this:

Problem: A child has died.
Solution: Take a trip. Try to forget.
Problem: Husband won't talk, won't share his grief.
Solution: Wife departs, talking divorce.

On Weekend 14, you'll move from problem and solution, gathering your insights to write a scenario, a narrative treatment of your novel. You'll focus on key scenes, on major actions, on the motivation for those actions. You'll aim your writing at the novel's climax, the moment of catharsis where all the major characters are present for the fireworks. Writing to closure in your scenario gives you the knowledge that you can write to the end of your novel.

• WEEKEND 11 •
KEY SCENES

Key scenes frame a novel. In Tyler's *Accidental Tourist*, we open in a car with Macon and Sarah in conflict. At the end of the novel, we close in a car with Macon telling the Paris taxi to stop for Muriel. Use this framing technique—repeating a key image—for your novel.

At key points in the book, other key scenes act as turning points, high points, or curtains to close off the acts of the linear novel.

Organize your novel into three acts, following Aristotle's advice about having a beginning, middle, and end. The book moves on a rising line of action to the climax, which Aristotle called "catharsis," a purging of emotion through symbolism. Each act should contribute to the rising action.

Act One is the setup, the beginning of your plot. You bring your characters onto your novel's stage, flashing their agenda cards, neon signs pulsing with detail that show the reader their problems in need of solutions. At the end of Act One, you close it off with a key scene containing a twist or a turning point.

Let's go back to *The Accidental Tourist* to flesh out the three-act structure and the key scenes necessary for smooth transition. Tyler ends Act One as Macon okays Muriel as the trainer for Edward. When Muriel, a dog trainer who doesn't get along with dogs, comes onstage in Chapter Seven, she's girded for action. The turning point, Macon's decision that ends Act One, is a key scene, event, or action called "plot point one."

Chapter Seven of *Tourist* (which we studied just last weekend) starts Act Two (the middle plot development), which is dominated by Muriel Pritchett. Muriel is driven to get close to Macon because she wants a provider, someone to pay the bills (her agenda). Her main weapon is dinner—she wants to cook for Macon—and the midpoint of Act Two, and of the book, occurs when Macon drives to her place on Singleton Street with an RSVP refusal. He winds up, not at Muriel's table, but in Muriel's bed, after blurting out a choked confession about Ethan's death the year before.

Following midpoint, Act Two winds into Rose's wedding in Chapter Sixteen as Macon, feeling right at home with Sarah and Rose and Mom, drifts away from Muriel and life on Singleton Street. The end of Act Two, which rings the curtain down on Macon and Muriel, is a key scene called plot point two.

Act Three contains three key scenes: 1. a *decision scene* that pushes the protagonist toward a resolution; 2. a *catharsis scene* where the protagonist, usually through high risk, reaches a resolution; 3. a *capping-off scene* containing a final image that sticks in the reader's mind. Using *The Accidental Tourist*, let's look at how Tyler handles these three scenes.

1. In the hotel room in Paris, Macon's decision scene comes when he decides not to take the pain pill. Instead, he will suffer pain from his injured back.

2. Not taking the pain pill leads to the catharsis scene, when Macon decides, in full deflector mode, to go back to Muriel: "I'm sorry, Sarah. I didn't want to decide this." Catharsis resolves the issue by solving the big problem of the book, Macon's isolation and policy of no personal growth.

3. Macon's decision to leave Sarah and go back to Muriel leads him into the early-morning Paris street, where he hails a taxi. When he tells the taxi to stop for Muriel, the sunlight gets brilliant, giving us a stunning final image to cap off the story.

Key scenes pace the book, giving you turning points for your story. You write a key scene the same way you write any scene, storyboarding the sketch, writing each part, then fitting the parts together so that you can place the scene in your story line. With plot points one and two you have a chance for a major dramatic connection that will lock Act Two into place. In *Tourist*, for example, plot point two shows us how natural it feels for Macon to be back among family and friends. Muriel is alien territory, after all; even though she's cracked his shell, her turf, so blue collar, is not his turf. Plot plot two reverses the good stuff, the healing that began after Macon's decision to hire her in plot point one.

Sometimes it helps to jot a quick list of action/motivation for each key scene. Here's what you might jot down about *The Accidental Tourist*.

1. *Opening Scene:* Macon wants to hide. Sarah wants him to open up. They bicker. Sarah asks for a divorce.

2. *The Scene at Plot Point One:* Macon wants to hold on to his last connection with Ethan: Edward the dog. Because Macon will do whatever is necessary to keep the connection alive, he lets Muriel in.

3. *The Scene at Midpoint:* Macon confesses to Muriel that his son is dead.

4. *The Scene at Plot Point Two:* Surrounded by women/family at Rose's wedding, Macon thinks of leaving Muriel.

5. *Catharsis Scene:* Macon decides not to take that pill.

6. *Wrap-up Scene:* Macon tells the taxi to stop to pick up Muriel. Macon shouting, *"Arretez,"* sunlight on the windshield, Muriel about to climb into the taxi with Macon—creates a memorable final image.

Guidelines for Plotting with Key Scenes

Frame your novel first. Sketch an opening scene and then sketch a wrap-up and then sketch your catharsis. Knowing the end of your novel now will give your unconscious a beacon to write toward, a North Star to guide you through the catharsis scene right up to the last line. Do the sketches in words, timing yourself. Here are sample sketches from *Tourist:*

Opening Scene: In the car coming home from the beach, Macon and Sarah Leary struggle with each other. It's raining. Sarah wants Macon to share his grief about the death of Ethan, their son. Macon, a systems guy, wants to stay buttoned up inside his glass cage. This opening sequence introduces Macon's isolation as the problem that needs solving. Sarah's solution—to leave Macon, to get a divorce—only makes his problem worse, driving him deeper inside his shell.

Wrap-up Scene: Riding along in the Paris taxi, Macon tells the driver to stop when he sees Muriel on the sidewalk. "A sudden flash of sunlight hit the windshield, and spangles flew across the glass." (Framing Note: Open with car, close with car.)

Cathartic Scene: On a plane to Paris, Macon discovers Muriel's a passenger too. He escapes, but she shows up at his hotel, guided by his travel agent and his handy guidebook on Paris. Evading Muriel puts Macon under stress and he twists his back. Phoning Julian about the pain, he reaches Rose, who's working for Julian, who has followed Macon's advice by asking Rose to organize things at the office. Phoning Rose, Macon alerts Sarah, who shows up at his hotel in Paris bearing pain pills, announcing in a cheery voice she'll make his day trips for him. This job is Macon's identity. Sarah wants to take over. Something has to give.

Macon's down, zonked on pain pills, so Sarah bombs him about Muriel. Why did he let her follow him? Why didn't he tell her to exit the plane before takeoff?

Macon palms the pill. In the climactic paragraph, he reflects on the lack of action in his life. He drops the pill. He jettisons *Miss Macintosh*, the book he's always used as a buffer zone between himself and fellow travelers. He tells Sarah he's going back to Muriel. Sitting up in bed, Sarah brings up the revenge theme: "Are you just trying to get even with me for the time I left you?"

No, Macon answers, deflecting like crazy. Then he exits.

As you sketch out your frame, moving the story toward your moment of release at the point of catharsis, stick tight to character and motivation. Your key word in the sketch is *wants*. Your key themes should be big: rebirth, love, fear, revenge. (A good example of revenge: In her dialogue line, Sarah asks if Macon is "getting even.")

Once you have framed the book, using opening and closing images, move on to sketch the key scenes that remain. Try starting in the middle.

The Scene at Midpoint: Recoiling from an invitation to dine at Muriel's house, Macon drives over to Singleton Street to pin a no-thank-you note on her door, only to end up in her arms, confessing the fact of Ethan's death. In Muriel's bed, their needy coupling picks up the thread of eroticism from Macon's dream from Chapter Seven. By sharing his grief with Muriel, Macon reveals the first tiny crack in his shell.

The Scene at Plot Point One: Edward attacks Julian, Macon's publisher, at the family home occupied by Rose and the boys. Edward tears up the screen door. The boys suggest getting rid of Edward, but Macon can't because he was Ethan's dog. Against his better judgment, Macon phones Muriel for help. Muriel, with her small-time sorcery, is the only person who can break Macon out of his shell.

The Scene at Plot Point Two: Macon escorts Muriel and Alexander to Rose's wedding, where he is surrounded by the four women in his life: wife, mistress, mother, sister. Since his confession at midpoint (Chapter Eleven), Macon has been living with Muriel. Now, standing with Sarah at the altar, Macon feels very much at home. The last line of the chapter is "It all felt so natural." If he goes back, the shell will fold over him again, and all of Muriel's work will be lost.

(After Rose's wedding, Macon slides away from Muriel to join Sarah in the house at the end of Chapter Eighteen.)

Act Two is where your book can jump the tracks. You hold it on with these key scenes. Midpoint is a good place for love, sex, or seduction. Plot point two (Macon drifts away from Muriel) is a good place to reverse the action of plot point one (Macon lets Muriel into his life).

WORKING THE NOVEL

Exercises

1. *Scenes for Your Novel.*
Jot down ideas for fifteen to twenty scenes for your novel, leaving a line or two between each scene. After you finish your list, add details to expand these scenes: time, place, temperature, season, lighting, who's onstage, who's coming onstage, purpose of the scene, action, dialogue, climax, exit line.

2. *Key Scenes for Your Novel.*
From this list of scenes, select half a dozen that feel weighty enough to become turning points. For each one, write a brief summary of action. Use the summaries in the analysis of *The Accidental Tourist* as models.

3. *Writing a Key Scene.*

From the smaller list, select a scene that turns you on. Sketch it out. Write it in parts. Fit the parts together.

Learning from Other Works

For a contrast to Tyler, here are some key scenes from "Cinderella," a fairy tale that keeps right on going:

1. *Opening Scene:* The King, having perceived his age, the state of his kingdom, and his unmarried son, decides to have a ball.

2. *The Scene at Plot Point One:* The Fairy Godmother, having outfitted the heroine with clothes and glass slippers, advises her to be back home by midnight.

3. *The Scene at Midpoint:* Dancing with our heroine, the Prince falls in love. Cinderella, in a swoon, forgets to mind the time.

4. *The Scene at Plot Point Two:* The clock strikes. The coach turns back into a pumpkin. Cinderella loses her slipper.

5. *Catharsis Scene:* Cinderella braves the wrath of the Wicked Stepmother to try on the shoe. It fits.

6. *Wrap-up Scene:* Her loyal subjects cheer the marriage of the new Princess.

If we step back for a wider view of "Cinderella," we see a problem in the throne room that's solved in the royal wedding. This linkage between problem and solution frames the story. The King is old; the Prince is unmarried; the kingdom has no heir. The King decides to throw a ball, which gives Cinderella a problem with wardrobe. The royal wedding solves the heir problem by making Cinderella into a Princess, which, unless socialist rebels storm the palace, solves our heroine's clothing problem.

A ticking plot device connects the scenes at plot points one and two, which precede the curtains for Acts One and Two. In an aside near the end of Act One, the Fairy Godmother warns Cinderella to be home by midnight. Our heroine, lifted aloft on dreams of romance and escape, hears but does not hear. Time slips by in Act Two. Midnight, the tolling of the royal clock, jolts Cinderella awake from her dream. A good story makes use of fact and detail introduced earlier.

There are two other key scenes, one at the middle of the work (the midpoint scene), halfway between the curtains for Acts One and Two—Cinderella waltzing with the Prince—and one at the peak of your story line. The peak scene is the cathartic scene, a moment of triumph where Cinderella gets her revenge with the glass slipper.

Research on Plotting

In his final chapter in *The Art of Fiction*, after identifying three ways to organize your plot—*energeic, juxtapositional, lyric*—John Gardner devotes several pages to the energeic: "The most common form of the novel is energeic. This is both the simplest and the hardest kind of novel to write—the simplest because it's the most inevitable and self-propelled, the hardest because it's by far the hardest to fake."

The energeic novel, drawn from *energeia*, a word coined by Aristotle, is the model to use when you're starting out. Compared to the juxtapositional (complex thematic linkups through deep symbol) and the lyric (layered rhythmic repetition analogized to mirror complex music), the energeic is relatively simple and straightforward. It has a rising action, and is built in three acts, Aristotle's beginning, middle, and end. These three acts are paced by specific turning points that act as helpful sign posts in your writing. If, for example, you are writing a novel of three hundred pages, and you come to page one hundred with no turning point, that's a signal for you to step back for a wider view. It's time to do a pencil sketch, time to study from afar the larger structure of your novel.

That sketch we call "Aristotle's incline."

DURING THE WEEK

Looking Ahead to Aristotle's Incline

Aristotle's incline—modified by the German philosopher Johann Gottlieb Fichte (1762–1814), and popularized by books on screenwriting—is a line that moves from left to right, through three acts, to a climax. The scenes follow Aristotle's dictum of beginning, middle, and end. Writers who find this too confining will design their own plot diagrams. Before you judge Aristotle too harshly, however, copy out his incline in your writer's notebook. If you *print* the letters, you'll allow your unconscious to absorb the pattern, which will speed up your understanding of just how well this technique works.

Copy the framework of this sketch into your notebook. Then add your key scenes.

Don't worry if you don't have everything nailed down at this point. A diagram is a sketch. You've already done one for Chapter Seven, where midpoint, Macon's dream, is a kind of turnstile for the appearance of Muriel. Let your diagrams grow slowly. Sketching your insights out plants the design in your unconscious where it works while you sleep.

· WEEKEND 12 ·
ARISTOTLE'S INCLINE

Doing a diagram of your structure—the arrangement of parts of your novel—plants the design of the book in your unconscious, and gives

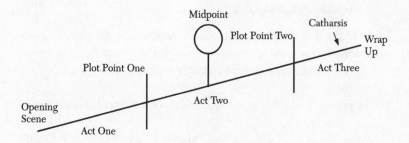

Fig. 2   Aristotle's Incline
Aristotle's incline helps you structure your plot with three acts—his idea of beginning, middle, and end—with rising action leading to catharsis at the climax of your tale. You can copy this diagram and try the structure of your novel on it now if you wish. Or you can wait until you're deeper into the writing.

you a comprehensive overview of your work. The first couple of diagrams might take longer while you accustom yourself to thinking visually about your story, but once you see the story line straighten itself out, once you feel the momentum building, you'll do diagrams for everything you write.

We're working with the structure of Tyler's *Tourist* because it is classical, three acts framed by key scenes that move the story along as Macon Leary, a reluctant hero who writes travel books, struggles not to solve his problem.

The diagram of Tyler's plot, highlighting the key scenes, shows you one reason *The Accidental Tourist* made a good movie. Each key scene highlights Macon's problem, isolation, which is not solved until the catharsis of the book, where he allows the pill to drop from his hand. Dropping the pill gets him out of Sarah's bed and headed back to Muriel, who has tugged and pulled to force him to rejoin society and the human race.

Muriel dominates Act Two with her quirky personality. Her need for Macon makes her vulnerable. When she chokes Edward in the opening of Act Two, Macon fires her, putting off his recovery even longer.

Guidelines for Plotting with Aristotle's Incline

On the *Tourist* diagram, the main problem of the plot, Macon's isolation, moves from left to right through the key scenes. Compress the scene, squeezing it down to a single statement of action:

Opening Scene: Because Macon can't share his grief, Sarah wants a divorce.

The Scene at Plot Point One: Macon okays Muriel as Edward's trainer.

The Scene at Midpoint: Macon confesses to Muriel about Ethan.

The Scene at Plot Point Two: Macon backslides into his old ways.

Cathartic Scene: Macon drops the pill; he's going back to Muriel.

Wrap-up Scene: Macon orders the taxi to stop for Muriel.

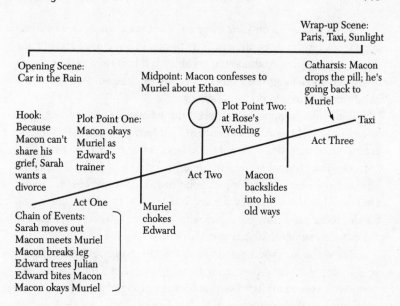

Wrap-up Scene:
Paris, Taxi, Sunlight

Opening Scene:
Car in the Rain

Catharsis: Macon
drops the pill; he's
going back to
Muriel

Midpoint: Macon confesses to
Muriel about Ethan

Plot Point Two:
at Rose's
Wedding

Taxi

Hook:
Because
Macon can't
share his
grief, Sarah
wants a
divorce

Plot Point One:
Macon okays
Muriel as
Edward's
trainer

Act Three

Act Two

Macon
backslides
into his
old ways

Act One

Muriel
chokes
Edward

Chain of Events:
Sarah moves out
Macon meets Muriel
Macon breaks leg
Edward trees Julian
Edward bites Macon
Macon okays Muriel

Fig. 3   Plotting with Aristotle's Incline

Aristotle's incline, divided into three acts, enables you to step back from the words to get a wider view of your story. If you start with Tyler's *Tourist* as a model, you can see the larger movement that begins in the car in the rain, with Sarah's request for a divorce, that ends inside another car, this one in sunlight, as Macon tells the Paris taxi to stop for Muriel. Stepping back allows us to see the story as one of replacement: Muriel takes Sarah's place. This replacement begins at plot point one, when Macon okays Muriel as Edward's trainer. It deepens at midpoint, as Macon confesses his loss to Muriel. It reverses at plot point two, as Macon backslides to his old ways, and to Sarah. It climaxes when Macon refuses the pain pill. The final image is a happy ending, filled with sunlight and confetti, that echoes the magical mood of a fairy tale. Tyler's Cinderella (zesty Muriel) has her Prince Macon at last. Listing chains of events (see above, under Act One) enables you to make connections between key scenes. Try using a sketch of your structure to help you create a solid plot for your novel.

You might start by copying the Tyler diagram down in your notebook, working slowly to allow time for your mind to assimilate the bare-bones structure. While you copy the diagram, let your mind focus on curtains used to close off the acts of your novel. Focus on rising action that leads to the catharsis scene.

When you write on your diagram, print your words slowly, using large block letters. According to Tony Buzan, in *Use Both Sides of Your Brain*, printing diverts the attention of the left hemisphere, which gets interested in making the letters look presentable, so that your right hemisphere is free to do its creative work.

To fill the diagram, you compress the action of the key scenes into a few words—"Macon Won't Share," "Macon Okays Muriel," et cetera—and then you print out these large actions above the main line. "Macon Won't Share" is your problem, so it goes first at the front of the line. Macon Okays Muriel is plot point one. It goes just before the Act One curtain. Above the key scenes, you can add the place, one locale for the scene, and the characters who are there. Macon and Sarah in the car, for example. Macon and Muriel on the phone.

Below the line you begin to work out the events that fill out each act. Under Act Two, part one (between the Act One curtain and midpoint), your chart lists Chapters Seven through Eleven from *Tourist*, along with the large action of each. A large action relates to the main problem-solution track of the book. Under the first part of Act Two, Tyler uses this sequence:

7. Macon Fires Muriel.
8. Macon Dines with Sarah.
9. Macon Calls for Help.
10. Muriel invites Macon to Dinner.
11. Macon Refuses, then Confesses.

Each large action deepens Macon's isolation, which shows in his refusal to share his grief, pushing and pushing until he confesses, showing Muriel he's human.

In Chapter Seven, when Macon fires Muriel, Edward the dog is still a biter and Macon the owner is still locked inside his glass cage. Things don't get better in Chapter Eight, dinner with Sarah, when Macon tries to discuss the past. This irritates Sarah, who, with her talk of legalities and dating, widens their separation. In Chapter Nine, at the top of a skyscraper in New York City, Macon has an attack of distance phobia (fear of getting too far away). Phoning home for help,

Macon discovers Charles trapped in the family pantry by Edward (still a problem). When Macon phones Muriel, she scolds him from her trainer persona, saying, "Things can't go on this way." Muriel's words refer not only to Edward's vicious biting, but also to the loose linkage between Muriel and Macon, a linkage that she wants tightened. In Chapter Ten, while Edward waits on the sidewalk, Muriel sandwiches in a dinner invitation between shopping and picking Alexander up. In Chapter Eleven, responding no to Muriel's invitation, Macon winds up in her bed.

If you aren't certain at this stage of what the scene-sequences will be in your novel, just fill in with scene sequences from last weekend. For example, under Act One you could print:

1. First Encounter
2. First Date
3. First Kiss
4. First Argument
5. First Separation
6. First Peace Overture
7. Second Date

You print the words—remember, they're not written in stone—and then you keep going until the diagram is finished. You set the diagram aside. Because you have done the actual work (not just thinking but the *physical act* of drawing), the sequences are now working deep inside your head. You'll be cooking, slicing onions for stew, and an idea will come to you. *Wrong sequence*, you'll say. *Wrong wrong wrong for my Act One*. And then you make a quick note about the right sequence and that new sequence ignites your story line. Sometimes it's easier to replace a wrong word with a right word than it is to write the exact right word in the first place. Replacement is easy. You've got something to work against. Filling a vacuum—or a blank page—is tough.

If you number your scenes, you increase your chances of deepening the sequence for each act. Using numbers helps your mind by keeping things simple as one-two-three. The scene sequences will come in handy as guides when you begin writing.

When you finish your diagram, or even a piece of it, set it aside and take a break. You've earned it. The design has been planted in your unconscious. When the structure shifts, you can do another diagram.

WORKING THE NOVEL

Exercises

1. *Aristotle's Incline.*
Copy the plot diagram. Make a couple of copies. Close your eyes and allow your mind to play across the key scenes of your story. Open your eyes and print your key scenes on the diagram. Don't despair if you don't do a perfect diagram in your first attempt. Writing is an act of discovery. The plot diagram is not the book; it's one more tool to help you build the book.

Try this: For each key scene, write the names of the characters who are there. As we discussed in Weekend 5, make sure you have a large action (or action plus reaction) for each key scene. "Muriel Chokes Edward" is good. The reaction, "Macon Fires Muriel," completes the unit of action and reaction.

2. *Scene Sequences.*
The key scene at midpoint halves Act Two, which gives you four sections to fill with scenes and scene sequences: Act One, Act Two (part one), Act Two (part two), and Act Three. Under each section, make a vertical list of the scenes (or main events) that appear in that section. List them sequentially. The purpose of these scenes will be to deepen the story.

Aristotle at the Movies

Study the way Syd Field handles diagrams of the three-act structure in either of his books on film writing: *Screenplay* or *The Screenwriter's Workbook*. Field calls his diagram the paradigm. He sees Act

One as setup, Act Two as complication (another concept borrowed from Aristotle's *Poetics*), and Act Three as resolution.

One of Field's main examples is the movie *Body Heat*, starring William Hurt and Kathleen Turner, the same duo who played Macon and Sarah in the movie version of *The Accidental Tourist*.

DURING THE WEEK

Looking Ahead to Story Line

The rhythm of story line is problem-solution, another example of one-two, one-two. Story line enables you to pull back from the words, where you see the larger patterns of your work. Before you tackle the story line of your novel, it might be helpful to learn from a famous story that's still alive in the culture. Name this story line:

Problem: Kingdom needs an heir.
Solution: Let's have a party.
Problem: Heroine has nothing to wear.
Solution: Magic. Fairy Godmother upgrades wardrobe. Changes pumpkin into a snazzy coach.
Problem: Magic has a time limit.
Solution: The heroine loses track of time.
Problem: Waltzing at the ball, the Hero falls for the Heroine.
Solution: The proposal is on his lips when . . .
Problem: Bong-bong, the clock strikes. It's midnight.
Solution: To save face, Heroine dashes for the coach.
Problem: Loses her slipper.
Solution: Search for foot that fits.
Problem: How to try on that slipper?
Solution: Courage. Stout heart. Character depth.
Problem: Slipper slips, almost breaks.
Solution: Helper catches slipper.
Ultimate Solution: Celebration, a royal wedding.

When the story line heats up, you move from problem-solution into writing prose: Cindy's need for a wardrobe brings on the Fairy Godmother who provides the glass slipper that fits only Cindy's foot which she loses dashing down the stairs because time's up and the magic has run out, but the Prince in hot pursuit snatches up the slipper and sends out the court flunky to try it on every female foot in the land.

· WEEKEND 13 ·
STORY LINE

Story line, a third plotting strategy, builds on the work you've already done on key scenes: 1) mapping out your scene sequence; and 2) diagraming your plot on Aristotle's incline. A story line is a written description of the obstacles that your characters must tangle with in the plot and the tactics they devise to combat them. By working through a problem-and-solution framework, you strengthen your plot. The key to writing believable and consistent story line comes when problems arise out of *apparent solutions*.

Tyler's story line is a good example for careful study. The first problem, Ethan's death in Burger Bonanza, before the book opens, forces the Learys to take a trip, a vacation on the beach, while they try to deal with what's happened. That apparent solution makes the problem worse, so they start home. In the car driving home, Sarah digs at Macon about his isolation, his unwillingness (Macon would see it as a gear in his systems) to share grief. Sarah gets away, solving the problem for herself, but deepening Macon's problem of self-centered isolation.

What saves him is another problem, Edward the biter, who forces Macon to try Meow-Bow, where he encounters Muriel. She's a problem on stilt heels—no money, weird taste, a sickly child. Muriel is the solution for Edward, but a problem for Macon. Muriel's training of Edward is a flimsy facade masking her real motives, finding a man to pay the bills. Macon, puzzled by her wild clothes and her wild personality, backs off, only to be pulled back by Edward's aggressive behavior.

Example

Story line for *The Accidental Tourist*:

Problem: A child has died.
Solution: Take a trip. Try to forget.
Problem: Macon won't talk, won't share his grief.
Solution: Sarah departs, talking divorce.
Problem: Edward the dog won't behave.
Solution: Take Edward to Muriel, the dog trainer.
Problem: Muriel's a pest.
Solution: Macon avoids Muriel.
Problem: Because of Edward and the cat, Macon breaks his leg.
Solution: For care, Macon lives with Rose and his two brothers.
Problem: Memories of Mom, who left.
Solution: Back to Muriel.
Problem: Muriel wants commitment.
Solution: Macon dives back inside.
Problem: Surrounded by women at Rose's wedding.
Solution: Escape to Europe.
Problem: Muriel tags along.
Solution: Macon hurts his back.
Problem: Sarah arrives to take over research chores.
Solution: To avoid pain, Macon takes pills.
Problem: Macon feels the heat from the Muriel-Sarah struggle.
Solution: He must choose. Refuses the last pill.
Problem: Paris taxi, driving fast, Muriel alone on the curb.
Solution: Macon tells the taxi to stop.

Guidelines for Plotting with Story Line

Burying a problem in Edward the dog is a great plot tactic, one you can think about for your novel. Instead of problems coming out of the blue, launched like a boomerang by the invisible hand of fate, attach a problem to a character, a human, an animal, a robot. You work the whims of the universe—in this case, to shape Macon up—through that character.

Creating a story line through problem and solution provides a dynamic framework that propels your book all the way to the climax, where your protagonist makes some tough decisions.

Trying to evade Muriel in Paris (Macon's problem revisited), Macon hurts his back. His solution, phoning Julian, brings Sarah to Paris, another problem, because she's after his job. A man's work is one key to his identity. Sarah brings pain pills for his back, a double-edged solution, because they ease the pain while they also knock him out. Behind every seeming perfection lurks a flaw.

Problem and solution, because it mirrors life's ambiguity, gives you a story line that feels real.

WORKING THE NOVEL

Exercises

1. *Problem-Solution.*
Close your eyes and take some deep breaths and let your mind focus on the story line from your favorite book or movie and then open your eyes and work out the story line in the form of problem and solution. *Don't worry if you miss a step.*

2. *Your Novel.*
Keep the hand moving as you work out a story line for your novel. Use the structure of problem and solution. Let your mind roam free. If you can't think of a problem, use money. It was good enough for Gatsby and Cinderella. You can use it too.

3. *Big Scenes.*
Locate the key scenes in your story line. Then circle them in colored pen or pencil. If you can't locate key scenes, go to generic terms: arrival, departure, discovery, escape, capture, trial, execu-

tion, first date, first kiss, party, birthday party, magic, wardrobe change, foreplay, love in June, argument, pregnancy, birth, divorce, remarriage, death, funeral, gravesite. Fill the space up and don't worry about where things go. It's idea time. Have fun. Then step back from your story line for the long view.

Learning from Other Writers

If you have a couple of minutes during the week, try working out a story line for another kind of novel. Since the mystery genre is plot heavy, here's a piece of the story line from *The Maltese Falcon* (1930), by Dashiell Hammett:

Problem: Miss Wonderly says follow Thursby; he has my sister.
Solution: Miles Archer says he'll follow Thursby.
Problem: The sister is a lie, a red herring.
Solution: Kill Archer; kill Thursby.
Problem: Cops brace Spade for double murder.
Solution: Spade toughs it out, questions Wonderly.
Problem: She lies.
Solution: Cairo diverts Spade from Wonderly/LeBlanc/Brigid.
Problem: Gunsel Wilmer Cook follows Cairo.
Solution: Wilmer leads Spade to Caspar Gutman.
Problem: Brigid slaps Cairo; they know each other.
Solution: His mind ratiocinating, Spade intervenes.

DURING THE WEEK

Looking Ahead to the Scenario

Building a scenario for your novel has at least two payoffs: writing it early in the process of writing the novel gives you a blueprint to follow; writing it later turns the scenario into a selling tool. When you're ready to get yourself an agent, you send off three chapters and your scenario. The term for this package is the partial.

The key word for the scenario is *wants*.

• WEEKEND 14 •
SCENARIO

The scenario, a narrative treatment of your story, gathers up the threads of your book—character, motivation, agenda, setting, conflict, large action, key scenes, story line—and combines them into a short treatment that gives you the first hint of the impact of the final book.

You write the scenario in three parts, mirroring the three-act structure of your book. You focus on large actions resulting from character motivation. For example, Sarah *wants* Macon to share his grief about the death of Ethan, their son. Macon, a systems guy, *wants* to stay buttoned up inside his glass cage. Sarah's motivation is strong enough to get her to ask for a divorce, to leave the house, thereby making their separation a reality. The act of asking for a divorce climaxes Chapter One, crystallizes her character, and forms a significant large action for the novel. Sarah, following her desires, leaves Macon alone in the house, thus deepening his isolation.

The word you use to display motivation is the verb *want*. Before you start writing the scenario, it's helpful to make a list of *wants* for your characters:

Sarah wants Macon to share his grief.
Macon wants to stay buttoned up.
Muriel wants a man to pay the bills.
Julian (Macon's boss) wants a family.
Rose (Macon's sister) wants order in her life.

Writing your scenario in three acts helps to organize your work. Act One, your setup for the novel, is where you introduce characters, who come onstage to work out their agendas. Agendas clash, creating problems that get worse in Act Two, your complication. In Act Two, things get worse for your protagonist. Obstacles keep rising up. Apparent solutions fail, forcing the protagonist to keep trying alternatives. Act Three is your resolution. With the protagonist weary and the goal fading from view, your protagonist makes a decision to give it one last try—Macon drops the pill; Cinderella in a last burst of courage tries on that slipper before it's smashed by the clumsy stepsisters—and succeeds. In popular fiction, your scenario ends with the problem solved.

Example: Scenario of *The Accidental Tourist*

Opening Scene—Macon wants to hide. Sarah wants him to open up, share his grief. They bicker. Sarah asks for a divorce.

Act I: Sarah moves out. Macon wanders the house. Edward the dog attacks people. The old kennel won't put up with Edward, so Macon tries a new place, where he runs into Muriel, a single mom who's attracted to Macon. For a fee, Muriel offers to train Edward. Macon, locked in his shell, refuses. Edward and the cat team up to break Macon's leg. At home with Rose and the boys, Macon stays isolated while his leg heals. Avoiding phone calls from Sarah, the Learys refuse to answer the phone. Edward trees Julian, Macon's publisher. Edward bites Macon. Edward's rage, plus family pressure, forces Macon to okay Muriel as a trainer for Edward.

Act II: Muriel comes onstage to help Macon train Edward with a choke chain. Muriel wants Macon, so she invites him to dinner. As he delivers his refusal note Muriel scares him, saying she's got a shotgun. He confesses to her about his dead son. Muriel lets him sleep. They make love. Redemption begins.

Macon sleeps over. He pays attention to Muriel's son, Alexander, a kid with bad allergies. He moves his writing gear to Muriel's apartment. He helps out with money. When he takes a research trip, gathering travel tips for his Accidental Tourist series, Muriel asks to come along. She's getting closer, introducing him to her family, sharing her back story.

At Rose's wedding—she's marrying Julian—Macon is charmed by the women in his life: Mom, sister Rose, wife Sarah, mistress Muriel. Musing how comfortable this feels, he backslides, away from Muriel, into his old ruts.

Act III: Macon's a compulsive guy who likes his ruts, so he goes back to Sarah, settling into the old house, leaving Muriel. When he heads for Paris on a business trip, Muriel, who asked in Chapter Seven to be taken along, now tags along. After all that's happened, she still wants Macon. In Paris, Macon hurts his back, a mirror injury to the breaking of his leg in Act I, and Sarah arrives to take over the research part of his trip. The symbolism is clear: Sarah wants to get back together again. She keeps Macon punchy with pain pills. If he's to get away, he's got to face the pain and avoid the pill.

The Big Decision: Macon palms the pill.

He leaves Sarah in his bed and creeps out of the hotel and hails a taxi and lo, there on the sidewalk is Muriel.

The taxi hurtles along. Macon can get away clear if he wants but instead he tells the taxi to stop. Muriel climbs in, radiant with love. The curtain falls.

This is Macon's story, but Muriel is Cinderella.

WORKING THE NOVEL

Exercises

1. *Wants List.*

Make a new wants list for your characters. This refreshes your mind about character agendas. If, during the making of this list, your hand feels like it wants to write sentences and paragraphs, don't stop it. That desire is your scenario, trying to get out.

2. *Writing the Scenario.*

Write your scenario in a series of timed writings. The time will vary, depending on how deep you are into an image of your structure. For starters, divide your scenario into five parts:

a. Opening sequence.
b. Act One.
c. Act Two, first half, to midpoint.
d. Act Two, second half, to plot point two.
e. Act Three.

Try writing for ten minutes on each part, letting the words fly. Push yourself to make it to the end, the final image. Allow yourself the freedom of discovery.

Use verbs like *want* and *need* because they show motivation. Aim your sentences at the key scenes. It's okay to write fat, because you can cut later. It's okay to write lean, because you can add later. Length is not important.

3. *Rewriting.*
After the words have had a chance to cool, you rewrite, starting with Act Three, then Act Two, Act One, and opening sequence. Rewriting from the end helps you stay fluid with your structure. Each time you enter the structure, each time you cross it with words, you become more intimate with the novel.

You're aiming for a length of five to ten pages. Concentrate on large actions growing from deep motives. Use dialogue sparingly.

A Scenario for Cinderella

The plot of Cinderella works in three acts. Act One sets up the problem, Cinderella's hopeless situation as she slaves all day cleaning her stepmother's house. News of the royal ball worsens her situation: she has nothing to wear; if she did, and if she could escape the house, she still has no transportation, no way of traveling to the castle. Cinderella wishes for help, which appears in the catalytic character of the

Fairy Godmother, a dimpled, absentminded sorceress who crowns the wardrobe with a pair of glass slippers as, with a wave of her wand, she turns a pumpkin into a coach. The curtain falls on Act One as Cinderella rides off in her fancy vehicle.

Act Two, marked by a dramatic scene change, takes place in the castle. It is light here—candles, lanterns, torches—the symbolism radiant in contrast to the gloom of Cinderella's situation in Act One. Suspense builds in the first half of Act Two as Cinderella and the Prince keep missing each other's arms. At last, they dance. At midpoint, the point of no return, the Prince is smitten (Cinderella, with the intuitive wisdom of a fairy-tale heroine, is already committed), and now the magic of the Fairy Godmother runs short on time, suspense building again as the clock strikes midnight. Cinderella, fearful of losing face, races away from the Prince and down the steps, with the coach already changing back into a pumpkin, and loses one glass slipper. The Prince, clutching the slipper, is bewildered. The curtain falls on Act Two.

Act Three is dominated by one scene: the trying on of the slipper. The Wicked Stepmother is ready to chop off toes to make the shoe fit one of her daughters, but Cinderella, helped by her helpers, tries on the shoe and it fits.

The plot wraps on a royal wedding.

Closing Thoughts

In an essay called "The Novelist; Guide to Getting Started," John Irving (author of *The World According to Garp*) advises novelists on the beauty of plot: "The authority in the storyteller's voice derives from foreknowledge. In my opinion, a novel is written with predestination . . . if you choose to write a novel without plot, I would hope three things for you: that your prose is gorgeous, that your insights into the human condition are inspirational, and that your book is short."

Looking Ahead to the Writing:
How Novelists Work

Anne Tyler keeps index cards, where she notes down snatches of conversation, daydreams, idle thoughts, a newspaper item. Her outline is a page long. She writes in longhand, then reads into a tape recorder. As the recorder gives her a playback, she reads along on the screen of her computer. The process reveals flaws she might have missed. Tyler revises a lot.

Raymond Chandler worked on the typewriter:

> Every day, from nine to twelve or one o'clock, Chandler typed out his fiction. He used half-sheets of yellow paper to reduce the amount of retyping necessary in case of mistakes. He worked rapidly, for the typing was the last stage of a procedure that took many hours of preliminary work. Often the night before he would work out in his head what he wanted to say, so that when he sat down to type it came spontaneously and fresh onto the page. Chandler said that the first draft was merely the material from which the story would be drawn, and he rarely fiddled with it, changing a sentence or phrase here or there. Instead, he rewrote the entire book, or passages of it, again and again. In that way he kept the language as alive as he could. When at last he had a book he thought he could stand by, he would give his stack of yellow half-pages to Mrs. Messick to be retyped on full sheets, eight inches by eleven. After this, there would rarely be any substantive revision. When the final copy was ready, it was sent to the publisher. Only at this stage, with the book in its final form, would he discuss it with Cissy [Mrs. Chandler] or anyone else. (MacShane, *The Life of Raymond Chandler*)

Henry James wrote scenarios for his novels of twenty thousand words. Robert Ludlum's outlines are a hundred pages, but he does not go past Act Two. Robert B. Parker writes scenarios of two hundred pages. Oakley Hall has done scenarios of five hundred pages.

PART · V

Weekends 15–20
Writing Your Key Scenes

If you drive an unfamiliar road, not knowing the landmarks, no map in hand, there's a chance that you'll make a couple of wrong turns. If you're in a rush—an important appointment, say, or night falling and potholes everywhere and you're tired and you need a stopping place—you might feel the road is against you, an obstacle to progress instead of a helpful corridor to your destination. If the road is too long, your joy of exploring new territory will fade, to be replaced by frustration growing out of your need to get somewhere.

Next day, however, driving back up the road, retracing your route from yesterday, you wonder what all the fuss was about. The landmarks are familiar. You're in control of your time.

That's the kind of journey you want for this first novel. You just drew a map—Aristotle's incline, the speed paced by your story line, the points of interest annotated by your scenario—and now, by writing your key scenes, you're going to establish way stations for your journey. The beacons are already burning, lit up by you on Weekend 11. Now, in the next six weekends, you're going to build scenes to guide your characters along the road.

Writing the Key Scenes

There are six key scenes in your book: The opening sequence and the final image work as frames or bookends for the story line; the climax is the high point of your story, Aristotle's catharsis, the moment of reader release; midpoint marks a turning point in the middle of your story; plot point one ends Act One; plot point two ends Act Two.

Before you tackle the word processor, storyboard each scene in your notebook. Write each scene in pieces—dialogue, main action, stage setup, climax, exit line—and when you finish a scene, connect it to your plot diagram. If you had just finished writing the climactic scene for Anne Tyler's *Tourist*, for example, you would print block letters something like these on your diagram: MACON DROPS PAIN PILL/ PACKS BAGS/DENIES SWEET REVENGE.

Adding scenes to your diagram has two functions: First, it gives you a visual display of measured accomplishment and progress; second, it gathers your writing, compressing it to a single page, a snapshot for your unconscious to work on.

After you write a scene, or a scene fragment, in your notebook, enter it into your word processor. Don't make too many changes on the printout. Read it over, make a couple of notes, then slip the printout into a manila folder. Label this folder "Key Scenes." This organizational work that you do now will pay off later, when the manuscript bulges with rewrites. A spiral notebook has its own order, its own limits. But a manuscript of loose pages can get out of control fast.

The key to being a successful Weekend Novelist is to work smart. Working smart means you prepare, digging deep before you write. Working smart means you allow time for discovery, trusting the process of writing. You've been working smart since the first exercise, where you sketched your Stranger in the Room, who is now transformed by magic and hard work into a major character in your novel.

Keep working smart.

The Next Six Weekends

On Weekend 15 you'll write the hook or opening sequence. My advice is to keep it short and dramatic.

On Weekend 16 you'll write the final wrap-up, reaching ahead to the end. These two scenes—opening sequence and wrap-up—frame the book.

On Weekend 17 you'll write the climax, the high point of the story.

On Weekend 18 you'll write the midpoint. Midpoint is the point of no return. You use it, not only as a turnstile for the action, but also to make the writing of Act Two easier by cutting it in half.

On Weekend 19, you'll write plot point one, which winds up Act One.

On Weekend 20, you'll write plot point two, which winds up Act Two.

• WEEKEND 15 •
WRITING YOUR OPENING SCENE

Your opening scene is a doorway into your novel's story. It's an invitation to a journey. With the first lines of your opening scene, you say: "Come on along, Reader, and let me entertain you, maybe even enlighten you."

The opening scene establishes tone, mood, situation, problem, and genre. You build the stage of your novel and bring on your characters, who enter with conflicting agendas. What do these people want? Why do they think they can get it here? What's in their way? How will they handle the obstacles?

With your opening scene, you make a promise to the reader, a sort of contract that guarantees you will fulfill in the rest of the book what you set up in the opening scene. Tyler's opening scene from *Tourist* sets up Macon Leary, Man in a Glass Box. His wife can't break him out, so she leaves, creating a vacuum that is, in Act Two, filled to bursting with the bubbly froth of Muriel Pritchett. At the end of *Tourist,* Macon, a newborn baby chick emerging from his transparent glass egg, chooses Muriel.

One change in your opening can alter the course of the book. What if Macon had died when their car slammed into a trailer van in the rain? Then it would have been Sarah's story. What if Macon had choked Sarah to death under the shelter of the Texaco overhang? Then it would have been a murder mystery. If Sarah pulls a gun on Macon, and the author describes it as a Walther 9mm with a fifteen-shot magazine equipped with a German-made silencer, the detail alone changes the genre: from psychological mainstream to crime thriller.

In his essay on getting started John Irving says: "Know the story— as much of the story as you can possibly know, if not the whole story—before you commit yourself to the first paragraph. Know the story—the whole story, if possible—before you fall in love with your first sentence, not to mention your first chapter."

Guidelines for Writing Your Opening Scene

You're in good shape. The plotting exercises, where you stretched your mind out to reach the end four times, enabled you to *know* the story. You know the ending, the climax, the turning points. Now, using Tyler as a model, think about writing the key start-up scene.

Beginners in my fiction classes often make the mistake of opening their books slowly, taking a long time to set things in motion. My advice is to begin the way Tyler begins, with a dramatic scene that sets up the characters and establishes the problem of the novel in a few well-written pages. Since half of Tyler's opening scene is made up of dialogue, pack your opener with dialogue—two characters talking—and use action to build to a climax and close off the scene with an exit line and move on to finish Act One.

Before beginning your opening scene, review the storyboard we created for Tyler's opening scene on Weekend 5, and then sketch out the parts for your scene on the storyboard:

Example

Stage Setup: inside the Learys' car; no specific make.

> *time/place:* Thursday morning, on the road.
> *temperature/season:* muggy heat, late summer.
> *lighting/sounds/smells:* sky darkens as rain approaches; rain hammers roof; mildew, dank smell.
> *symbols/images:* rain (water images), car, road, sight/ blindness.

Characters/relationships: Macon and Sarah Leary, a married couple in their mid-thirties.

Dialogue

> *subjects:* rain, comfort, systems, the past.
> *subtext:* anger that child is dead.

Action

> *large:* Macon driving the car; Sarah asking for a divorce.
> *supporting:* passing cars, gripping dashboard, sitting up straight; turning on windshield wipers.

Point of View: third person omniscient.

Climax: Sarah's line, "I want a divorce."

Exit line: rain drumming on the roof.

In *The Art of Fiction*, John Gardner says: "A good writer can get anything at all across through action and dialogue. . . ."

WORKING THE NOVEL

Exercises

1. *Storyboard.*
Using the sketch from Weekend 11, work out a storyboard for your opening scene.

> *Stage Setup*:
>> *time/place*:
>> *temperature/season*:
>> *lighting/sounds/smells*:
>> *symbols/images*:
> *Characters/relationships*:
> *Dialogue*
>> *subjects*:
>> *subtext*:

Action
  large:
  supporting:
Point of View:
Climax:
Exit line:

2. *Dialogue.*
Write dialogue for ten to fifteen minutes, timing yourself. Write minimal stage directions or none at all. Give the characters room to talk while you take notes. Who are these people? What agendas to they pack onto your stage? Have they just met? Do they know each other from the past?

3. *Action.*
Write action for ten minutes. Use strong verbs and allow your sentences to expand until they are out of control: for example, ". . . and then he blew the lid off and the lid, hell, it's turning into a wafer, a caramel-colored wafer, turning and turning, that's a line from Yeats, Falcon, dapple-dawn drawn, poetry, rhythm, and the he blew the lid off, the shards of lid splattering and . . ."

4. *Stage Setup.*
Write stage setup for fifteen minutes as you frame the action and the dialogue with time, place, and temperature. Let yourself go with color and sound and texture touched by your characters. Allow symbols to bubble to the surface.

5. *Rewrite.*
Read your pieces aloud, either to a friend or into a tape recorder. After the reading, close your eyes and take some deep breaths. Open your eyes and make a few notes to yourself. Then rewrite for twenty minutes, allowing the scene to build itself from the parts. Type it up. Slip it into your key-scenes folder.

Tip: As you write your opening sequence, recall T. S. Eliot's line from *Four Quartets,* "In my end is my beginning." When you reach the end of your novel and loop back across the story line to rewrite your opening sequence, you will know so much more about the book, and you will feel it so much more deeply, that you'll wish you'd written the book backwards.

DURING THE WEEK

Learning from Other Writers

Your opening sequence is important. A reader in a bookstore will read your first page, maybe your second. Readers are busy. They like to be hooked on page one. Knowing this, a busy editor in a publishing house will read your first page to decide whether or not she'll read page two.

Find half a dozen successful opening scenes written by other writers. Read them over quickly, as if you were a browser in a bookstore. Divide them into two piles—the ones that grab you, the ones that don't. Analyze what grabs you. Circle the verbs. Check the adjectives in the stage setup. How much dialogue is there? How does the writer handle subtext? What's the main action/central image? Where's the climax?

Now that you have written an opening scene, what did you learn from these writers that will make yours better?

Looking Ahead to the Wrap-up Scene

Since the opening scene and the wrap-up scene frame your story, take your cue from Tyler and read the last couple of pages of Chapter Twenty again. Track Macon as he leaves the hotel to enter the street, past the boy and into the taxi where he sees sunlight on the windshield, a final image of hope and beauty. To probe the language, circle the nouns and box the verbs and underline the adjectives in red.

· WEEKEND 16 ·
WRITING YOUR WRAP-UP SCENE

The wrap-up scene caps off your novel. To make the wrap-up memorable, you create an unforgettable final image that sticks in the reader's mind.

F. Scott Fitzgerald's final image in *The Great Gatsby* is the green light, blinking on and off from the tip end of Daisy's dock in East Egg. The green light represents Gatsby's hope of capturing Daisy, the Girl from East Egg. Hope, tinged with irony, still lingers as the book closes. But by the book's end most hope has died.

In *Museum Pieces*, by Elizabeth Tallent, the final image shows a man and woman in bed. As the man wishes for a cigarette, the woman's hair fans across his shoulders. This moment of beauty does not mute his desire for a cigarette. Life goes on, mired in irony.

In Melville's *Moby Dick*, the final image is Queequeg's coffin rising from the vortex of the sea to save Ishmael: "Round and round, then, and ever contracting towards the button-like black bubble at the axis of that slowly wheeling circle, like another Ixion did I revolve . . . and now, liberated by reason of its cunning spring, and owing to its great buoyancy, rising with great force, the coffin life-buoy shot lengthwise from the sea. . . ."

In Tyler's *Tourist*, the final image of the wrap-up scene is sunlight on the windshield, an omen of good fortune, spangles as bright and festive as confetti. The story ends where it began, with Macon in a closed car watching through the windshield. But his life has changed. This systems guy is in love.

Guidelines for Writing the Wrap-up Scene

To reach your wrap-up scene, gather images and key words from your manuscript as you think through the development of your novel.

Example: The Storyboard for Tyler's Wrap-up in *The Accidental Tourist*.

Stage Setup: Macon leaves the hotel, hits the street.

> *time/place*: morning in Paris.
> *temperature/season*: coolish; feels like autumn.
> *lighting/sounds/smells*: sunlight.
> *symbols/images*: bag/taxi/boy/luggage/cartons/sunlight.

Characters/relationships: Macon wants Muriel.

Dialogue (minimal)

> *subjects: Attendez/Arretez* (Wait! Stop!)

Large Action: Leaving Sarah, returning to Muriel.

Point of View: third person omniscient.

Climax: Macon orders the taxi to stop.

Final Image: sunlight like confetti on the windshield.

To re-create Tyler's wrap-up, you might begin with Macon in the street. His back hurts, so he leaves the bag, which appeared in Chapter Three as an essential piece of equipment for his work, writing the Accidental Tourist guidebooks.

The boy in the street tickles his memory of how Ethan would have been if he had lived. Macon's lost again, recalling the problems with sense of direction we saw with geographic dyslexia in Chapter Seven. Pausing for the last time, Tyler echoes her opening scene: "And if dead people aged, wouldn't it be a comfort?" *Comfort*, you recall, is a key word in the opening scene from Weekend 5. The taxi passes the hotel where Sarah lies in bed. Then Muriel appears.

WORKING THE NOVEL

Exercises

1. *Storyboard.*
Working from the sketch in Weekend 11, storyboard your wrap-up scene, sketching out action, dialogue, stage setup, et cetera.

2. *Writing the Wrap-up Scene.*
In ten minutes, write a wrap-up scene containing a memorable final image.

3. *Rewriting.*
On your rewrite, echo images and ideas from your opening scene.

Closing Thoughts

Since you learn more when your learning window is open, study some wrap-up scenes from writers you like. How do they close their novels? What's the tone? At the end of *The Sun Also Rises*, Hemingway puts Brett and Jake in a taxicab in Madrid, another closed-car scene. Brett has a line of dialogue that echoes her bitchy behavior with men in general and the bullfighter Pedro Romero in particular: "Oh, Jake, we could have had such a damned good time together." And Jake responds with a line edged with irony: "Yes, isn't it pretty to think so?" And in between there is the *image* of a policeman raising his baton.

The baton slows the taxi, throwing Brett up against Jake. They're close, but they're apart: the human condition.

DURING THE WEEK

Looking Ahead to Writing Your Climax

In *The Art of Fiction*, John Gardner writes: "The writer works out plot in one of three ways: by borrowing some traditional plot or an action from real life (the method of the Greek tragedians, Shakespeare, Dostoevsky, and many other writers, ancient and modern); by working his way back from his story's climax; or by groping his way forward from an initial situation." (pp. 57–58)

Beginning writers balk at writing the climax before the story is complete. They argue from a swirling pool of nervousness. Fearing the unknown, they forget the process. Have faith in the process. Keep the hand moving and build a scene for your climax now, knowing you can change it later on your rewrite. Give it a try. Be prepared to be surprised.

Writing the climax now fills a vacuum in your story. It frees your mind to work on connecting scenes.

• WEEKEND 17 •
WRITING YOUR CATHARSIS SCENE

The action of your book rises toward climax, the high point, the culmination, the moment of resolution in your story that explodes while it reveals and releases. This is catharsis for your reader, a purging of emotion because of your expert handling of theme and symbol and character.

At the cathartic high point of Moby Dick, Captain Ahab plunges in his harpoon (*"Thus,"* he grunts in italics, "I give up the spear"), and he realizes, and we realize with him, that his harpoon, dripping with vengeance and green with bile, is just one more mosquito bite in the thick white hide of Moby Dick. Ahab dies, the crew dies, the good ship *Pequod* is lost to the deep. Ahab has been aiming at this moment since long before he stepped onstage in Act One. To arrive here, at his big moment of revenge, he crushes all obstacles in his path. Then he dies.

Build your novel in an upward sloping structure, represented on your drawing of Aristotle's incline as a line of rising action with hot spots and turning points controlling the story. The novel's catharsis is the highest point and the hottest spot and from here you can look back over your shoulder at the story line. Writing the climax now helps to anchor your novel and will help your unconscious to track the book.

As a reader, you read to see what happens, to see how the story comes out, to see how the dragon/ogre is dispatched and who winds up with whom in a relationship. As a writer, you sweat to *create* a cathartic moment with your imagination.

Chain of Events

As we saw in Tyler's *Accidental Tourist*, a novel's high point caps a chain of events that builds as it gathers momentum. In your writing, you work toward a fundamental decision made by the protagonist—a decision to resolve conflict. The decision must have consequences. Macon drops his pain pill; the consequence is pain. Fitzgerald's protagonist, Jay Gatsby, thinking it will smooth Daisy's delicate East Eggian nerves, decides to let her drive his yellow car back from the city; the consequence is the death of Myrtle Wilson.

Practice constructing this chain of events by studying professionals. Here's how you learn from Fitzgerald by charting his chain of events in *The Great Gatsby*: The protagonist (Jay Gatsby), faced with a multitude of obstacles (Western rube innocence, bootlegger past, Tom, Old Money, East Egg), grabs the prize (Daisy, who represents Old Money), taking the consequences (Daisy kills Myrtle Wilson, Tom's mistress, with Gatsby's yellow car; Tom deflects Wilson away from Daisy to Gatsby; Gatsby does not rat to the cops on Daisy), made personal by his gallant vigil that defines his innocence. After the collision that killed Myrtle, Gatsby as knight errant keeps watch outside Daisy's house, waiting for Daisy to return to his side. Wilson kills Gatsby, then commits suicide. On the day of his funeral, the irony of Gatsby's arduous pilgrimage from Out West to Back East is highlighted by his dad's words: "Jimmy always liked it better down East."

Guidelines for Writing Your Climax

Let's look at the chain of events from Macon's trip to Paris, which we pick up from the story line we created on Weekend 13:

Problem: Muriel tags along.
Solution: Macon hurts his back.
Problem: Sarah arrives to take over research chores.
Solution: To avoid pain, Macon takes pills.
Problem: Macon feels the heat from the Muriel-Sarah struggle.
Solution: He must choose. Refuses the last pill.

Problem: Paris taxi, driving fast, Muriel alone on the curb.
Solution: Macon tells the taxi to stop.

To get momentum, you can follow the model we used for *Gatsby*, compressing your chain of events into a couple of sentences. Let's try that now for Macon Leary:

> The protagonist (Macon Leary), faced with a multitude of obstacles (Sarah, pain, fear of change), decides to push ahead (drops the pill), taking the consequences (increased pain, Sarah's ironic ire), which leads to his decision (he's going back to Muriel), made personal by a character trait that is still part of his problem (the old deflector reflex): "I didn't want to *decide* this." [Italics mine]

Sometimes the hardest part is getting your hand moving, so take the time to copy down part of your story line and pretty soon you're writing.

From story line, you create a chain of events to build your way into the climax for your book. Remember that it's just a list—it doesn't have to be perfect or even smooth—and no one will see it but you. Play with scenes and events as if they were colored building blocks, moving them around to see where they might fit.

One key to discovering catharsis is to reach back to character work to find the motive that works itself out in actions that produce conflict. Macon Leary's conflict, for example, is between the Old (Sarah, family, suffocation in the glass box) and the New (Muriel, Alexander, chance for change). At the moment of catharsis, he chooses the New (a fundamental decision). Because change is hard work and because we avoid it, we like to see change at work in our stories. Change gives the reader hope.

Use this tip from Tyler. Knowing what your character wants, match that desire up with the character's strengths and weaknesses and obstacles in the plot and you write your way toward catharsis. Sometimes it helps to write down the big moment—in *Moby Dick*, Ahab stabs the whale; in *The Great Gatsby*, Wilson kills Gatsby; in *The Accidental*

Tourist, Macon drops the pill—and print the words carefully onto the plot diagram you worked on in Weekend 12.

WORKING THE NOVEL

Exercises

1. *Chain of Events.*
In your notebook, copy out a piece of your story line from Weekend 13. From that story line, following the model we used for *Tourist* and *Gatsby*, create a chain of events leading up to your climax. Try this model, expanding the parentheses to fit your own detail:

—the protagonist (_____)
—faced with a multitude of obstacles (_____)
—grabs the prize (_____)
—taking the consequences (_____)
—made personal by (_____)
—as he/she acts/reacts/awaits (_____)
—and the final twist is (_____)

2. *Storyboard Your Cathartic Scene.*
Using the storyboard technique from Weekend 5 (stage setup, action, et cetera), sketch out the parts of your cathartic scene. Make certain your protagonist is present. Make sure each character coming onstage has a clear agenda.

3. *Timed Writing.*
Write the cathartic scene in a fifteen-minute timed writing. Keep the hand moving and let your imagination go. Remember, this is a discovery process in which you explore with sentences.

4. *Rewrite.*
After letting your scene cool, read it over, brooding a bit, and then rewrite it. Start by copying a few lines from what you have written in exercise 3, above, and allow your sentences to dig deeper.

DURING THE WEEK

Learning from Other Writers

Explore the work of other novelists to see how they handle the moment of a novel's climax. Melville, for example, puts us inside Ahab's ultimate monologue, close enough to feel the symbols of death bumping against our gunwales: "Sink all coffins and all hearses to one common pool! and since neither can be mine, let me then tow to pieces, while still chasing thee, though tied to thee, thou damned whale! *Thus*, I give up the spear!"

At the climax of *The Sun Also Rises*, Hemingway reveals his aficionado's tribute to the ritual of bullfighting as Jake and his pals, sober for a moment in Pamplona, watch from the safety of the stands while Pedro Romero, hurt by his fight with Robert Cohn the night before, becomes "one with the bull."

For a clue to the nature of catharsis after Aristotle, consider for a moment what Melville and Hemingway have done. Melville pits man against monster in a mythic struggle at the symbolic end of the world's oceans. Hemingway pits torero Pedro Romero against animal in a mythic struggle in a symbolic ringed sandpit in Spain. If you want your catharsis to produce heavy emotion in the reader, and not merely weariness and despair, write your way to a struggle that evokes myth.

Looking Ahead to Midpoint

In Chapter Eleven of his *Screenwriter's Workbook*, Syd Field tells the story of his discovery of midpoint. Students in one of his early screenwriting workshops did wonderful first acts, Field says, but went off the tracks when they arrived at Act Two. When Field asked for help, veteran screenwriter Paul Schrader came up with this tip: "Something happens," Schrader said, about page 60, which is midway through a script of 120 pages. Chasing that elusive *something*, Field explored three films: *An Unmarried Woman, Manhattan*, and *Body Heat*. At the end of that chase he found Midpoint.

In *An Unmarried Woman*, for example, Jill Clayburgh's therapist advises our heroine to experiment with her life. She can't tell Clayburgh what to do, she says, but "I know what I would do. . . . I would go out and get laid." That line, advice from the therapist, is on page 60: midpoint. At page 85, enter Alan Bates, the "mad artist" Clayburgh falls for . . . but only after being released at midpoint.

In *Manhattan*, Mary (Diane Keaton) and Ike (Woody Allen) move from being friends to being lovers. Their love scene, on page 60, is the midpoint.

In *Body Heat*, Ned (William Hurt) kills Hubby (Richard Crenna) aided by the wife (Kathleen Turner). The murder is on page 60, halfway through the script.

Notice how midpoint determines (or is determined by) the type of movie. *An Unmarried Woman* is a rebirth story; the midpoint is a dialogue line by a therapist that triggers action in the protagonist. *Manhattan* is a relationship story; midpoint is a love scene, a turnstile that transforms friends into lovers. *Body Heat* is a *film noir* mystery thriller; midpoint is an act of violence that digs the protagonist's grave another three feet down.

If midpoint is that important to movie genre, wouldn't it be safe to say it's also that important to your novel?

• WEEKEND 18 •
WRITING YOUR SCENE
AT MIDPOINT

In his *Screenwriter's Workbook*, Syd Field calls midpoint a pit stop: "The midpoint is a pit stop, a destination, a beacon that guides you and keeps you on course during the execution of your story line."

Until movies got shorter, it was easier to find the midpoint because you could time it on your watch. A film script moves about a page a minute, so page 60 in the script was usually about an hour into the movie: sixty pages, sixty minutes. In today's feature films, look for midpoint about fifty or sixty minutes in.

Novelists can learn from screenwriters because they use the same Aristotelian structure—beginning, middle, and end—and because they encounter the same problems: a sagging somewhere near the middle of an extended work. A solid understanding for midpoint could save your novel.

Something must happen at midpoint. Record that happening with action. If you're writing a mystery, there's a good chance you'll have a violent act around midpoint. If you're writing a rebirth novel—a man, newly separated, foundering, refuses Help from Without—you should initiate a change in direction at midpoint.

The midpoint of *The Accidental Tourist*, for example, occurs in Chapter Eleven. Muriel (Help from Without) has invited Macon to dinner and he fusses about, writing a note declining her invitation. It's the day of the dinner, too late for the mails, so Macon braves the city streets to deliver the note in person. After threatening him with a fake shotgun, Muriel lets Macon in, and he burbles out a confession about Ethan. Whispering, "Sleep, sleep, sleep," Muriel leads Macon to bed. In response to Macon's question, "Will you take this off?" they make love. Their relationship is transformed from business—dog trainer and dog owner—to a level of deeper intimacy. At midpoint, having changed course through action, Macon begins to heal.

Guidelines for Writing Your Midpoint

Focus on action that initiates a big change in your characters. If they're in love, they fall out of love. If they're friends or have a business connection, they become lovers. Things change at midpoint.

Macon's action in Chapter Eleven is confession. He's come almost two hundred pages since the opening scene in the car, when Sarah badgered him about not caring (with the heavy subtext of Ethan's death like a rancid pool between them), and now, at midpoint, he chooses to confess, not to Sarah, but to dizzy Muriel Pritchett. Confessing to Sarah could have ended the book.

Midpoint anchors two other chains of events: one leading up to the midpoint action; the other leading away from it. These chains of events dramatize the change in direction initiated at midpoint. For example, events leading up to the midpoint in Tyler's *Tourist* include: training Edward to curb sit while Macon shops; a dinner invitation from Muriel; Macon, uncertain, in full deflector mode; Macon meets Alexander; Muriel keeps pushing her invitation, shoving it in his face; midpoint section, Macon declines the invitation to dinner; ends up confessing his sorrow.

Events leading away from the midpoint: Rose badgers Macon about his new schedule (part time at Leary House, part time at Muriel's); Macon delivers pizza to Muriel and Alexander; Macon has new energy for his work; Macon takes Muriel on a business trip.

Think about this technique from Tyler. Before the midpoint, your character withdraws; after the midpoint, your character charges ahead with new energy.

At midpoint of his story, Macon Leary makes a good effort to leave the confines of the glass box. Think about what your protagonist does.

Study what you discovered for your characters in character work, Weekends 1–4. Line up their motives, their fears, their strengths, their weaknesses. Check your wants list. What do they want? How close are they to getting it? What decision do they make that takes them deeper? You want to construct a midpoint that transforms them.

WORKING THE NOVEL

Exercises

1. *Chains of Events.*
Develop two chains of events: one leading up to midpoint; the other leading away from it. Write long lists for both chains of events. Lists are easy. They don't commit you the way paragraphs do.

2. *Storyboard Your Scene at Midpoint.*
Using the storyboard technique from Weekend 5 (stage setup, action, et cetera), sketch out the parts of your midpoint scene. Make certain your protagonist is present. Make sure each character coming onstage has a clear agenda.

3. *Timed Writing.*
Write the midpoint scene in a fifteen-minute timed writing. Keep the hand moving and let your imagination go. Remember, this is a discovery process where you explore with sentences.

4. *Rewrite.*
After letting your scene cool, read it over, brooding a bit, and then rewrite it. Start by copying what you have written in exercise 3 above, and allow your sentences to work deeper. Enter the rewrite into your computer.

Learning from Other Writers

At the midpoint of *Oedipus Rex*, Oedipus and his mother, Jocasta, compare back stories as both recall details that deepen the grave for Oedipus. Jocasta recalls dumping her newborn baby with his ankles pinned together because of the curse (the son will murder the father and marry the mother) that drives the story. Jocasta recalls that Laius, her husband and King of Thebes before Oedipus, was killed at a place where three roads meet. Oedipus, who, as a grown man, still walks with a limp from having had his ankles pinned, recalls leaving Corinth because of the same curse that had made Jocasta dump her newborn baby, thereby saving him from Laius, who was acting under the same curse. Now, as Oedipus recalls having killed a rude old man at a place where three roads meet, we can see he's trapped himself. The rude old man was Laius. With the blind strength of youth, Oedipus murdered his dad and three faithful retainers.

That is some midpoint.

DURING THE WEEK

Looking Ahead to Plot Point One

Plot point one, as the name suggests, ends Act One. A plot point is a scene or a moment in a scene that grabs the action, hooks into it, and flings it in a new direction. As plot point one ends Act One, so it throws the action into Act Two.

Plot point one, like any key scene, is a target to guide your writing. Let's see how this works to help you write your book. Some novelists set arbitrary numerical goals to help them guide their writing. If your novel manuscript is 300 pages long, and if you want acts of equal length, then you divide by three, and plot point one would come around page 100 in your manuscript.

If it helps you to think of specific page numbers as goals, use Tyler for a model: Act Two, at 168 pages, is the longest; Act One, at 95 pages, is shorter than Act Two and longer than Tyler's Act Three, which is 79 pages long. If you're aiming at a book of 300 manuscript pages, you need to reach plot point one somewhere between page 80 and page 100.

If you reach page 110 and there's no plot point one to contain Act One, there's a good chance you need to rethink your story line.

· WEEKEND 19 ·
WRITING THE SCENE
AT PLOT POINT ONE

Plot point one is the key scene (or a hot action spot contained by the scene) that ends Act One. It wraps up the action of your setup—where you introduce characters and the problematical situations fired by their conflicting agendas—and shoves the rest of the story into Act Two. If there is a big scene change, from a small town in Kansas, say, to the bullet-torn streets of Beirut, plot point one functions as a curtain for Act One of your novel.

In *Tender Is the Night*, which is divided into three books, Fitzgerald uses his plot point one to drop us backward in time. Book 1/Act One opens on the French Riviera in 1925. The action of Book One ends with plot point one in Paris, where Nicole Diver, distraught after seeing a corpse in the hotel hallway and jealous of youthful Rosemary Hoyt, a budding film actress, goes bonkers in the bathroom. Rosemary has the point of view. We see Nicole through her young eyes. The curtain falls.

When the curtain opens on Book 2 we see Dr. Richard Diver, age twenty-six, arriving in Zurich in 1917. In this time of war, he has come to Switzerland to complete his studies in psychiatry. Before she becomes Mrs. Diver, Nicole will be a patient of his. There is a tone change as Fitzgerald stands back, increasing the psychic distance, to speak as Author: "In the spring of 1917, when Doctor Richard Diver first arrived in Zurich, he was twenty-six years old, a fine age for a man, indeed the very acme of bachelorhood."

Fitzgerald was smart: he saved his flashbacks for Act Two.

If you don't change scenes or make a big time-jump between acts, you can use plot point one to shift the mood, which in turn will change the pace. That's what Tyler does at the end of Chapter Six, which is plot point one for *Tourist*: Macon okays Muriel as Edward's dog trainer.

Tracking the chain of events leading to Tyler's shift at plot point one starts in Chapter Three, where Macon is forced to take Edward to Meow-Bow. Edward's foul temper, much worse by Chapter Six, propels Macon to his decision to hire Muriel—a decision made in response to the preceding chain of events.

Model your chain of events after Tyler's.

Guidelines for Writing Plot Point One

Use a chain of events to develop momentum for writing the scene that contains plot point one. Since the plot point in *The Accidental Tourist* occurs in Chapter Six, let's track the chain of events leading to Macon's decision to hire Muriel:

—Edward trees Julian. (A subplot starts here.)
—Flashback: Macon's first meeting with Julian because of Macon's hot dog article for *Watchbird* magazine. ("Hot dog" could be a humorous reference to Edward's fiery temper.)
—Edward bites Macon. (This is serious.)
—Rose bandages the bite.
—Charles advises Macon to give Edward away.
—Macon can't; Edward was Ethan's dog.
—Edward tears open the screen door.
—Macon, giving in, hires Muriel.

When you work with a chain of events, you can add detail that develops into a subplot. The subplot of *Tourist* is the romance of Julian, Macon's boss, and Rose, Macon's sister. It starts here, with Julian's visit in Chapter Six. It culminates at the end of Act Two, with their marriage at Leary House becoming the container for plot point two.

WORKING THE NOVEL

Exercises

1. *Chains of Events.*
From the story line you developed on Weekend 13, develop a chain of events leading up to plot point one. Begin as deep in Act One as you can. Then add links in your chain as you move toward the curtain.

2. *Storyboard Your Plot Point One.*
Using the storyboard technique from Weekend 5 (stage setup, action, and so on), sketch out the parts of the scene at plot point one. Make certain your protagonist is present. Make sure each character coming onstage has a clear agenda.

3. *Timed Writing.*
Write plot point one in a fifteen-minute timed writing. Keep the hand moving and let your imagination go. Remember, this is a discovery process where you explore with sentences.

4. *Rewrite.*
After letting your scene cool, read it over, brooding a bit, and then rewrite it. Start by copying what you have written in exercise 3, above, and allow your sentences to work deeper.

Learning from Other Writers

In *The Great Gatsby* near the end of Act One, Nick Carraway discovers that Daisy's husband, Tom, has a mistress named Myrtle Wilson. That's a big scene, a setup for Daisy's decision in Act Three to drive Gatsby's yellow car, which she slams into Myrtle at the climax.

Nick's discovery of Myrtle in Act One shows a crack in the Old Money Establishment that Tom represents. Daisy's killing of Myrtle, followed by the cover-up that points the finger at Gatsby, seals the crack, making East Egg a safe place to live once again. Myrtle, a minor character from the lower class and the subplot, is the link in the chain of events that connects those scenes.

DURING THE WEEK

Looking Ahead to Plot Point Two

Plot point two closes Act Two the way plot point one closes Act One. Plot point two is a miniclimax that whirls the action of your story into Act Three, where everything is resolved. The complication peaks at plot point two, but does not unwind from here. Near the end of Act Two in the movie *Body Heat*, for example, Ned Racine finally realizes that "someone" is out to get him. In Act Three, he finds out that "someone" is Matty, the lady he broke the glass door for at plot point one.

There are two keys to writing a solid Act Two, which is the key to writing a solid novel. First, using your midpoint, you divide Act Two into two equal parts, thus removing the awesome pressure of writing a huge sprawling thing. Second, you forge a connection (action, character, motive, symbol, theme) between plot point one and plot point two. At plot point one, we watch Ned Racine break glass to get close to Matty. At plot point two, we know (though he's not sure yet) that Matty is out to get him. Breaking the glass was not smart, but, given his character, he had no choice.

· WEEKEND 20 ·
WRITING THE SCENE
AT PLOT POINT TWO

Plot point two, the last key scene before you start the discovery draft, stands like a beacon at the close of Act Two. It is a high point and a turning point. You use it to wind the action up, twisting the strands of your story together, making a tight knot, so that they can be unwound in Act Three, sometimes called the denouement.

(*Denouement* comes from *desnouer*, which means "to undo." *Des* means reversal; *nouer*, meaning "to tie," comes from the Latin *nodare*, also meaning "to tie." *Nodus* is Latin for "knot.")

You use plot point two to close off Act Two while you raise the curtain on Act Three.

The scene that contains plot point two is important. In *The Accidental Tourist*, Anne Tyler uses Rose's wedding to close off Act Two and to link up with Act Three, which opens with Muriel pushing Macon about getting married. Rose's wedding forces Macon to bring Muriel to meet his family. At the wedding, the gathering of Learys forces Macon to compare his life *with* Muriel—on full display in the second half of Act Two—with his life *before* Muriel.

Life Before Muriel is represented not only by Sarah, but also by Rose, Julian, the Boys, and, out of the deep past, Macon's mom. The season is spring, a time for buds and blossoms. Sarah looks good. As Julian's best man, Macon gets sucked into the marriage ritual. Sarah, matron of honor, stares at Macon across a tiny space. She is still his wife. Macon has come home. With her last line, "It all felt so natural," Tyler signals us that Macon, in Act Three, will reverse the healing process begun in Act Two. He's going to leave Muriel and backslide into his old ways.

This is spiritually disastrous—only with Muriel can Macon heal— but a great suspense builder.

Guidelines for Writing Plot Point Two

Follow Tyler and use a chain of events to catapult your book into plot point two. Since the plot point is contained in the wedding scene, which results from the Julian-Rose subplot, you track the chain back to Chapter Six, when Edward trees Julian.

—Edward trees Julian. Julian meets Rose. (Chapter Six)
—Julian asks to be invited to dinner. (Chapter Seven)

—Julian drops by for coffee. (Chapter Eight)
—Julian takes Rose to dinner. (Chapter Nine)
—Julian eats Rose's underdone turkey. (Chapter Ten)
—Rose eats Christmas dinner at Julian's. (Chapter Twelve)
—Julian announces his engagement to Rose. (Chapter Fifteen)
—The wedding. (Chapter Sixteen)

This is a good technique for you to try in your scene at plot point two. Tyler uses Rose's wedding as a backdrop to highlight Macon's live-in relationship with Muriel. The ironies compound as more characters come onstage. Rose, his sister, is getting married to his boss. Macon's still married to Sarah, but living with Muriel, a blue-collar person looked down on by Macon's family. Family has a feeling of permanence, especially as Mom comes onstage to reinvent Macon's past. The permanence is looking good right now, which edges Muriel into the shadows as Macon gets deflective, edging back to Sarah. For the moment, he forgets that Sarah is the antagonist.

When you storyboard this scene, don't forget to bring on all your major characters.

WORKING THE NOVEL

Exercises

1. *Chain of Events.*
Develop a chain of events leading up to plot point two. Begin as deep in the book as you can. Then add links in your chain as you move toward the curtain.

2. *Storyboard Your Plot Point Two.*
Using the storyboard technique from Weekend 5 (stage setup, action, et cetera), sketch out the parts of your scene. Make certain your protagonist is present. Make sure each character coming onstage has a clear agenda.

3. *Timed Writing.*

Write plot point two in a fifteen-minute timed writing. Keep the hand moving and let your imagination go. Remember, this is a discovery process where you explore with sentences.

4. *Rewrite.*

After letting your scene cool, read it over, brooding a bit, and then rewrite it. Start by copying what you have written in exercise 3 above, and allow your sentences to work deeper.

Learning from Other Writers

At plot point one of *All the King's Men*, by Robert Penn Warren, the governor (Willie Stark) orders Jack Burden to get some dirt to use as blackmail on the judge. The judge is Old Money and the governor, who wants to be president, needs the Old Money support to win the next election. To get this dirt, Burden dives into the past, finding the dirt at midpoint. He brings it back. The dirt, a smirch on the past, shows the judge was not totally upright in his back story. Burden shows the dirt to the judge and the judge commits suicide because of it and that's plot point two. The plot points define Burden's journey into the past. Plot point one is his doorway in; plot point two is his doorway back out, bearing dirt.

Closing Thoughts

If you think in scenes, you can practice your craft all day long. Say you're sitting in a coffee shop watching a man and woman arguing. You jot down action and dialogue. You list the items in the room. A scene builds in your mind. The woman leaves in a huff. The man turns, catching the eye of the waitress, who gives him a sympathetic smile. You block out the scene on your storyboard, not thinking about where it goes until you've written it out, until the woman climbs into her car and drives away. Would it make a good opening? A good ending? A good midpoint?

The answer rests in the writing. Keep writing scenes and you'll write many novels.

Looking Ahead to Writing the First Draft

Ernest Hemingway wrote the first draft of *The Sun Also Rises* in a series of small notebooks called *cahiers*. He and his wife, Hadley, were living in Europe. The year was 1925, the summer following a trip to Pamplona to see the bulls, and the Hemingways had moved from Madrid to San Sebastian and then to Hendaye, across the border in France. "By August 12th," writes Carlos Baker in *Ernest Hemingway: A Life Story*, "Ernest had filled two *cahiers* with his boyish longhand . . . he was working harder than he had ever worked in his life, often until three or four in the morning. Then he would fall asleep, his head feeling like a frozen cabbage, only to jump awake again a few hours later, with the words already stirring themselves into sentences, clamoring to be set down. By August 19th when he left for Paris his first draft covered more than 250 of the small notebook pages and he thought that the end was almost in sight."

PART · VI

Weekends 21–31
Writing the Discovery Draft

"At some point," writes Gardner in *The Art of Fiction*, "the writer stops planning and starts writing. . . . Here, too, he is partly in control and partly controlled by the fiction process. Again and again, in the process of writing, he will find himself forced to new *discoveries*." [italics mine]

Your main goal in the next eleven weekends is to write your discovery draft all the way through to the end. In the discovery draft, write fast, speedballing along, skipping, leaping deep chasms, laughing at the words in your wake. In the discovery draft you are a child at play in the vast field of your fiction, using technique *as* discovery.

Don't think too much. Thinking comes later, when you write the meditation draft. Don't stop for research. Don't stop to fix a sentence or to monkey around changing words or fixing metaphors. Don't stop to polish up an image. Don't worry about form.

Your internal editor, that voice inside your head, will urge you to stop. "Listen up, dummy," the editor will say. "You can't write a novel this way, without rewriting. It's too messy. Its formlessness makes me sick. Fix your spelling now. Edit your sentences now."

Don't listen and don't stop. Keep the hand moving while you write scenes, and if you can't finish a scene, jot down a couple of key ideas and push on ahead to the next scene. Keep the eye of your imagination locked on that last line, that final image, that gives your book closure.

Sink into your novel. Settle into the warmth of words. Get to know your characters. Go again into closet and bedroom and desk drawer and mind and memory and poke around. Gather the images. Hold them in your arms. Knit them into your book. Keep filling up the well of your unconscious.

Try not to worry about what you are writing while you are writing. This is the discovery draft of your first novel. You're learning as you go, making discoveries about character and plot that you could never make if you hadn't come this far. Every day of writing increases your writing power.

Write this discovery draft with momentum. Write with heart and write with heat and when you get punchy from writing, slow down by using all caps: B-R-E-A-T-H-E while you write. Let your mind become the P-E-N-P-O-I-N-T. . . .

Write dialogue and attach it to action and watch the scene grow, almost by itself. Build your scene's stage and watch the lights come on and feel the temperature change and bring on a character dressed by your wardrobe people and nail down your point of view with a touch or a sharp smell or the *tick*-swoosh of rubber wiper blades on the windshield and let your action peak and write an exit line and suddenly you've got a scene which is a bucket for drama which is what readers pay for.

Write in a notebook for most of your draft. Filling the notebook will give you confidence so that, when you come to enter the novel into your word processor, many of the scenes will be fully formed. If you must, enter a couple of scenes into the word processor. Print them out, assuring yourself that they are real, but don't edit. Use these eleven weekends to write the discovery draft. Push yourself to make it all the way to the end. Stay up late and get up early and when you lose your way, map your scene sequences on Aristotle's incline.

Mapping helps you step back for a breather so that you can keep going.

The Next Eleven Weekends

You can divide your work something like this: Spend three weekends drafting Act One; spend five weekends on Act Two; spend three weekends on Act Three.

If you're following the guidelines suggested earlier, Act One will run around a hundred manuscript pages. If your scenes average ten pages (some might be five pages, some might be twelve), that means you'll need ten to fourteen scenes for Act One. Some writers like to contain scenes by numbers of pages.

In Act Two, which can run longer, your scenes might deepen and also expand. You could use twenty to twenty-five scenes here, which leaves you ten to twelve scenes for Act Three. As you move to the end of the book and closure—capping off characters, ending the subplot— you'll write tighter and tighter scenes. You're aiming for a novel manu- script of just under three hundred pages, which, at this writing, will keep the cost of your hardback book under twenty dollars. The key to writing three hundred pages is to keep a steady pace.

Your preparation is done—characters primed, acts framed by key scenes, key scenes extended by chains of events. If you're careful to create your storyboards before you start writing each scene, you should have no trouble completing, at least in rough form, three to four scenes per weekend.

This is a discovery draft. Remember that the scenes don't have to be perfect. You're writing to reach the end while you fill in what you can. You can always fix the language when you rewrite.

Let's move on to Act One.

• WEEKENDS 21–23 • DISCOVERY DRAFT: ACT ONE

The discovery draft is an exploratory writing containing scenes, scene sketches, snatches of dialogue, snippets of action, new faces, and stage setups that are overwritten on purpose as you root for symbols.

As you write, speeding along, new characters (strangers never seen before) will come onstage. Since they're new, they won't have back stories. Since they don't have back stories, you're not sure of their motivation, where they're coming from, so you make a note to yourself,

"During the Week: Prepare Back Story on Character F," and then you keep writing.

That's your goal in this discovery draft: to keep writing.

Give yourself room to grow while you produce a lot of manuscript. Make a list of scenes, keeping it fluid, to give yourself a track, a chain of events to follow. Act One is your setup, just as it was Tyler's setup, or Hemingway's or Herman Melville's. Act One begins with your opening scene and builds to the first structural peak, plot point one. In Act One you introduce your characters, who come onstage brandishing their individual agendas. In Act One you set up your scenes, writing stage setups to establish place, time of day, temperature, season, and lighting. As you write these stage setups, stay open to symbols and images popping up, stuff you never thought of, so you can develop some of them into central images. In Act One you allow large actions to spring from the motivations of your characters. Cinderella *wants* to go to the ball so she dials the universe for help and, because it's a fairy story, the Fairy Godmother enters from stage right, where she's been waiting in the wings. One of the large actions in "Cinderella" is her transformation, via the magic of the Fairy Godmother, into the Belle of the Ball. This large action forms the center of plot point one.

As you write Act One, bring on the characters from your character work in Weekends 1–4.

Guidelines for Writing Act One

Because of the careful preparation you've been doing for the last twenty weekends, you've already assembled most of what you need for writing Act One. Some of your characters are onstage; others, dressed and expectant, wait in the wings. Your wants list reminds you what they're after in the story. You've recorded their speech and mentally videotaped their actions and gestures. You've poked around in their closets; you've probed their back stories.

You've built stages and furnished them. You've written key scenes built around large actions. A quick look at the problem-solution rhythm of your story line written in Weekend 13 will remind you of things you need to accomplish in Act One.

Before you start writing, you might take the time to create a list of scenes. This is a quickie list that works as a road map for your writing. The creative self creates the list; reading the list calms the editorial self down so that the creative self can keep working.

As an example to follow, here's a list of scenes for Act One of Tyler's *Tourist*:

Inside the Car (Hook)
Coming home from a trip, after bugging Macon about comfort, systems, and getting out of the rain, Sarah asks for a divorce.

Home Alone
Macon wanders the house, which seems to be closing in. Empty spaces remind him of where Sarah's stuff used to be.

Phone Call
Sarah bugs Macon about the separation.

Running the House with a System
Laundry, washing the dishes, making the bed—all done with Macon's system. No system could keep Ethan alive, as Macon, in a tense interior monologue, blames the world for his son's death.

Phone Call
Sarah, phoning about a rug, vents her anger at Ethan's killer.

Meow-Bow
When the old kennel refuses Edward space, Macon takes him to Meow-Bow, where he has a first encounter with Muriel.

Airplane
On a flight to London for his work, Macon relives a back story trip with Ethan.

London
Macon surveys hotels and restaurants. He thinks Sarah might meet him in New York. No luck.

Meow-Bow
Muriel offers to train Edward. Macon hedges.

Phone Call
Julian, Macon's boss, wants copy for the new edition of *Tourist*.

Back Story
Macon remembers meeting Sarah. Dates in Grandfather Leary's long black Buick. Engagement, marriage, work at the bottle-cap factory. Love troubles.

Phone Call
Muriel, her true purpose veiled, asks about Edward. Asks Macon to supper. He says no.

Building the System (Miniclimax)
Working with a new system of laundry, Macon gets tangled between Edward and the cat and breaks his leg.

Leary House
At home with Rose and the boys, Macon defends Edward (he was Ethan's).

Back Story
Flaky Alicia, Macon's mom, who married an engineer and sent the Leary children off to live with grandparents. Close-up of a photo on page 66.

Decision
Since Sarah might call, they decide not to answer the phone. Garner Bolt, a neighbor, informs Macon that mail is piling up.

Leary Family Lore
Back story on the boys. They play a Leary family card game called "vaccination." The phone rings; no one answers.

Leary House
Edward trees Julian, who gets a quick crush on Rose.

Back Story
How Macon and Julian met.

Action (Plot Point One)
Edward bites Macon. Family wants Edward to go. Macon okays Muriel. This is plot point one, as Muriel takes over in Act Two.

Threads run through this list of scenes, tying events together. Sarah's request for a divorce, *Inside the Car*, causes Macon to be alone in *Home Alone*, which echoes with the silence caused by Sarah's departure, which gets worse when she calls him up in *Phone Call*. Since Edward won't behave, Macon takes him to *Meow-Bow*, where he has a first encounter with Muriel, whom he hires to train Edward in *Action* (plot point one). At the Meow-Bow, clashing agendas lurk in the subtext: Macon wants a place for Edward; Muriel, a blue-collar Cinderella, wants Macon. What Muriel wants, so invisible to Macon, seems clear to the reader, providing a nice dramatic irony for Act One.

Edward, onstage with great fanfare in the scene called *Building the System*, is the cosmic agent who gets Macon out of the house by breaking his master's leg. For care, Macon retreats to *Leary House*, where Edward trees Julian, who initiates the subplot (Romance with Rose), which gives us a lovely plot point two, Rose's wedding, in Act Two.

Good things happen if you stay fluid and keep the hand moving across the page.

WORKING THE NOVEL

Exercises

1. *List of Scenes.*
Following the form used for Tyler—an opening line describing the kind of scene (Leary family lore), the setting (Leary family house), the action (phone call), or a switch to an exotic locale (London)— create a list of scenes for your discovery draft. If your goal is to write a book with forty to fifty scenes (making an easy transition from book to film), then you'll list a dozen or so scenes for Act One. If you list more than that, don't worry. You can compress them later, after you get a sense of the rest of the novel.

2. *Storyboarding.*
Using your storyboard, sketch at least four scenes from your list. Your best bet is to sketch a sequence of scenes that lock together. A sequence will build your momentum while it marches through the

act toward plot point one. Name your characters early. Use only one name to refer to each character. Macon is Macon. Sarah is Sarah. In the narrative, don't switch from Macon to Leary and back to Macon.

3. *Write the Scenes.*
In timed writings of fifteen to twenty minutes, write the scenes from your storyboards. The easiest way to start a scene is to write dialogue, then fill in with action and stage setup. Your goal is three to four scenes per weekend.

4. *Getting to Plot Point One.*
Write as many scenes as you can, but don't enter them into your word processor until you have half a dozen scenes tucked away in the notebook. Writing in notebooks creates the energy in your discovery draft. Writing in the notebook moves you toward your goal—to write toward closure at plot point one. For lots of writers, the word processor is a mind tool. Writing in the notebook keeps the writing physical.

DURING THE WEEK

Preparing Back Stories

During the week, prepare back stories for new characters who come onstage in Act One. For each character, do a quick chronology and then a back story, ten to fifteen minutes on your lunch break. Doing the back stories now, focusing on childhood trauma that produces motivation, will save you hours of time as you continue on with the discovery draft.

Looking Ahead to Writing Act Two

Act Two is fun to write because your momentum is building. The setup is behind you and now you go for broke. By the time you reach midpoint, your discoveries will be popping like fireworks.

By the time he reached midpoint in *Tender Is the Night* (1934), the novel that followed *Gatsby*, Fitzgerald had his momentum. In her interior monologue, you can feel Nicole Diver emerging from her cocoon of madness, gaining strength from her husband. Once she was upside down. Now she sees her husband, symbolically and socially, upside down: "If you want to turn things topsy-turvy, all right, but must your Nicole follow you walking on her hands, darling?"

From her realization at midpoint, Nicole keeps gaining strength until, at the climax of the novel, in bed with Tommy Barban (the sexy animal guy who provides, with his physical stamina, a healthy contrast for Dr. Diver), she has enough strength to stand alone against the ruined mind-doctor.

Writing Act Two is wonderful because, with your setup behind you, you can feel the momentum building as you push toward your midpoint.

• WEEKENDS 24–28 •
DISCOVERY DRAFT: ACT TWO

Act Two is important because it's long. It contains the center of your book, the focal point, the omphalos. You write it by cutting the problem down to size, halving Act Two at midpoint, and by framing it with plot points at each end.

Act Two is where things get complicated. Your protagonist, trying to battle through the obstacles, digs in deeper.

Act Two is fun to write because you keep gaining momentum as you push deeper into your story. Ideas pop in Act Two the way they never popped before and you realize that this is why you prepared, giving yourself a base so that you could arrive at the writing desk ready to write.

Guidelines for Writing the
First Draft of Act Two

Divide your work at midpoint. Write the first half, then the second half. Put labels on the movement of both halves of Act Two. For example, in the first half of Act Two of *Tourist*, Macon dances with

Muriel in an on-again, off-again rhythm. "Dancing with Muriel" is your metaphor for what's happening to them. She closes in. He pushes her away. She waits to be asked. He asks, but only when he's desperate. Dance, then, could be used as a controlling image for the first half of Act Two. If you had written *Tourist*, you could have used "Dancing with Muriel" to guide your writing.

The second half of Act Two weaves a kind of domestic web around Macon, as he begins sleeping over at Muriel's house, giving her a chance to court him, while he brings home pizza and trains Alexander in plumbing repair techniques. The metaphor to use here might be "At Home with Muriel," which begins to fade at plot point two, Rose's wedding.

Develop the past in your book now. Load those flashbacks and narratives about childhood into Act Two. Used right, they can help you here.

In handling the past, follow Tyler's lead. In Chapter Seven, for example, she gives us Macon's erotic dream, pulling us back to the past with Grandfather Leary's 1957 Buick. In Chapter Eight, when Sarah calls for a chummy divorce chat, she suggests they meet at the Old Bay Restaurant, a favorite of Macon's grandfather and also his great-grandfather. In their dialogue, the Learys evoke their shared past ("You liked Betty Grand. You told me when we first went out"), while talking of divorce and separation.

From the scene at the Old Bay, Tyler moves to memories of Grandfather Leary, a neat old guy who foreshadows the spirit of his eccentric grandchildren. The memories end in a dream, a good technique to try in Act Two, once your story gets rolling, especially if it moves the plot: "Sarah," cries Grandfather Leary from Macon's dream. "[She's] the best of all of us!" And just before midpoint, when Macon confesses Ethan's death (in the past) to Muriel (in the present), he remembers Ethan learning to ride a bicycle: "one of those memories that dent the skin." (p. 184)

When you write your flashbacks, make them shimmer by locking them down with similar metaphors of perception. *Dent the skin* evokes touch.

Echo your strategy for Act One and create a list of scenes for Act

Two. You'll need ten to twelve scenes for the first half, the same number for the second half.

Keep the scenes bristling with action, drama, and complication. For example, here's a list of scenes for part of Act Two of Tyler's *Tourist*, which we pick up from the climax of Chapter Seven, where Muriel chokes Edward:

Muriel Chokes Edward
Fighting for her economic life and enraged that Macon now knows about Alexander, Muriel chokes Edward. Macon and Muriel tussle. Result: Macon fires Muriel.

Phone Call
While Julian visits, Sarah phones to invite Macon to dinner.

Old Bay Restaurant
Sarah dumps on Macon. She's seeing someone.

Macon's Dream
In a dream, Grandfather Leary, hearing that Sarah is gone, says: "Sarah's the best of all of us." Macon's under pressure.

New York Skyscraper
Trapped in an attack of distance phobia (fear of getting too far from things), Macon phones home, only to find his brother Charles is trapped by Edward. Focusing on the problem, Macon calls Muriel, back in Baltimore, for help with Edward.

Give twists to your list of scenes: When Macon fires Muriel, his problem gets worse. He can't leave Edward at the Meow-Bow anymore because he doesn't want to see Muriel, who still works there. Because Edward is not yet trained (more work for Muriel to do), he traps Charles in the Leary family pantry, which Macon finds out about when he phones home for help (family sympathy) with his sudden attack of distance phobia, which is related thematically to the "geographic dyslexia" defined by Macon in Chapter Seven. Since Macon is tied to Edward by the memory of Ethan, he is forced to call Muriel to rescue Charles.

The price Macon pays is the return of Muriel—as it turns out, a blessing in disguise.

WORKING THE NOVEL

Exercises

1. *Divide Act Two and Apply Labels.*
Cut your work in half by dividing Act Two. On your plot diagram, apply metaphoric labels ("Dancing with Muriel," "At Home with Muriel") covering the theme for the first half and the second half. Below the line on your diagram, jot down ideas for scenes.

2. *List of Scenes.*
Following the form we used for Tyler, create a list of scenes for both halves of Act Two. If your goal is to write a book with forty to fifty scenes (making an easy transition from book to film), then you'll list twenty to twenty-four scenes for Act Two. Draw boxes around scenes taking place in the past.

3. *Storyboarding.*
Using your storyboard (stage setup, action, dialogue, climax, etc.), sketch half a dozen scenes from your list. Your goal is to write four to five scenes per weekend. Your best bet is to sketch a sequence of scenes that lock together. A sequence will build your momentum while it marches through the act, first toward midpoint, then toward plot point two.

4. *Write the Scenes.*
In timed writings of fifteen to twenty minutes, write the scenes from your storyboards. The easiest way to start is to write dialogue, then fill in with action and stage setup.

5. *Getting to Midpoint, then to Plot Point Two.*
Your first goal is to reach midpoint. If you don't finish drafting all the scenes, sketch the rest and stay on schedule. Reaching

midpoint should give your momentum a boost. After that, you move on to plot point two. Use your notebook first, your word processor later. When new scenes appear, sketch them quickly on your storyboard and keep writing toward the end.

DURING THE WEEK

Learning from Other Art Forms

In Chapter 13 of *The Screenwriter's Workbook*, Syd Field explores strategies for building Act Two. "All you need," he says, "is one key scene to hold the entire first half of Act II in place." In *Chinatown*, for example, the key scene is Hollis Mulwray's murder, which occurs in the script on page 45. In *Body Heat*, the key scene is Matty Walker's announcement that she wants her husband dead, also on page 45. Field calls this scene "the pinch" (perhaps a metaphor for waking up your audience or reader). In *Tourist*, the "pinch" could be the scene referred to above, Macon's attack of distance phobia atop a skyscraper in Chapter Nine: he calls home, only to find Charles trapped in the pantry by Edward, which forces Macon to phone Muriel to rescue Charles. The skyscraper scene occurs about halfway between the beginning of Act Two and midpoint.

You can learn a lot about structure by studying film and theater.

Looking Ahead to Act Three

In his chapter on plotting in *The Art of Fiction*, John Gardner offers good advice on writing Act Three. You're trapped, Gardner maintains, by what has come before. That, of course, is why you did all the preparation before starting your novel, so that you know, not only by sight, but also by touch and smell and footfall, the walls of your novelist's cave. "The writer," Gardner says, "is more servant than master of his story. He can almost never use important details only once: They are sure to call out for repetition. . . . It is this quality of the novel, its built-in need to return and repeat, that forms the physical basis of the novel's chief glory, its resonant close. . . . What rings and resounds at the end of a novel is not just physical, however. What moves us is not just that characters, images, and events get some form of recapitulation or recall; we are moved by the increasing connectedness of things, ultimately a connectedness of values."

Because of all that has come before, Act Three almost writes itself.

· WEEKENDS 29–31 ·
DISCOVERY DRAFT: ACT THREE

Act Three is the closing movement of your novel. Here, with the dramatic climax, you bring your action to a conclusion that satisfies the reader. If you're writing a love story, the lovers, having been split apart for much of Act Two, get together at last. If you follow Tyler's lead and deepen the love story with a psychological rebirth of a reluctant passive hero, you could wind up your story in Paris in the early morning with sunlight and confetti.

Act Three, which contains the catharsis of the novel, is framed by plot point two and the wrap-up scene. Since all three of these scenes are written, you can speed through Act Three, writing with a confidence bordering on abandon because more of the book lies behind you than lies ahead.

A look at Tyler's Act Three offers some great strategies for your work: At plot point two, Rose's wedding, we watched Macon think about turning away from Muriel. Macon is a systems guy. For him, action, made passive by multiple deflections, is always preceded, not just by thought, but by weighty analysis. He is a writer, after all.

So he *thinks* about turning away and Muriel, a female in touch with the cosmos (and also with her economic needs), jumps on him about Sarah and marriage. Her energy drives him away, and by the middle of Act Three, he's back with Sarah. This return to the rituals of the past has a comforting feel to Macon, and perhaps to us. It doesn't last because Sarah's still on her power trip, dumping on Macon with more verve than she used in Chapter One. In Paris, Tyler turns Sarah into a witch doctor, drugging Macon on pain pills while she takes over his work. For Macon, the systems guy who gains his identity from work, this is the last straw. In a major action, he drops the pain pill without a long analysis preceding the action. He's leaving Sarah. He's going back to Muriel. Bang.

You want this same thrill of triumph, brought about through cathartic change, in your Act Three.

Macon Leary, a protagonist gritting his teeth over the back pain, is Tyler's tough-guy hero. His wound is psychological, a metaphor for our neurotic age. Like Ike McCaslin, Faulkner's hero in *The Bear* (who leaves gun and compass at the edge of the wilderness so that he can meet the bear unencumbered by the trappings of civilization), Macon Leary leaves his leather travel bag on a curb in Paris so he can make it to the taxi to pick up Muriel and start a new life. He has made a fundamental decision and chooses to change his life dramatically.

Guidelines for Writing Act Three

Scenes in Act Three will be shorter because you'll be driving old roads, returning to old haunts and rooms already decorated. You're on the final stretch, where you echo themes already in place. To locate your scenes for Act Three, you might start with chains of events. Here, for example, is a chain of events connecting Macon as he drifts from Muriel at Rose's wedding to Sarah's phone call in Chapter Eighteen. Sarah wants to move back to their house. Now that she's back, the door is left open for Macon.

From Muriel to Sarah

—Muriel, with marriage on her mind, bugs Macon about eloping with someone else.

—Muriel quits Meow-Bow so she can travel, echoing with action her desire to see Paris, first mentioned in Chapter Seven. In Chapter Twenty, she follows Macon to Paris.

—In an argument about Alexander's education, Muriel demands commitment from Macon. Stop drifting, she says.

—Through the mail, Muriel sends Macon a calendar with the word *Wedding* scribbled in red across a Saturday in June.

—Munching a familiar pâté at Rose's house, Macon realizes it's Sarah's recipe as he is embarrassed, in the next bite, by Muriel's presence.

—Sarah, closing in, phones Macon at a hotel in Winnipeg. Her lease is up. She wants to move back into the house. The symbolism is clear: So long, Muriel.

By adding stage setups—Muriel's apartment, Rose's apartment—you can see which events need to be turned into full scenes. Take the time to storyboard the scenes. Because you have written several scenes already, you'll be smoother at the writing now. Instead of building the pieces first—dialogue, action, stage setup, and so on—you'll write the full scene at one burst of speed, integrating the parts as you go. Should you have a problem with a particular scene, you can always break it down into parts and work on them separately, later in the meditation draft.

If your novel contains a subplot, you need to cap off these subplot characters before you reach the climax, thus clearing the deck for your major characters in the final struggle of clashing agendas.

In Act Three of *Tourist*, for example, Tyler uses the dinner with Rose and Julian (the "Happy Marriage" subplot) to reinforce Macon's embarrassment with Muriel. On a visit to Leary House, Macon and Sarah find Rose back with the boys: "I kept losing that apartment [Julian's] every time I turned around." When Julian asks for help to get Rose back, Macon advises him to give her a job organizing the office. That sets up a nice cause-effect sequence for capping them off. When Macon calls Julian from Paris about the work slowdown because of his back pain, Rose answers the office phone. She has taken over Julian's office, getting things in order, she says.

With that phone call, Rose fades into the wings, leaving the stage clear for Macon, Muriel, and Sarah, who arrives in Paris on the next available flight.

WORKING THE NOVEL

Exercises

1. *Chain of Events.*
Following the form used in the guidelines, create a chain of events connecting plot point one with your climax, and your climax with the final image. Make sure each event has a core action that connects to the earlier parts of the book.

2. *List of Scenes.*
Add stage setups—Muriel's apartment, Paris hotel—to each of these events. This helps you determine which scenes will be full scenes.

3. *Storyboarding.*
Using your storyboard, sketch your scenes. If you need momentum, sketch a scene sequence that works with a chain of events to bind Act Three together.

4. *Write the Scenes.*
In timed writings of fifteen to twenty minutes, write the scenes from your storyboards. By now you should be able to write full scenes, integrating the parts as you go. If you have problems, storyboard the scenes. Your goal is three to four scenes per weekend.

5. *Finishing the Draft.*
Write as many scenes as you can, working in the notebook before entering them into your word processor. As you print each scene out, allow yourself to feel a sense of completion. Your goal is to push yourself to reach the end.

Wrapping Up the Discovery Draft

Using Aristotle's incline, a woman in one of my fiction seminars diagramed her novel on the board. The story was about a woman who loses her husband in a car accident. As she reaches the dramatic climax, the woman pauses: "My heroine dies here," she announces. "She kills herself."

A downer ending brings a groan from the group.

As a strategy, I advise the woman to plug into Greek myth. Read some Bullfinch, I say, and come back next week with a different ending, something that smacks of redemption. She comes back with the story of Laodamia and Protesilaus, a warrior killed by Hector at the battle of Troy. "When Laodamia heard about her husband's death," the woman said, "she asked the gods for a boon. She wanted three hours to talk to him and they said okay. Mercury brought him back to the upper world. When he died a second time Laodamia died with him. Isn't it beautiful?"

Dipping into Greek myth gave her a better ending for her story. The death of her protagonist, which reunited her with her husband, now made story sense.

Be careful of those downer endings.

Closing Thoughts

Looking Ahead to the Meditation Draft

In the discovery draft, you are a wild child flying free, arms flung wide, open to all things. In the meditation draft, you mature into an artist, brooding upon your creation. You write. You print out pages. You seek feedback from trusted friends who understand the pain and pleasure of the writing process. In the meditation draft, you might write even when you're not writing.

"I never know when I'm not writing," said James Thurber. "Sometimes my wife comes up to me at a dinner party and says, 'Dammit, Thurber, stop writing.' She usually catches me in the middle of a paragraph. Or my daughter will look up from the dinner table and ask, 'Is he sick?' 'No,' my wife says, 'he's writing.' I have to do it that way on account of my eyes."

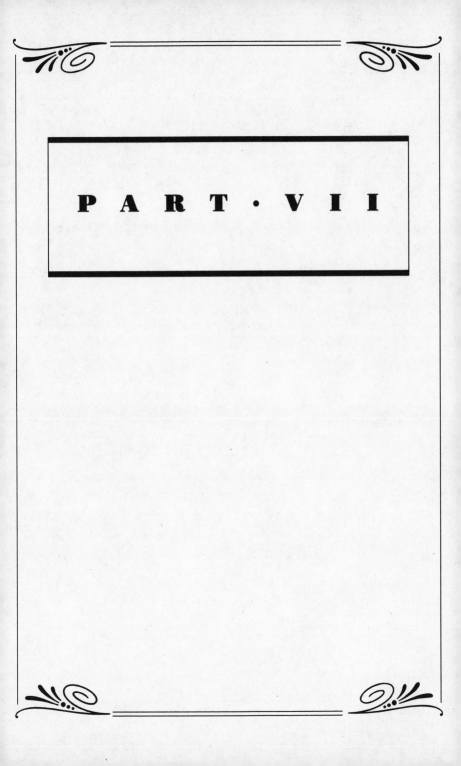

PART · VII

Weekends 32–45
Writing the Meditation
Draft

In his introduction to *Writers at Work* (the first Paris Review interview series), Malcolm Cowley explores the second stage of writing a book: "The book or story shapes up—assumes its own specific form—during a process of meditation that is the second stage in composition. . . . The meditation may be, or seem to be, wholly conscious. The writer asks himself questions—'What should the characters do at this point? How can I build to a climax?—and answers them in various fashions. . . ."

John Gardner calls this process of meditation a kind of *brooding*. When the novelist finishes a first draft, Gardner says, he "begins to brood over what he's written, reading it over and over, patiently, end-lessly, letting his mind wander, sometimes to Picasso or the Great Pyramid. . . . Reading in this strange way lines he has known by heart for weeks, he discovers odd tics his unconscious has sent up to him, perhaps curious accidental repetitions of imagery. . . ."

In the meditation draft, you brood over what you have discovered. As you brood, you write to reshape parts of the book. You rework dialogue and tighten action and rebuild your stage setups until the novel hums. You breathe deeply while you write, in and out, in and out, and breathing infuses your writing with the rhythms of life.

In the meditation draft you give yourself permission to invent (or to borrow or to steal) some helpful fictional forms.

You know these forms already. They rise up from life, from the street or the stage or the movie screen, from the room around you. Take close-up, for example. A close-up is a fictional form we associate with film and camera movement, but Flaubert uses a close-up in the opening sequence of *Madame Bovary* (1854), as he zooms in on a funny hat that makes Charles Bovary the laughingstock of his classmates at school. We have already seen how Tyler moves in for a close-up of Sarah: ". . . but if you looked closely you'd notice the tension at the corners of her eyes."

In the meditation draft, you enable your imagination to transform the everyday objects in the world (hats, clothes, notes, letters, diaries, documents, dossiers, et cetera) into the significant detail of fiction. In Chapter Eleven of *Tourist,* for example, before Macon writes his refusal note to Muriel, he looks *closely* at his fountain pen: "It was a Parker, a swirly tortoiseshell lacquer with a complicated gold nib. . . ." The note in closeup (*"Dear Muriel . . . I am very sorry,* he wrote. . . .") becomes a plot device to get Macon within range of Muriel's powers. On her doorstep on Singleton Street, Macon blurts out his confession about the fact, not the pain, of Ethan's death: "I lost my son. . . . He was just . . . he went to a hamburger joint and then . . ."

Macon's note guides us to the midpoint of the story, where Muriel, her healing powers churning, guides Macon's hand to her Caesarean scar: *"We're all scarred. You are not the only one."*

The refusal note, a simple plot device, leads us to the wound, one of the key symbols of our age. Follow Tyler's example and supply your novel with notes, reports, diaries, letters, dossiers. Borrow freely from other art forms. The monologue comes from theater. Flashback comes from film.

In the meditation draft, allow your meditative imagination to transform exploratory sentences from the discovery draft into drama. Let's say you're writing a story about a girl in a doctor's office. She's fourteen and alone. The purpose of her visit is an operation. As she waits for the doctor, the girl sits, thinking to herself. "Her mother wasn't coming, she reflected" is the way you've written it. Since you've delivered information without making drama, it's now time to brood on your choice. Time to play what if. What if you moved that line from inside her head into dialogue? What if, instead of writing "Her mother wasn't coming, she reflected," you wrote dialogue: "She's not coming" or "She's not here." Writing dialogue brings the doctor onto your novel's stage, which gets you into a scene.

Try it now. He's an old guy, gray hair, eyeglasses, his face smooth and baby-pink. He wears a white doctor coat. He looks at the girl.

> "She's not here," she says.
> "Who?" the doctor says.
> "My mother. She's not here. She's not coming."
> "Your mother." The doctor studies his chart, shuffling loose papers inside a manila folder. "And you're Trudy, right?"
> "She can't come. She works. This is . . . just between you and I, okay?"
> "Me," the doctor says.
> "What?"
> "Between you and me. Didn't they teach you the objective case in school?"
> "Want me to undress now?" she says. "I'm real nervous."

By moving the line about Mom out of the character's head into dialogue, by allowing Trudy to talk *to* someone instead of to herself, you reveal anxiety, giving her another dimension. She's not just a writerly mind doing random teenage thoughts. Now, on your novel's stage, she's a person with a problem. The problem drives the story.

Playing what-if is a systematic way of brooding. Brooding is a form of meditation. Writing practice in timed intervals is meditation through keeping the hand moving.

The Next Fourteen Weekends

Key scenes control your pace, so it's smart to reshape key scenes first. My advice on reshaping key scenes is to let them grow larger, especially midpoint and climax and plot points one and two. Let them extend via chains of events, until the key scenes seem to link up with each other. Extending your key scenes will help you make your novel's transitions more fluid.

Reshaping the key scenes takes three weekends. After that, you reshape the acts, starting with Act One, then moving through to Act Three. This reshaping of the three acts takes eleven weeks. Your goal is to brood and to meditate on the shape of your novel while you write your way to the end, building a computer printout. Working through to the end gives you a feeling of closure. With the book contained, you'll finish in no time.

· WEEKENDS 32–34 ·
MEDITATION DRAFT:
DEEPENING KEY SCENES

Your goal in the next three weekends is to deepen and expand your six key scenes: opening scene, plot point one, midpoint, plot point two, catharsis, and wrap-up scene. Using these scenes as focal points stabilizes your structure. When you connect the scenes with chains of events, you produce a structure that is strong and solid, a house well built.

The key scenes of your novel are connected by the work they do. The opening scene and the wrap-up scene *frame* the book, like bookends framing a shelf of books. The action at midpoint determines the resolution at the catharsis with the inevitability of an *IF-THEN structure* (IF X happens, THEN the protagonist must make a choice at catharsis to resolve the conflict). Finally, plot point two *reverses* plot point one.

Bookends Frame the Book

If you step back for a wider view of *Tourist,* you see the car in the beginning and the taxi at the end. In the beginning, Macon drives, controlling the car, exercising his systems, and Sarah's with him, gripping the dashboard. In the end Macon has moved to the backseat, giving up control, and Muriel is about to replace Sarah at his side.

Construct this same kind of connection in your book, as a resonance or mirror image between beginning and end. The best way to connect is with images—car in the Maryland rain, car in the Paris sunlight.

Reversal

If plot points one and two work together you have a tighter book. At plot point one of *Tourist,* Macon okays Muriel as Edward's trainer, and Muriel swoops in to envelop Macon's life. Plot point two *reverses* this trend as Macon, at Rose's wedding, eases away from Muriel in his favorite reflex, the Macon Leary deflector mode.

If-Then

At the climax of *Tourist,* Macon chooses Muriel—sort of. At the midpoint of *Tourist,* Macon confesses to Muriel about Ethan's death. If he hadn't confessed, then there wouldn't have been the scene with the pill or the scene inside the Paris taxi, Muriel waiting on the curb.

Midpoint is the turnstile that gets you to the end of Act Two, which gets you to the climax, which gets you to the end. You can tighten the connection by using an IF-THEN structure.

Try it: IF Macon confesses to Muriel at midpoint, letting her into his life, THEN he has a chance to choose her at the climax.

Guidelines for Deepening Key Scenes

1. Take the time to go over the storyboard for all six of your key scenes. Because we live in a world of television screens, we often skip the stage setup. On TV, the camera sets the stage. If you omit the stage setup from your novel, your characters don't have a place to stand, or to *be.* The result is unexciting talking heads.

2. Check to make sure your central image/key symbol expands into the central event of each scene. The central image in the opening passage of *Tourist* is rain, which acts as a force, increasing Sarah's discomfort until she blurts out that she wants a divorce. The central image of the midpoint is Macon's abortive note. It's too late to mail it, forcing Macon to deliver it in person, which plops him down on Muriel's doorstep. Muriel, waiting in the wings, is ready with a fake shotgun. Gotcha, she says, drawing Macon inside, then upstairs, to her bed.

3. Repeat images from one key scene to another. Rain, dominant in the opening, reappears again at plot point two. The taxi in Paris echoes Macon's car in the opening. Edward the causal dog links plot point one to the dog-choking scene in Act Two.

4. Fix the language of each key scene, starting with the verbs. Comb through your pages, circling weak verbs. In fiction, *was* and *were* are weak. Subjunctives like *could, should, would, might,* and *may* are weak. Temporal auxiliaries like *had* (as in *had seen*) and *had been* (as in *had been seen shopping*), which drop your reader through a trapdoor into the past, are weak. Verbs of the mind—*understood, knew, thought, reflected, imagined, realized, wondered*—shuttle the narrative from the stage into the mind of the author, leaving the reader outside. *Appears* and *seems* soften perception, forcing us to peer at the scene through gauze. When you join two weak verbs, *seemed to have wondered* (soft verb *seemed* with passive infinitive *to have wondered*), action loses its zip and what remains of your writing power oozes away.

In a chapter called "The Action of Sentences" from *Writing Down the Bones,* Natalie Goldberg hands over her secret of locating strong verbs: Think of an occupation; for example, a carpenter, doctor, flight attendant. List fifteen verbs ... to go with that occupation." Her occupation, cook, brings verbs like these: *sauté, chop, mince, slice, cut, heat, broil, taste.* Like Goldberg, you get strong verbs when you connect with process. List verbs for tennis (*stroke, lob, slice, chop, smash*) or the observed flight of a bird (*soar, swoop, sail, float, dive*). Be bold with your language. Instead of writing, "Desdemona felt wonderful when she saw him," you try writing with a good verb: "Desdemona exploded when she saw him. Her blood buzzed."

For good verbs, look at any passage by Tyler. Here are verbs from Chapter Eleven, midpoint in her story, as Muriel undresses Macon: *removed, hung, knelt, untied, stepped, rose to unbutton, stood, hung, dropped, covered, smelled.*

5. Deepen the drama of each key scene now. To give drama a chance, convert interior passages (inside the narrator's head) to dialogue. Use your explanatory passages to shift psychic distance. Have a purpose (close-up for change of pace; pulling back for a wider view) for each shift in tone or rhythm. Tighten your action, using the one-two rhythm of action and reaction. Have at least one major character onstage in all key scenes. If possible, have two. Make certain your characters come onstage with clear agendas.

WORKING THE NOVEL

Exercises

1. *Meditation.*
Close your eyes and watch your breathing, chest rising and falling, as you brood on the key scenes of your novel. Allow your mind to play over lines of dialogue, actions, details in the stage setup, a narrative line that would go better as a dialogue line.

2. *Warm-up.*
Write for five minutes on "My favorite key scene is . . ." Then write for five minutes on "The key scene that really needs work is . . ."

3. *Stage Setup.*
List parts of each stage setup outlined in Weekend 6 for each key scene (time, place, temperature, season, lighting, props, who's on, who's coming on). Let the images cluster and the symbols deepen. Make sure your verbs evoke sense perception: "[Muriel] covered him with a thin, withered quilt that smelled of bacon grease." Do timed writings on each stage setup, allowing the symbols to deepen and take root.

4. *Dialogue.*
Using the dialogue checklist from Weekend 7 (rhythm, attaching to stage setup, evoking the past, echo lines, et cetera), reshape your dialogue.

5. *Action.*

Using the guideline of action and reaction from Weekend 8, re-write your action chain. Replace all weak verbs (*think, know, wonder, seemed to appear to have been seen reflecting*) with strong verbs (*buzz, explode, chop, singe*).

6. *Chains of Events.*

List the chain of events leading up to and/or away from each key scene. The moment you finish the list, write about the chain for ten minutes. This will allow you to flow into the key scene that you are deepening through rewriting.

7. *Computer Work.*

Enter the changes into your computer. Print out your scenes. File the new material in your folder.

DURING THE WEEK

Learning from Other Writers

If you want to write a tight book, you'll want to frame it. Look again and again at the structural devices you choose to open and close the novel. Here's the opening of *Rebecca,* where Daphne du Maurier, with a dream sequence, paints a big house called Manderley: ". . . I could not enter for the way was barred to me. I called in my dream to the lodge-keeper, and had no answer, and peering closer through the rusted spokes of the gate I saw that the lodge was uninhabited. No smoke came from the chimney, and the little lattice windows gaped forlorn."

Manderley, its people, its secrets, contains the novel. At the end, the house burns: "The road to Manderley lay ahead. There was no moon. The sky above our heads was inkly black. But the sky on the horizon was not dark at all. It was shot with crimson, like a splash of blood. And the ashes blew towards us with the salt wind from the sea."

End of house, end of story: a novel perfectly framed. Think about using this bookend technique (opening and closing with the same image) for your book.

The work that you do here—deepening scenes—is a prelude to the work for the next several weekends. As long as you are a writer, you'll practice rebuilding and shaping to deepen your scenes. And you won't be alone. Here's Virginia Woolf: "And I have just finished . . . the last sentence of *The Waves*. . . . But I have never written a book so full of holes and patches; that will need *rebuilding* [italics mine] yes, not only remodeling." (*A Writer's Diary*)

In an early draft of *A Farewell to Arms*, Ernest Hemingway tried an interior passage held together, but not tightly, with parallel repetitions of the phrase *I could tell:* "I could tell you what I have done since March nineteen hundred and eighteen and when I walked that night in the rain alone, and always from then on alone, through the streets of Lausanne back to the hotel where Catherine and I had lived. . . . I could tell what has happened then but that is the end of the story." (Michael Reynolds, *Hemingway's First War*)

But in the final version, Hemingway shifted from writing woeful interior narrative to building a *short scene*. In the hospital, the protagonist, Frederic Henry, talks to the doctor about the operation that has just killed Catherine Barkley. The doctor, concerned, says:

> "I would like to take you to your hotel."
> "No, thank you."
> He went down the hall. I went to the door of the room.
> "You can't come in now," one of the nurses said.
> "Yes I can," I said.
> "You can't come in yet."
> "You get out," I said. "The other one too."
> But after I had got them out and shut the door and turned off the light it wasn't any good. It was like saying good-by to a statue. After a while I went out and left the hospital and walked back to the hotel in the rain. (*A Farewell to Arms*)

Try this from Hemingway: Turn your narrator's interior observations into a scene.

· WEEKENDS 35–45 ·
MEDITATION DRAFT:
ACTS ONE, TWO, AND THREE

In the meditation draft, you step back for a breather as you take a wider view of your work. In your mind, you stretch out across the body of your novel, feeling for rough spots, shallow spots, scratchy spots, spots that need rebuilding. In your mind, you whirl away from the book; in your mind, you spiral back, brooding and writing, writing and brooding. Curious about a word or a phrase, you zoom in for a close-up, detail you never saw before, tossed up by your subconscious.

As you reshape the book, look at the world around you. Let's say you're writing in a notebook. Give a notebook to a character in your story. There's a photo on your wall. Describe the photo, changing it to fit a scene from your story. If your character walks down a long hallway, footsteps echoing, describe the paintings on the walls. Portraits of soldiers, tycoons, explorers, a small boy sitting on a horse, three women in ball gowns. Who are these people? What's the story here? Be creative with your detail. Moving into form in your reshaping is smart because form not only gives you boundaries—a diary entry cannot run on too long without taking over the book—but it can also provide a central image for a scene.

Make everything count in this draft. Make use of whatever you have introduced. If you've got a short scene of someone watching TV, you could deepen this scene with a weather person in front of a weather map. Whether it shows rain in Maryland or wind sweeping across Idaho, the weather map informs the reader about the facts of your novel's landscape. Once you know the weather, you know how to dress your characters. If you repeat a weather word, the way Tyler repeated rain in her opening scene, you'll build symbolic meaning into your book.

· WEEKENDS 35–37 ·
MEDITATION DRAFT: ACT ONE

As we discussed in Weekends 21 and 22, Act One is your setup.

In the setup you introduce your characters. You establish time and place for scene and story. You develop stage setups to unearth symbols. You display character motivations through involving action. You have your characters speak. If there's a subplot, you start the subplot in Act One.

In the meditation draft, for every scene in Act One, you write and then you brood, focusing on doing more work with action and dialogue. For example, let's say you wrote a scene early in your discovery draft, a man and woman eating dinner, and the doorbell rings. The man answers. The caller is a process server who hands the man legal papers. He's being sued. The plaintiff is his mistress. In the discovery draft, the man hides the papers under a stack of mail on a marble-topped table in the foyer. Back at the table, the wife asks who it was. No one important, the man says. Just a kid selling something.

In the meditation draft, you rethink the man's actions. Have him fold the papers, palms sweaty, hands trembling. He slips the folded papers into his jacket pocket. He wasn't wearing a jacket in the discovery draft, so you give him a jacket now, a silk dressing gown, dark blue, with a monogram. The man hears movement behind him. Turning, he sees no one. But perfume lingers on the air, and in the dining room he can hear the staccato tap-tap of his wife's high heels. Did she see him? Back at the table you write dialogue:

> "Who was it, dear?"
> "That boy, collecting for the paper."
> "Are you feeling all right, dear?"
> "I don't trust him, if that's what you mean. Something in the eyes."
> "Your face, it's pale. Are you all right?"
> "I said I'm fine." He pours wine. His hand still shakes.

Setup is important, and in the meditation draft you think about your lines critically, retooling them to see what works best as you play what-if. In the scene above, for example, what if the wife asks, "Who was it?" and the man answers with a line like this: "The Avon lady. I ordered perfume." And with one line, you change his character from stuffy gentleman to wise-guy joker.

Characters Onstage

Bringing your characters onto the stage of your novel is your main job in Act One. And the way you bring them on is determined by your style, what kind of writer you are, the kind of book you're writing, and the time in which you write. To bring Captain Ahab onstage in *Moby Dick* (1851), Herman Melville wrapped his description, roughly three hundred words, around the image of Ahab's scar: "Threading its way out from among his gray hairs, and continuing right down one side of his tawny scorched face and neck, till it disappeared in his clothing, you saw a slender rod-like mark." The weight of words, the sheer mass of detail, tells the reader Ahab is important.

Do the same thing with your characters. Bringing a character on with 100–150 words indicates a character of more importance than one you bring on with a dozen words. While writing the discovery draft, you probably found new characters coming into the story in Acts Two and Three. Now, in the meditation draft, you have a chance to rewrite descriptions (dress, vehicle, hairdo, gesture, makeup) to deepen these characters.

By the end of Act One, you want to have introduced all of the key characters. Since *Tourist* is our model, let's look at Tyler:

Macon and Sarah come onstage in the first word, the pronoun *They*, of Act One. "They were supposed to stay at the beach a week, but . . ." Macon is the protagonist; Sarah is the antagonist.

Muriel, the helper, comes onstage in Chapter Three, when the boarding kennel refuses Edward because he's a biter. Muriel, a dog trainer who doesn't like dogs, works at Meow-Bow. Muriel enters around the middle of Act One, which has six chapters.

Rose and the boys come onstage in Chapter Five, when Macon moves back to Leary House after Edward, displaying to the world his need for training, breaks Macon's leg in the basement. Rose, Macon's old-maid sister, is important for the romance-marriage subplot.

Julian Edge, Macon's publisher, comes onstage in Chapter Six, precipitating plot point one when Edward trees him in the Leary front yard. Julian joins Rose in the romance-marriage subplot.

You can follow Tyler's use of subplot, counterpointing the separation of one married couple (Macon and Sarah) with the coming connection of another (Rose and Julian).

Guidelines for Reworking Act One

1. Take the time to make a list of scenes from the discovery draft. Include in your list the central image/key symbol and the main action for each scene. Studying the list will help you decide which scenes need to be expanded, which scenes can be cut. Cutting scenes now saves you time.

2. Rework your character wants list (from Weekends 2 and 14), tying each want, if you can, to a specific line from the discovery draft. In Tyler's wants list, Macon wants to be left alone. Here's a line from Chapter Eight of *Tourist:* "Sometimes he wished he could stay in his cast forever. In fact, he wished it covered him from head to foot."

3. Use the wants list to shape your characters as they come onstage. If you didn't take the time in the discovery draft to dress them, do that now. Your scenes will work better if each character has an agenda.

4. Probe your stage setups for symbols that need to get strengthened.

5. If your novel has a subplot, start it before the end of Act One.

WORKING THE NOVEL

Exercises

1. *Meditation.*
Close your eyes and watch your breathing, chest rising and falling, as you brood over the entire expanse of Act One. Allow your mind to play over character entrances, stage setups, large actions,

central images, long passages of explanation, a line inside the narrator's head that you could change to dialogue.

2. *Warm-up.*
Write for five minutes on "The shape of Act One looks (feels) like . . ."

3. *List of Scenes.*
Each weekend, before you start work, write down the list of scenes for Act One. Making a list is fast; it gets you back in touch with the scope of the work. A list of scenes charts your progress and gives you a sense of accomplishment. In your list, include pieces of scenes, bits of scenes, snippets, whatever you've written, no matter how tiny it seems. If a scene is complete and whole, write "Done" in red pencil near your entry. If a scene is incomplete, write "Still to Write" or "More to Come." When your list is done, examine the story line (written on Weekend 13) for holes. Can an old scene be expanded to cover the hole? Or do you need a new scene? If there are scenes you can cut now, do so. Cutting the excess now can close gaps in Act One.

4. *Rebuilding Pivotal Scenes.*
From your list, select a pivotal scene from Act One. This scene could be a turning point in the protagonist's life, such as Macon's first encounter with Muriel at the Meow-Bow. First encounters are important as starters. As we saw on Weekend 10, on building a chapter, this meeting opened the door, just a crack, into Macon's life.

Identify at least one pivotal scene and rebuild it, working, as always, in parts: dialogue, action, stage setup. Time yourself, doing as much as you can in ten to fifteen minutes on each part. If you need to step back, use the storyboard technique for a view of the whole.

5. *Chain of Events.*
Link the scene you just rebuilt to scenes that follow and scenes that come before with chains of events, discussed in Weekend 17.

6. *Rebuilding Connecting Scenes.*

Work at your scenes one piece at a time. Stop in between writings to brood. Try not to edit while you write.

7. *Computer Work.*

Enter the changes into your computer. Print out your scenes for Act One. File the new pages in your folder.

DURING THE WEEK

Learning from Other Writers

In a 1919 essay called "Modern Fiction," the novelist Virginia Woolf writes about the need to keep going:

> Nevertheless, we go on perseveringly, conscientiously, constructing our two and thirty chapters after a design which more and more ceases to resemble the vision in our minds. So much of the enormous labour of providing the solidity, the likeness of life, of the story is not merely labour thrown away but labour misplaced to the extent of obscuring and blotting out the lights of the conception. The writer seems constrained, not by his own free will, but by some powerful and unscrupulous tyrant who has him in thrall, to provide plot, to provide comedy, tragedy, love interest, and an air of probability embalming the whole so impeccable that if all his figures were to come to life they would find themselves dressed down to the last button of their coats in the fashion of the hour. . . .

Woolf went on, after this essay, to write more novels.

Looking Ahead to Act Two

In *The Art and Craft of Novel Writing,* Oakley Hall offers some excellent tips for keeping going. Here's one:

> Characters, as they begin to curve into roundness, will contribute to the progress of the novel. Decisions as to their personalities, relationships, and fates may have to be rethought because of demands of the

characters themselves. Each will have his *through-line*—his overall objective, as well as his objective in a particular scene. In that scene will be other characters with their own objectives, and if those characters quarrel, we will get to know their objectives and their natures more rapidly than if they merely chat.

In *The Accidental Tourist*, Tyler uses Muriel's through-line to develop Act Two. Muriel's overall objective is to marry Macon. Her objective in Chapter Seven, which begins Act Two, is to show Macon what a neat person she is by training Edward to obey. At the end of Chapter Seven, Muriel kills her chances by choking Edward. In Chapter Nine, her through-line picks up again when Macon is forced to call Muriel for help when Edward traps Charles in the pantry.

Follow Hall's advice and let your characters lead you through Act Two.

· WEEKENDS 38–42 ·
MEDITATION DRAFT: ACT TWO

Act Two is your complication.

Here the problems for the protagonist get tougher, the holes get deeper, the obstacles get worse. In Act Two, in between the problems, you have a chance to explore the past, where more problems lurk. In the past, you unearth images that connect to images from Act One. If you need to explore back stories for your main characters, this is the place.

In Act Two you have room to expand your work with myth and symbol. In Act Two, you advance by rebuilding the Syd Field "pinch" scenes, used in screenwriting, that we talked about in Weekends 24–28. Pinch scene number one is located halfway between plot point one and midpoint. Pinch scene number two is located halfway between midpoint and plot point two.

Ritual

The focus of your meditation for Act One was characters, their agendas, the way they came onto the stage of your novel.

The focus of your meditation for Act Two is ritual. Ritual, a process repeated over and over, sometimes with sacred significance, can hold your Act Two together. Ritual is something you might have zipped across in your discovery draft, so you have a chance to explore it now with more depth. Hemingway develops Book Two (Act Two) of *The Sun Also Rises* with different rituals: drinking in Paris; fishing in Burguete; running with the bulls; watching the English; bullfighting; being an aficionado about bullfighting.

In Act Two of *Tourist,* Tyler uses ritual to move through the plot. The main ritual for the first half of Act Two, for example, is Muriel's *training* of Edward, and then Macon. When Macon gripes about his crutches, Muriel says: "Listen, I've taught a man with no legs at all." When Muriel exits, the memory of her training methods lingers: "Macon wished he could change the gestures of command—the palm, the pointed finger, all vestiges of the heartless trainer—but he supposed it was too late." (p. 120)

Other rituals from *The Accidental Tourist:*

- Dinner with Sarah at the Old Bay is a ritual from the past that doesn't work when dragged into the present.
- Macon's trip to New York, which starts as just another ritual journey to gather information for his work, results in his skyscraper distance phobia, which brings Muriel back into his life.
- At Thanksgiving, Macon and the boys refuse to eat Rose's underdone turkey, a ritual with a deep past, thus allowing Julian to play white knight: he eats the turkey and survives.

The second half of Act Two begins with Julian's announcement that he wants to marry Rose. This announcement culminates in the wedding, a marriage ritual to cap Act Two. At home with Muriel, Macon teaches Alexander (father-son ritual) how to fix a leaky faucet. Macon and Muriel eat ritual Christmas dinner at her parents' house at Foxhunt Acres in Timonium. As the New Year dawns, Macon ritualizes Muriel's life: "So every morning, Macon rose and dressed before Alexander woke. He started fixing breakfast and then roused him. 'Seven o'clock! Time to get up!' " (p. 223) Macon's ritual shopping tour with Alexander ends on an upbeat note: "Actually, I find shopping for boys is a pleasure."

Since every reader is familiar with ritual, use it to lock the reader into the longest and most difficult part of the novel, Act Two.

Guidelines for Reworking Act Two

1. Take the time to make a list of scenes for both halves of Act Two from the discovery draft. Include in your list the central image/key symbol and large action for each scene. Studying the list will help you decide which scenes need to be expanded, which scenes can be cut. Cutting scenes now saves you time.

2. Study your character wants list, jotting notes down. For each want, jot down two obstacles in Act Two that stand in the way of the want. Macon wants to be left alone. The obstacles are Muriel and Edward. Muriel wants someone to pay the bills. The obstacles are Macon's desire to be alone and Macon's family.

3. Connect your characters and their traits to the past, using back story scenes in Act Two. Macon's odd Leary world-view is inherited from Grandfather Leary, who invents a nonexistent Indian tribe, the Lassaquans, whom he plans to visit. In a flashback, Macon and Grandfather Leary hunt without success for the Lassaquans in the encyclopedia.

4. When in doubt, dip into ritual. Ritual includes training, teaching, learning, cooking, eating, drinking, shopping, praying, fishing, sewing, bullfighting, bathing, washing up, applying makeup. Use ritual to deepen your scenes and to connect the chains of events in Act Two.

WORKING THE NOVEL

Exercises

1. *Meditation.*
Close your eyes and watch your breathing, chest rising and falling, as you brood over both halves of Act Two. Allow your mind to play over ritual, the past, wants, obstacles, images, character agendas.

As always, keep a sharp eye out for a line inside the narrator's head that would go better as a dialogue line.

2. *Warm-up.*
Write for five minutes on "The shape of Act Two looks (feels) like . . ."

3. *List of Scenes.*
Make two lists of scenes, one for the first half of Act Two, one for the second half. Include pieces of scenes, bits of scenes, snippets. If a scene is finished, write "Done" in red pencil near your entry. If a scene is unfinished, write "Still to Write." When your list is done, examine it for holes in the plot. Can an old scene be expanded to cover the hole? Do you need a new scene? If there are scenes you can cut now, do so. Cutting sometimes opens up new territory that's easier to work. From your list, select the two Syd Field "pinch scenes," one from the first half of Act Two, one from the second half.

4. *Rebuilding the Pinch Scenes.*
Rebuild the "pinch" scenes first, working from the parts to the whole: dialogue, action, stage setup. Time yourself, doing as much as you can in fifteen minutes per scene. If you need to step back, use the storyboard technique.

5. *Chain of Events.*
Link the scenes you've just rebuilt to scenes that follow and scenes that come before with chains of events.

6. *Rebuilding Connecting Scenes.*
Rebuild the remaining scenes. Tighten the first half first, then the second half. Work at scenes one piece at a time. Stop in between writings to brood. Try not to edit while you write. Your goal is to finish Act Two, not to have completely realized scenes.

230 •••••••••••••••••••••••••••••••• Weekends 32–45

7. *Computer Work.*

Enter the changes to Act Two into your computer. Print out your scenes for Act Two. File the new pages in your folder. Keep going until you have pushed through to the end of Act Two on Weekend 42.

DURING THE WEEK

Learning from Other Writers

Study other novelists for keys to unlock the rituals in Act Two.

In Act Two of *Rebecca,* Daphne du Maurier describes the tea ritual: "The performance of the day before was repeated, the placing of the table, the laying of the snow-white cloth, the putting down of cakes and crumpets, the silver kettle of hot water placed on its little frame. . . ."

In Act Two of Elizabeth Tallent's *Museum Pieces,* Peter Barnes watches a woman in the ritual of chopping wood: "She swings gracefully and the chunk splits in two. She quarters each of these halves with increasingly quick small blows of the ax."

In Act Two of *Moby Dick,* Melville deepens the symbol of whiteness with two fulsome chapters ("Moby Dick" and "The Whiteness of the Whale"), and then weaves the ritual of the whale hunt with a parade of nine ships met by the good ship *Pequod* on the open sea. These meetings, beginning with the *Jeroboam* in Act Two and ending with the *Rachel* just before the climax in Act Three, form a bridge that keeps the story moving as Ahab and crew approach the final and deadly confrontation with the White Whale.

Looking Ahead to Act Three

"By the nature of our mortality," Gardner writes in *The Art of Fiction,* ". . . we care about what we know and might possibly lose, dislike that which threatens what we care about, and feel indifferent toward that which has no visible bearing on our safety or the safety of what we love. Though we do not read fiction primarily in order to find rules on how to live or, indeed, to find anything that is directly useful, we do sympathetically engage ourselves in the struggle that produces the fictional events. Reading a piece of fiction that ends up nowhere— no win, no loss; life as a treadmill—is like discovering, after we have run our hearts out against the timekeeper's clock, that the timekeeper forgot to switch his clock on."

Translation: make your story count by caring about everything— plot, characters, scenes, language.

• WEEKENDS 43–45 •
MEDITATION DRAFT: ACT THREE

In the discovery draft, when you were writing Act Three, you went for speed. Your goal was making it to the end no matter what, a wild, breathless sprint for the finish line. In the meditation draft of Act Three you're going for torque, a slow and powerful gathering together of all the elements of your story.

In Act Three, you move with relentless resolve toward resolution. You cap off minor characters. You cap off the subplot before you arrive at the climax. As the climax starts, you want the major characters either on your novel's stage or waiting in the wings to come on. In Act Three, as you move toward resolution, you can keep the conflict going by letting your characters move at different speeds. Character A, for example, wants to rush forward toward resolution while Character B, working a different agenda, dawdles, stopping for a meal, a coffee, a bit of window shopping.

To find the best strategy for Act Three, you look back at what you did for Acts One and Two.

In the meditation draft of Act One, for example, you focused on the problem of *characters onstage*—getting them on, dressed, faces prepared and agendas pulsing—to drive your book through to plot point one. If a character popped up in Act Two or Three of your discovery draft, you used the meditation draft to bring that character onstage earlier in Act One.

In the meditation draft of Act Two, you focused on *ritual*—teaching and training and the painful process of learning—as you deepened symbols and explored the past.

In the meditation draft for Act Three, you'll focus on *echoes that resound*—echoing images, echoing lines, echoing incidents—repetitions that replay themselves in your novel as you move, in the end, toward John Gardner's symphonic effect, one of your goals from "Writing Tips," in the introduction to this book.

Example: Echoes

Rain opens Act Three of *Tourist*. It's almost a year after the rain of Chapter One, where Sarah, in the closed set of the car, asked Macon for a divorce, kicking off the separation that continues as we start Act Three. Macon's living with Muriel, who was introduced at the middle of Act One in a memorable first encounter. But repetition can mean change—Muriel has quit her job at the Meow-Bow—and her passport photos tell Macon she's ready, as suggested in Chapter Seven, to fly with him to romantic Paris. On the phone with her mom, Muriel recalls her training of Edward (the ritual strategy that brought her close to Macon) as she chats about a current dog-training project.

Muriel has changed, but when the phone rings in Winnipeg, Macon finds that Sarah, who wants to move back into their old house, is much the same. At the end of Chapter Eighteen, Macon goes home too.

With Macon's return to the old house and the old wife (they're not divorced yet), his healing stops. In a dressing-room scene in Chapter Nineteen, Tyler echoes the opening scene in the car from Chapter One, with Sarah on the attack, Macon a half step quicker in mounting his defenses:

> "You never asked me if I slept with anyone while we were sepa-
> rated."
> Macon paused, halfway into one sleeve.

> "Don't you want to know?" she asked him.
>
> "No," he said.
>
> He put on the shirt and buttoned the cuffs.
>
> "I would think you'd wonder."
>
> "Well, I don't," he said.
>
> "The trouble with you is, Macon—"
>
> It was astonishing, the instantaneous flare of anger he felt. "Sarah," he said. "Don't even start. By God, if that doesn't sum up every single thing that's wrong with being married. 'The trouble with you is, Macon . . .' "
>
> "The trouble with you is," she continued steadily, "you think people should stay in their own sealed packages. You don't believe in opening up. . . ." (p. 311)

Images are so important. With his *instantaneous flare of anger,* Macon shows us that he's capable of change. Sarah, on the other hand, is not. Her experiences—separation from Macon, living alone, seeing someone, reclaiming the house—did not change her. As we see in this dressing scene, she's quoting Macon again, echoing herself in the opening chapter, when she told him: "You said, 'Honey, to tell the truth, it never seemed to me there was that much point to begin with.' Those were your exact words." Macon's defensive behavior, while still deflective, is more abrupt, a sure sign of Muriel's influence in Act Two.

In this scene so fraught with the echoes resounding in the marriage, Tyler shows you, with imagery and character, how to keep the conflict going: Sarah, still the tough one, is still winning battles by attacking; Macon, changed by life with Muriel, is more willing to feel his emotions. He's better. Sarah is the rigid one now, and the echoes let the reader *feel* the change.

Guidelines for Reworking Act Three

1. If you take the time, before plunging ahead, to make a list of scenes for the entire novel while searching for the echoes, you'll save yourself a lot of writing time. In your list of scenes, you might include names of characters, along with their exit lines as you cap them off. It might be helpful, in the plot diagram you drew on Weekend 12, to note where these characters exit the story line, and to cap off your subplot.

Reading over your work, what has come before, you jot down images that have grouped in clusters or grown to form symbols. In *The Art of Fiction*, Gardner has this advice: "Read the story over and over . . . watching for subtle meanings, connections, accidental repetitions, psychological significance. Leave nothing—no slightest detail—unexamined; and when you discover implications in some image or event, oonch those implications toward the surface."

A good writer's word, *oonch*.

2. Study the list you made for Act Two, "Wants" plus "Obstacles," and add a third column called "Resolution." Macon wants to be left alone. His obstacles are Sarah, Muriel, and Edward. The resolution—we've already seen hints of it in the echo section above—is that Macon changes.

3. Except for echoes, leave the past behind, in Act Two, where it belongs. Act Three is no place for more back story.

WORKING THE NOVEL

Exercises

1. *Meditation.*

Close your eyes and watch your breathing, chest rising and falling, as you brood over Act Three. Allow your mind to play across echoes, repetitions, recapitulations. Who comes back onstage? Who stays? Who gets capped off? As always, keep a sharp eye out for a narrative line that would go better as a dialogue line.

2. *Warm-up.*

Write for five minutes on "The shape of Act Three looks (feels) like . . ."

3. *List of Scenes.*

Make a list of scenes for Act Three. Include pieces of scenes, bits of scenes, snippets. If a scene is finished, write "Done" in red pencil near your entry. If a scene is unfinished, write "Still to

Write" or "More to Come." When your list is done, examine it for holes in the plot. Can an old scene be expanded to cover the hole? Do you need a new scene? If there are scenes you can cut now, do so.

4. *Rebuilding an Echo Scene.*
The dressing scene in Chapter Nineteen, where Sarah echoes herself from Chapter One, is a turning point in Act Three. Find a similar scene in your work—a scene from Act Three echoes a scene from Act One—and rebuild it. Work from the parts to the whole: dialogue, action, stage setup. Time yourself, doing as much as you can in ten to fifteen minutes per writing. If you need to step back, use the storyboard technique.

5. *Chain of Events.*
Link the scene you have just rebuilt to scenes that follow and scenes that come before with chains of events.

6. *Rebuilding Scenes.*
Rebuild the remaining scenes in Act Three. Work at scenes one piece at a time. Stop in between writings to brood. Try not to edit while you write.

7. *Computer Work.*
Enter the changes to Act Three into your computer. Print out your scenes for Act Three. File the new pages in your folder.

DURING THE WEEK

Learning from Other Writers

Echoes in a novel can glitter with the tinsel of romantic, Cinderella-ized happiness or they can fall with dead sounds, hollowed and empty. In Act Three/Book 3 of *Tender Is the Night*, Dr. Richard Diver, in his downhill slide on his leg of the big X plot structure, has a final meeting with Rosemary Hoyt, his inamorata from Book 1. The year is 1930. Five years have passed since their first encounter.

> *Dr. Diver:* "Five years ago you came here. And what a funny little thing you were, in one of those hotel peignoirs."
> *Rosemary:* "I'm going to pretend it's five years ago and I'm a girl of eighteen again."

The scene is the beach, an echo from Book 1, and Dr. Diver, trying to show off on an aquaplane towed behind a speedboat, cannot lift himself out of the water. Last year on the Zugersee, his wife remembers, he "lifted a two-hundred-pound man from the board onto his shoulders and stood up." Panting, Dr. Diver says: "I couldn't have lifted a paper doll that time."

And Rosemary says: "The first drink I ever had was with you."

And Dr. Diver says: "Did you hear I'd gone into a process of deterioration?"

Mrs. Diver has the point of view, showing us it's her story now. And as her husband evokes the past by flirting with Rosemary, we watch a man dive deeper into ruin. Here, near the end of Act Three, Dr. Diver is about to make his last dive.

Closing Thoughts

Natalie Goldberg, a writer who sat Zen (meditated) for fifteen years, and who uses writing as her practice, remembers how it was to wrap up *Writing Down the Bones:*

> I finished typing Sunday night at eleven. . . . I took a bath, climbed out of the tub, dressed, walked alone at midnight to the Lone Wolf Café in downtown Santa Fe. I ordered a glass of white wine and two scoops of toffee ice cream. I looked at everyone, spoke to no one, and kept smiling. . . . On Tuesday I told my class: "The book took a year and a half to write. At least half the chapters came out whole the first time. The biggest struggle was not with the actual writing, but working out the fear of success, the fear of failure, and finally burning through to just pure activity." The last month and a half I wrote seven days a week. . . .

Looking Ahead to the Final Draft

Once when I sent a final draft to an editor, the manuscript came back with all the dreams deleted. They were lyrical dreams, I remember, packed with symbols and touched with the mysterious blend of dream time and shadowy shivers of eroticism. I had worked hard; the dreams were well written. I stayed miffed about the deletion of dreams all through the final copy edit and the galley stage and I was still miffed until I saw the manuscript turned into a book with a handsome cover, a product for the marketplace, and then, reading it over, searching for the holes I had patched after cutting those dreams, I realized that my editor, once again, had been right.

The dreams, though beautiful, were excess baggage. In novel writing, in this day and age, you cut the excess and save a tree.

PART · VIII

Weekends 46–52
Writing the Final Draft

Writing a novel, you have probably discovered, is a series of creative actions and deep processes where you keep changing speed. When you know something for sure, you run wild and free, writing hot, writing like mad. When you're learning as you go, you slow to a crawl, digging your toes into the mud of creation as your writing hand probes for depth.

In the discovery draft, you zipped along, skipping from scene to scene, your writing eye and your writing heart tugged along by the lure of reaching the finish line. In the discovery draft, you were both wild child and breathless athlete.

In the meditation draft, you stepped back for a wider view of your work. Using your telescope, you swept over the hummocks and hills of your novel, brooding until something caught your eye, an image, a line of dialogue, a bracelet glittering on the arm of a character, and then you zoomed in for a closer look. Getting close during meditation gave you a hands-on feeling, a touch of possession. *This is mine*, you might have thought. *This thing was born out of me*.

In the meditation draft, you were an artist, a writer, a Zen master, a sculptor, a sentient architect.

In the final draft, you become an editor. You cut and prune and edge and shape the best parts of the manuscript into a product for the marketplace.

In the final draft, you scrutinize and analyze and measure, weighing the value of each scene, each image, each line of dialogue. Too many repetitions? Take some out. Image too bushy? Trim it down to size. A monologue that goes on and on, slowing the dialogue? Collapse it, compressing it down to bare essentials, leaving only mood and information.

"Simenon," writes Malcolm Cowley in his introduction to *Writers at Work*, "spends exactly three days in revising each of his short novels. Most of that time is devoted to tracking down and crossing out the literary touches—'adjectives, adverbs, and every word which is there just to make an effect. Every sentence which is there just for the sentence. You know, you have a beautiful sentence—cut it.' " Cowley quotes Joyce Cary on cutting: "I work over the whole book," Cary says, "and cut out anything that does not belong to the emotional development, the texture of feeling."

The Last Seven Weekends

Spend the first weekend reading your manuscript. Take notes while you read, but don't do any serious rewriting. What you're after is an editorial view of the whole book.

Spend the next weekend cutting the excess. Cut scenes that don't belong. Cut passages that wander from the story line.

Spend the next four weekends rewriting what you didn't cut. You want to rewrite for power and depth. Your job here is to range across the full manuscript, working at paragraphs and sentences through specific images, specific parts of speech.

The last weekend you'll edit your work. Once you're at this stage, editing is a matter of changing a word here, a word there. The hard work is behind you. Compared to the road you've come down, this is easy.

• WEEKEND 46 •
READING

Now that the writing is almost done, you need to read your novel before you start your last task, editing.

1. Dedicate a fresh notebook to editing. Call it something like *The Edit Book*.

2. Take notes, gathering them in your edit book, noting page numbers from the manuscript where you encounter problems. These notes are communications with your internal editor. The fresh notebook gives you a fresh look.

3. Don't mark on the manuscript pages too much. Marking stalls your reading and sucks you into rewriting sentences before you get a sense of the whole.

4. Map each act as you read. Chart the main events. Make sure the key scenes are connected by character, symbol, and action.

WORKING THE NOVEL

Exercise

Set up a reading schedule—Act One, Saturday morning; Act Two, Part One, Saturday afternoon, et cetera—and stick with it. In your edit book, make notes on pages of the book that still need work. Sometimes it's helpful at this stage to redo your character wants list, to make sure your character agendas are still in force.

DURING THE WEEK

Learning from Other Writers

Here's Virginia Woolf writing to her friend Clive Bell, about her first novel, called *The Voyage Out:* "When I read the thing over (one very gray evening) I thought it so flat and monotonous that I did not even feel 'the atmosphere': certainly there was no character in it. Next morning I proceeded to slash and rewrite, in the hope of animating it; and (as I suspect for I have not reread it) destroyed the one virtue it had—a kind of continuity; for I wrote it originally in a dreamlike state, which was at any rate, unbroken. . . . I have kept all the pages I cut out; so the thing can be reconstructed precisely as it was." (*The Letters of Virginia Woolf*)

The edit book helps you preserve the energy of the creative process, what Woolf calls the "dreamlike state."

· WEEKEND 47 ·
CUTTING

Before you cut, get a fresh look at the entire book by making a new list of all your novel's scenes. If you have more than fifty scenes, try to cut some out, the way my editor deleted my dreams, before you rewrite.

Cut scenes and then cut paragraphs. Cut out monologues and wordy passages of explanation. Cut lines of dialogue that don't work. Pare down the book early because once you begin writing again, the grooves will fill with words and the material will swell with promise.

Cut sentences down, taking out adverbs first. An adverb is an adjective to which the suffix *ly* has been added: *waspishly, uneventfully, gorgeously, intermittently*. If the base adjective is strong (*waspish* comes from *wasp*, a stinging insect), then the adverb has more punch. If the base adjective is weak, like *intermittent*, which comes from the verb *intermit* (the dictionary definition, "to suspend activity temporarily," contains its own adverb), excise it before it dies on the page. In your first novel manuscript, the last thing you want is a vast plain of words filled with decomposing adverbs.

Sometimes you have to cut the words you love. This will hurt. You've invested time and care getting those words on the page. Because of the investment, you might feel they are just right, perfect for this moment in the story. You might think of cutting as making a place for new words. You might think of cutting as faith. Here's Susan Griffin from "Thoughts on Writing: A Diary:" *"Here (I say) the words are too thin. I have heard this before, I say, and there is more to this than is being revealed. I have said the obvious and expected. But beyond this must be something shocking, something satisfying.* And so I mark out these old words and write again. I cross out all the words except those that affect me deeply. . . . I keep those and build again. And again. All the while knowing that deeper meaning will rise to the surface like the form in a piece of stone. . . ." (*The Writer on Her Work*)

WORKING THE NOVEL

Exercises

1. *List of scenes.*
Make a fresh list of scenes. Be terse. Include stage setup, characters onstage, core action, central event.

2. *Cutting.*
Cut scenes that don't do any work in the novel. Be tough.

3. *Cutting.*
Cut paragraphs of explanation that don't do any work in the novel, no matter how lovely, no matter how much time you invested in writing them.

4. *Cutting.*
Cut sentences that don't work.

5. *Cutting.*
Cut old words. Cut all the words that don't affect you deeply. Have faith. Keep writing.

DURING THE WEEK

Learning from Other Writers

In *The Writing Life*, Annie Dillard offers some Zen-like advice on writing, acting with the pen to fill the page, and cutting. "Acting," says, Dillard, "is better than being here in mere opacity; the page, which you cover slowly with the crabbed thread of your gut; the page in the purity of its possibilities; the page of your death, against which you pit such flawed excellences as you can muster with all your life's strength: that page will teach you to write.

"There is another way of saying this. Aim for the chopping block. If you aim for the wood, you will have nothing. Aim past the wood, aim through the wood; aim for the chopping block."

In her chapter "The Samurai" in *Writing Down the Bones*, Natalie Goldberg says: "Be willing to look at your work honestly. If something works, it works. If it doesn't, quit beating an old horse. Go on writing. Something else will turn up. There's enough bad writing in the world. Write one good line, you'll be famous."

· WEEKENDS 48–51 ·
REWRITING

Since the language of fiction is word pictures, most of your rewriting will be making your word pictures sharper for the reader. As you discovered early in this book, making word pictures works well if you write with rhythm (discussed in Weekend 5), a basic one-two of telling and showing:

Telling: She stared at the lake.
Showing: Hot orange sun and blue water and white rocks on the opposite shore and behind the rocks a rim of trees, green against the hot blue sky.

Telling is the *one* of rhythm; showing is the *two*.

Since English works best when it runs in a straight line, moving from left to right, you simplify your work as a writer by writing lots of sentences that follow this model—"She stared at the lake"—which gives you a subject (she), a verb (stared), and an object (lake). This tight unit of subject plus verb plus object creates a consistent center for each sentence.

That same pattern, subject-verb-object, keeps you out of trouble whether you're writing about the weather ("Rain flattened the grass") or writing about politics (VEEP LAYS EGG ON TV) or about a marriage foundering on the rocks ("WIFE STABS ERRANT HUSBAND WITH GRANNY'S HEIRLOOM BROOCH").

To embellish your telling, you can hang clauses on either end of the subject-verb-object structure: "Naked to the waist, she stared at the lake, raising the pistol until the muzzle pointed at . . ." A change of weather means a change in the clothing clause: "Shivering, her face buried in the parka fur, she stared at the lake." To emphasize the pistol, put it up front in the sentence: "Raising the pistol, a Walther PPK 9mm, retailing for $450 at your better gun stores, she stared at the lake." In the second clause, beginning with *retailing*, you have added, along with the information, a new tone. The simple picture, Woman Staring at Lake, now has a voiceover. The voice belongs to the author and the tone veers into irony, a picture drawn with the writer's tongue-in-cheek.

Three Simple Rules for Rewriting

The first rule of rewriting: Sharpen your word pictures.

Breaking this rule tears you away from objective writing and shoves you into fuzzy abstraction. The picture, embellished by the author's voice, fuzzes up, sometimes even goes away. To fix the sentence about the Woman Staring at the Lake you return to the word picture. Chop out the clause about retailing, and add physical detail: "Raising the pistol, a Walther PPK 9mm that glinted in the sun, she stared at the lake. Hot orange sun and blue water and . . . The gun felt hot in her hand."

The second rule of rewriting: Keep the language simple by making sure every sentence has a subject (she), a verb (stared), and an object (lake).

Breaking rule two takes you into fragments, complexity, and reader confusion. A sentence *fragment* is a string of words posing as a sentence but which does not contain a verb to make it a sentence. This string of words, "She *staring* at the lake," is a sentence fragment. The word *staring*, made from joining *stare* with an -*ing* suffix, is a verbal, an almost verb. To make it a verb, you cut the -*ing* suffix and add -*es* (*stares* is present tense) or -*ed* (*stared* is past tense). If you add *is* to *staring*, you create a verb that extends the action, making it feel longer and, sometimes, smoother: "She is staring at the lake." Sometimes, those *ing*-words can add a sense of singing to your prose: "Humming to herself, sweating, seething with sun, she stared at the lake."

Complexity comes from using a passive-voice verb to reverse the key words in your sentence: "The lake was stared at by the woman."

Reader confusion comes when you toss the picture, filling the page with author voiceover while reversing the sentence with passive-voice verbs: "The pistol was purchased, retailing for somewhere around four, perhaps five hundred, dollars, at your better gun emporiums, which was thought of while the lake was being stared at by this awfully peculiar-seeming woman."

(When you toss the picture, your eye backs away for a wider view from inside the author's head where, sometimes, readers cannot follow.)

The third rule of rewriting: Wait to rewrite until you have a solid manuscript.

Rewriting, as you can see from our work on the Woman Who Stared at the Lake, is a left-brain activity. Rewriting engages your internal editor, who is also judge and executioner. Activated too early, your internal editor can smother your creative child, killing all desire to play and create. Once the book is done, however, once you have a solid manuscript built on character work, solid scenes, careful plotting, discovery, and meditation, you can let the editor out of the cage.

Three rules are enough: One, make word pictures. Two, keep it simple. Three, make the internal editor wait.

Guidelines for Rewriting

Fix your verbs first. Verbs help you make word pictures. Make lists of verbs associated with action and process: athletes doing their thing, dancers, carpenters, musicians, tailors, doctors. Tack the lists on your wall. An activity that produces strong verbs is slicing onions or cutting meat: skin, slice, chop, mince, et cetera.

Fix your sentences by making sure they work rhythmically. If one sentence tells, make sure the next one shows. One-two, one-two, until the end of the novel.

Fix your sentences by sharpening word pictures. Use detail that connects the character via sense perception (touch, taste, smell, sound, sight). This keeps the point of view steady, a camera mounted on a tripod. If you use fragments ("Hot orange sun and blue water and . . ."), use good detail.

To move your sentence along, use simple connectors like *and, so, then, when, and so, and then*, et cetera. To slow your sentence, pulling back to increase the distance between reader and story, use connectors that take your sentence into the more formal word-arena of subordination: *if-then, not only–but also, either-or, neither-nor, more-than*.

Never never never use cliches associated with academe. The worst of these cliches is the *it-that* construction: "IT is interesting to note THAT . . . IT is further interesting to note THAT . . ."

In fiction, padding is out.

WORKING THE NOVEL

Exercises

1. *Combing.*
Comb the manuscript for passages that still need work. Make a list. Then write little notes to your internal editor: "Action passage, scene 10, Summerhouse: Night, right before plot point one. Sentences seem choppy. Replace weak verbs. Add reactions to complete actions in the one-two." Combing the manuscript reacquaints you with words the way a list of scenes reacquaints you with structure. Writing notes gives your internal editor focus.

2. *Rhythm.*
Fix your rhythm where it needs fixing. A patch of dialogue might need help with clearer one-two's. An action sequence (where you moved too fast) might need reactions.

3. *Word Pictures.*
Sharpen your word pictures to make an easy read for your reader.

4. *Verbs.*
Circle verbs in passages that need work. Replace weak verbs with strong verbs. Weak verbs can be passive voice ("could have been said to have been resubmitted"), or mushy verbs from the interior like *thought, knew, opined, assumed, understood*, and *questioned*. One tactic I use for getting rid of interior verbs is to view the mind like a stage. Stage demands a stage setup: "Inside her mind, Trudy smells . . ."

5. *Detail.*
If fixing verbs doesn't make the passage better, fix the nouns and modifiers. Get specific. Instead of *flower*, write *orchid, rose, calendula.* Instead of *tree*, write *elm, eucalyptus, pine, sycamore.* Instead of *color*, write *fuchsia, puce, mauve, vermilion.*

6. *Sentences.*
Change sentences to make sure the center is solid subject-verb-object, with clauses clamped on at the beginning or draped on at the end. Remember, words ending in *-ing* might feel like verbs, but they are really verbals. A verbal works to extend the verb, sometimes into continuous, or repeated, action—"She's *staring* at that doggone lake again"—or as a modifier—"The *staring* woman, stripped to the waist, raised her Walther and . . ."—or to form a phrase: "*Staring* hard at the lake, the woman in the fur parka raised the pistol and fired."

Definition of a verbal: feels like a verb and acts like a verb but isn't.

DURING THE WEEK

Learning from Other Writers

To make word pictures in English, we build little stacks of modifiers. Tyler's opening passage shows us Macon in a neat little stack: "a tall, pale, gray-eyed man." Three modifiers is a good stack. For a better visual grasp, you can pull the modifiers out of the sentence line, stacking them up in your notebook:

tall
pale
gray-eyed
   MAN

One modifier added to this stack, while piling on information about Macon, would also change the rhythm. Just for fun, let's pile on *odd:* "a tall, pale, odd, gray-eyed man." Remember what happened to the Woman Who Stared at the Lake when we added another clause? The author's voice crept in. That same thing just happened here, with *odd.* Does a deeper stack always mean author's voice? Here's a four-word stack from the opening pages of *All the King's Men*, where narrator Jack Burden describes a cow. "I knew that they were the eyes of a cow," Burden says:

a
poor
dear
stoic
old
   COW
      with a cud

With modifiers like *poor, dear,* and *stoic,* Warren's stack builds into heavy irony. But *behind* the noun, Warren gets back to objective, cowlike things: "cow with a cud."

This is the lesson of modifiers: after you try for depth by writing your stack, try leapfrogging a couple of modifiers *behind* the noun. Keep your internal editor busy while you allow your image to deepen. After you write a stack like "The nervous spavined jittery-handed old gray-haired man," you jump a modifier out of the stack to a position *behind* the noun:

The old man, nervous as a starved spider, moved on spavined legs to the coffee machine. "Help you, lady?" The woman, her throat flushed with blood, stopped hammering on the machine. "What?"

Your words now have room to breathe. The stack collapses. A scene starts to build. And, suddenly, you have turned your internal editor into a creative force.

To see how this works in the hands of a professional, let's look at a passage from "The Undefeated" (1936), a short story by Ernest Hemingway. The protagonist is an aging bullfighter named Manuel. He opens the passage, then steps aside to turn the stage over to Zurito, his picador. Hemingway gives you a lesson in staying with the image:

> Four times he swung with the bull, lifting the cape so it billowed full, and each time bringing the bull around to charge again. Then, at the end of the fifth swing, he held the cape against his hip and pivoted, so the cape swung out like a ballet dancer's skirt and wound the bull around himself like a belt, to step clear, leaving the bull facing Zurito on the white horse, come up and planted firm, the horse facing the bull, its ears forward, its lips nervous, Zurito, his hat over his eyes, leaning forward, the long pole sticking out before and behind in a sharp angle under his right arm, held halfway down, the triangular iron point facing the bull.

This passage starts in slow motion, like a movie clip. In the first frames, the bullfighter controls the bull with the cape and Hemingway slows down to let the images synchronize into various swirling objects (cape, skirt, bull, belt):

- the cape billowing full
- cape like a ballet dancer's skirt
- winding the bull about him like a belt

At the same time Hemingway moves our reader's eyeball through the images with numbers, four swings of the cape mentioned, with the first three swings implied, until, at the end of the fifth swing, with the infinitive *to step clear*, the bullfighter exits the frame, leaving the bull to face Zurito the picador. Zurito is the man holding the lance, the man sitting the white horse. The almost-verb verbals (*facing, facing, leaning, sticking, facing*) slow the action, smoothing the picture into a kind of freeze-frame in prose.

As the camera shifts to Zurito, the images connect bull, man, and horse in a word picture that deepens because of Hemingway's careful modification. It could have been a stack—the nervous-eared, nervous-lipped, firmly planted horse—but Hemingway gave each image, and each piece of the image, a syntactic unit all to itself. The image deepens this way: Zurito sitting the horse, the horse facing the bull as the lance links man and horse and bull in a still life built on five levels.

If we break the passage, we can see the levels of modification that deepen the image:

1 Zurito on the white horse,
  2 come up and planted firm,
    3 the horse facing the bull,
      4 its ears forward,
      4 its lips nervous,

1 Zurito . . . leaning forward,
      4 his hat over his eyes
      4 the long pole sticking out . . . under his right arm,
        5 held halfway down,
        5 the triangular iron point facing the bull.

There are three key nouns—*Zurito, horse, bull*—and five levels of interlocked detail.

Zurito takes the top position in the passage, sitting the horse. *Firm*, a modifier, implies the legs and feet of the horse. Ears and lips are connected with parallel *its*, reinforcing the tension and fear in the horse, and the camera swings back to Zurito, leaning now, as separate images outline this figure of a picador hard at work: hat, pole, sticking, right arm, angle of the pole, iron point, triangular. As we reach the last two images, feeling the iron strength of Zurito, we know this bull will be dead.

When you rewrite, working on passages, try leapfrogging a modifier from a stack to a position *behind* your noun.

· WEEKEND 52 ·
EDITING

The verb *edit* comes from *editor*, a noun, which comes from the Latin verb *edere*, meaning "to publish, to bring forth." *Edition*, the thing brought forth, comes from *edictus*, the past participle of the verb *edere*.

As a writer, you become a keeper of the language. Acting as your own editor, you bring forth from the jungle of words a story. The form of this story is your first novel, not your last, for you'll write a second now that this one is done.

On this last weekend you'll touch the book up. Cut a word here. Fix a verb that you missed in your rewrite. Compress one last image. Rewrite a sentence that won't behave, even after all these rewrites.

On this last weekend, you'll roam the book, tightening the manuscript, as you hum passages from your novelist's symphony. A year ago, you had no idea you could come this far, running this deep, or that you could grow so fast as a writer. A year ago, you were a different person from the editor-writer who sits here before this heap of novel manuscript.

You are to be congratulated. You've done it. You have come through.

WORKING THE NOVEL

Exercise

Roam the book, reading passages at random, as you cut words or tighten sentences. Read for style, not story. Read for detail that illuminates motivation. If you write fat, your prose tending to excess, keep on cutting. If you're a spare writer, one who trims as she goes, you'll need to make sure your images are lean without seeming skeletal and stark.

Have fun with this final edit. You deserve it.

Closing Thoughts

Once you start rewriting, your internal editor will urge you to keep on, and on, and on. "I keep on rewriting," says Frank O'Connor, "and after it's published, and then after it's published in book form, I usually rewrite it again. I've rewritten versions of my early stories, and one of these days, God help, I'll publish these as well."

This happened to F. Scott Fitzgerald with *Tender Is the Night* (1934), the novel that followed his success with *The Great Gatsby*. He couldn't stop working on it, messing with it. The project took him nine long years, from 1925 to 1934, and the book, an ambitious novel about emotional bankruptcy, drew dings from critics on publication. Fitzgerald, weak, disillusioned, and depressed, wanted to revise the book, opening with Dr. Richard Diver in 1917 instead of Rosemary Hoyt in 1925.

So he brought out a "revised" edition, based on chronology, beginning with the arrival of his protagonist in Switzerland in 1917. The revised edition is not better than his original. The best writing in the book is still Nicole's interior monologue, which sits at midpoint, where Fitzgerald understood the structure of his novel, perhaps for the first time.

Learn from Fitzgerald. Plot your book early. Revising after it's published probably won't help.

Looking Ahead to Finding a Publisher

Manuscript preparation means double-spaced copy with professional margins, an inch or so all the way around. The left margin should be straight down the page; the right-hand margin, in contrast, should be ragged for submission, not justified. Page numbers go in the upper right-hand corner, making it easy for the agent or editor to flip through. Across the page, in the upper left, you print your last name and a title line. If your name is Mary Louise Smith and your title is *The Woman Who Stared at the Lake*, you write "Smith: Lake" on every page. The reason: agents and editors are busy. If they lose pages in the office, your name on the page makes recovery easier.

Print your manuscript on white paper, twenty-pound weight. For suggestions on finding a publisher, see the Appendix.

Appendix: Finding a Publisher

When the book is done, when your teachers and writing friends have pronounced it ready for the marketplace, you make contact with literary agents. A literary agent acts as your go-between, your link with a particular editor in a particular publishing house. An agent negotiates your contract—advances against sales, royalties, payment schedules, rights (subsidiary, foreign, film), et cetera—and keeps an eye on the marketplace so that he or she can help to guide your writing career.

An agent's job is selling. Your job is writing. Agents read the fine print so you can keep your hand moving on the next manuscript.

There are three ways to make contact with literary agents: 1) a personal link; 2) a writer's conference; or 3) by mail. Let's look at them in order.

Personal Link

You know someone who knows someone who has an agent. This link could be a writing instructor or a fellow writer. You make connections in writing the same way you do in other endeavors—by networking. My first agent came from a colleague in an English department.

Writer's Conferences

Agents on the lookout for new clients appear at writer's conferences. Most writer's conferences are held in the summer and there's a great list in the March or April issue of *Writer's Digest* (9933 Alliance

Road, Cincinnati, OH 45242; phone 800 Information for their toll-free number). If your manuscript is ready, you take along copies of your plot scenario, written on Weekend 10, and your first chapter. If you make a connection, the agent will ask to see some work. Some agents read on site. Some ask you to send it by mail.

By Mail

Writer's Market, published each year by the same people who publish *Writer's Digest*, has a list of agents. *Literary Marketplace* (the industry abbreviation is the *LMP*), available in most libraries, lists editors and agents. Author Aid Associates (340 East 52nd Street, New York NY 10022) publishes *Literary Agents of North America*, which lists over four hundred agencies in the U.S. and Canada, has handy subject-matter breakdowns and information on manuscript submissions. Some agents want a query first; some want a partial (two or three chapters and a scenario); some want scenarios only; some want the full manuscript.

If you live in a big city, you might find agents listed under Literary Services in the Yellow Pages. Check your library for Literary Services listings for Manhattan and Los Angeles.

When writing to a literary agent, always send along an SASE—the industry acronym for self-addressed stamped envelope.

Finding a Publisher

Finding a publisher means finding an editor who likes your work. The personal touch is best. If you have a friend who has an editor who can recommend you, you can bypass the agent for now, writing the editor to check the interest level on books like yours. You'll do better if you're a marketeer, and if you can compress your book into a high-concept sentence: "This is the story about a fish that eats people."

If you're not a marketeer, you connect with an agent and the agent connects you with a publisher.

Since you're a first-time writer, your agent will probably want the full manuscript before contacting a publisher. Knowing how tough the writing game is, they'll want to make sure you can push through to the end. Because of the way you've learned to work, you have pushed through to the end of your novel many times during the writing process.

The Contract

When an editor acquires your book, the agent will negotiate a contract for you. For fiction, the writer usually gets half of the advance on signing the contract, the other half when the revised manuscript is accepted by the editor. After the royalties earned by the book pay back the advance, you receive what's left over. All of this is specified in the contract. If you're keen on contracts, you can read about them in any number of books on publishing.

Working with Editors

Editors move around. They work for peanuts and a love of literature. Editors are people. They have tastes, likes, dislikes, specialties. At one publishing house, the editor might handle fiction and travel books. At a larger house, she might carve out a specialty in mystery fiction, with an emphasis on the trendy female sleuth.

Editors work hard. Your best bet as a budding writer is to make your editor's job easier by being professional at your job. Have a tight plot driven by great characters. Prepare a professional manuscript. Use your spell checker to clean up spelling. If you don't know grammar, hire a free-lance editor to go over the manuscript before you send it off.

If you were interviewing for a job, you would present yourself as neat and professional so that you could make the best impression possible. The manuscript you send to the editor makes the impression for you.

A year ago, when you started reading this book, you were an amateur. Now you have a chance to become a professional writer.

Be a pro.

Glossary

Act

A distinctive and framed section of a play, drama, opera, or novel. The word *act* comes from the Latin *agere,* meaning "to drive, to do." For your first novel, write in three acts.

Antagonist

The character who opposes your protagonist. *Ante* means "against" and *agonist(es)* means "one who competes."

Aristotle

Greek philosopher (384–322 B.C.) who gave us catharsis, denouement, and complication, three keys to dramatic action.

Aristotle's Incline

A visual diagram that demonstrates, with rising action and three acts, how plot structure works to provide emotional release.

Back Story

Events, sometimes traumatic, that have happened to your character(s) before the opening of the story. In novel construction, back story often holds the key to character motivation.

Catharsis

The high point of action for a dramatic structure.

Characters

The people in your story. For a novel you need at least three main characters: protagonist, antagonist, helper.

Character Chart

A technique for character development which contains information that is both demographic (age, sex, income) and psychographic (tastes, habits, et cetera).

Character Sketch

A brief one-page list of observed character traits—hairdo, eyes, eye makeup, jewelry, clothing—that stimulates a writer's creative guesswork about what motivates characters.

Chronology

A ladder of key dates reaching up from the past into the heart of the story that highlights a moment of trauma for a character.

Climax

The high point of a scene or chapter.

Compound Verb

Two or more verbs paired by *and* that work from a single subject. For example, in the following sentence, built on a compound verb, you have speed but not much for the reader to grab on to: "He [the subject] *came* [verb 1] into the room AND *looked* [verb 2] AND *saw* [verb 3]. . . ." Compound verbs speed up action, but hinder rhythm in your writing. Use them sparingly.

Denouement

The final unraveling of a plot. *Denouement* comes from the Old French *desnouement,* from *desnouer,* reversing the tying, meaning to "undo." In Latin, *nodus* means "the knot" and *nodare* means "to tie."

Dialogue

Two characters talking, usually in a one-two rhythm. One: I hope it doesn't rain. Two: I don't mind a little rain.

Discovery Draft

The first writing of your novel all the way through, from beginning through the middle to the end.

Final Image

A stunning image to make the reader recall the final moments of your book. Examples of memorable final images: the green light at the end of *The Great Gatsby*; the coffin in the vortex at the end of *Moby Dick*; the royal wedding at the end of "Cinderella."

First Person

A point of view operating from the first person pronouns *I/we*.

Helper

One of three main characters for your novel. The helper acts as a catalyst, a force for change.

Image Cluster

A group of images clumped together in the writing that help the writer deliver indirect messages to the reader. For example, Anne Tyler uses sight/blindness metaphors *(see, glasses, windshield, focus)* in her opening chapter of *The Accidental Tourist* to suggest that the characters are blind to one another's needs.

Key Scene

A turning point, high point, or hot spot in a novel's plot.

Meditation Draft

Stage Two of your novel-writing process, where you brood over your earlier work to deepen and tighten the construction.

Midpoint

A key scene in the middle of a novel's second act.

Motivation

The force that drives your characters. The best source for motivation is Back Story.

Parallel Structure

A powerful rhetorical device you can use to enhance the rhythm in your writing. Parallel structure—repetition of key phrases at strategic locations in your syntax—comes into English from the Bible ("Blessed are the poor in spirit. . . . Blessed are they that mourn. . . . Blessed are the meek. . . .") and from Greek rhetoric.

A great book on Greek rhetoric is Edward P. F. Corbett's *Classical Rhetoric for the Modern Student*. These two examples come from Corbett:

Anaphora repeats words at the beginning of phrases: "We shall fight on the beaches, we shall fight on the landing fields. . . ." (Churchill)

Epistrophe repeats words at the end:

In a cake nothing tastes like real butter
" " " nothing moistens like real butter
" " " nothing enriches like real butter. . . .

(Pillsbury ad)

Plot
A blueprint of your novel's action, sketched out with Aristotle's incline.

Plot Point One
The key scene that occurs right before the end of Act One.

Plot Point Two
The key scene that occurs right before the end of Act Two.

Point of View
The frame of reference from which your story is told.

Protagonist
The lead character in a novel. *Protagonist* is derived from the Greek. *Protos* means "first, foremost" and *agonist(es)* means "one who competes" for the prize.

Psychic Distance
The distance between the reader and the events in the story.

For example:

Much Distance: It was summer of the year 1991. A woman wearing a shirt looked out at the lake.

Less Distance: Maria had never much cared for hot sun.

Even Less: Maria hated the sun.

Closer Yet: God, how she hated the sweat running down her belly.

Scene

A container that holds a novel's dramatic action. The word *scene* comes from the Greek *skaena,* meaning "tent," and from the Latin *scaena,* meaning "stage" or "theater."

Stage Setup

A term borrowed from theater to suggest that novelists must do the work of set designers and stagehands. The parts of a stage setup are: time, place, temperature, season, lighting, props. The function of stage setup is to alert the reader not only about time and place, but also about mood, atmosphere, and depth of scene. Stage setup is important because it contains symbols and images that can give the writer's work an added dimension.

Storyboard

A technique for sketching the parts of a scene before the writing starts. A storyboard includes stage setup (time, place, temperature, season, lighting, sounds, smells, symbols, images), characters and their relationships, dialogue (subjects and subtext), action (large action and supporting actions), point of view, climax, and exit line.

Story Line

A bare-bones description of a novel's plot.

Third Person Omniscient

A point of view using third person pronouns *(he/she/they)* that enables the author to change the narrative frame of reference.

Third Person Multiple

A planned expansion of the third person omniscient point of view into more than one frame of reference.

Writing Practice

Writing like an athlete trains; writing every day, whether you feel like it or not; writing under the clock, timing yourself to distract the internal editor; writing with these rules: Keep the hand moving, don't cross out, don't edit, go for the jugular, go for first thoughts, don't think, lose control, spend it all.

Bibliography

Baker, Carlos. *Ernest Hemingway: A Life Story*. New York: Charles Scribner's Sons, 1969.

Berg, A. Scott. *Max Perkins: Editor of Genius*. New York: E. P. Dutton, 1978.

Burroway, Janet. *Writing Fiction: A Guide to Narrative Craft*. Glenview, Ill.: Scott, Foresman & Co., 1987.

Cowley, Malcolm, ed. *Writers at Work: The Paris Review Interviews*, First Series. New York: The Viking Press, 1958.

Dillard, Annie. *The Writing Life*. New York: Harper & Row, 1989.

Du Maurier, Daphne. *Rebecca*. Garden City, New York: Doubleday and Co., Inc, 1938.

Field, Syd. *The Screenwriter's Workbook*. New York: Dell Publishing, 1988.

Fitzgerald, F. Scott. *The Great Gatsby*. New York: Charles Scribner's Sons, 1925.

Fitzgerald, F. Scott. *Tender Is the Night*. New York: Charles Scribner's Sons, 1934.

Forster, E. M. *Aspects of the Novel*. New York: Harcourt, Brace, 1954.

Gardner, John. *The Art of Fiction: Notes of Craft for Young Writers*. New York: Alfred A. Knopf, 1984.

Goldberg, Natalie. *Long Quiet Highway: Waking Up in America*. New York: Bantam, 1993.

Goldberg, Natalie. *Writing Down the Bones: Freeing the Writer Within*. Boston: Shambhala, 1986.

Hall, Oakley. *The Art and Craft of Novel Writing*. Cincinnati: Writer's Digest Books, 1989.

Hemingway, Ernest. *The Complete Short Stories of Ernest Hemingway*. New York: Charles Scribner's Sons, 1987.

Hemingway, Ernest. *A Farewell to Arms*. New York: Charles Scribner's Sons, 1929.

Hemingway, Ernest. *The Sun Also Rises*. New York: Charles Scribner's Sons, 1926.

Joyce, James. *Ulysses*. New York: The Modern Library, 1961.

Lessing, Doris. *The Four-Gated City*. New York: Alfred A. Knopf, 1969.

MacShane, Frank. *The Life of Raymond Chandler*. New York: E. P. Dutton & Co., 1976.

Nicholson, Nigel, ed. *The Letters of Virginia Woolf, Volume I*. New York: Harcourt Brace Jovanovich, 1975.

Rose, Phyllis. *Woman of Letters: A Life of Virginia Woolf*. New York: Oxford University Press, 1978.

Sternberg, Janet, ed. *The Writer on Her Work*, Volume I. New York: W. W. Norton & Co., 1980.

Sternberg, Janet, ed. *The Writer on Her Work*: Volume II: *New Essays in New Territory*. New York: W. W. Norton & Co., 1991.

Tallent, Elizabeth. *Museum Pieces*. New York: Alfred A. Knopf, 1985.

Tannen, Deborah. *You Just Don't Understand: Women and Men in Conversation*. New York: William Morrow & Co., 1990.

Thompson, Joyce. *Bones*. New York: William Morrow & Co., 1991.

Walker, Barbara. *The Woman's Encyclopedia of Myths and Secrets*. San Francisco: Harper San Francisco, 1983.